White Women Writers and Their African Invention

Florida A&M University, Tallahassee
Florida Atlantic University, Boca Raton
Florida Gulf Coast University, Ft. Myers
Florida International University, Miami
Florida State University, Tallahassee
University of Central Florida, Orlando
University of Florida, Gainesville
University of North Florida, Jacksonville
University of South Florida, Tampa
University of West Florida, Pensacola

White Women Writers
and Their African Invention

Simon Lewis

University Press of Florida
Gainesville · Tallahassee · Tampa · Boca Raton
Pensacola · Orlando · Miami · Jacksonville · Ft. Myers

08   07   06   05   04   03   6   5   4   3   2   1

Library of Congress Cataloging-in-Publication Data
Lewis, Simon, 1960–
White women writers and their African invention /
Simon Lewis.
p. cm.
Includes bibliographical references and index.
ISBN 0-8130-2652-0 (acid-free paper)
1. Schreiner, Olive, 1855–1920—Knowledge—Africa.
2. Dinesen, Isak, 1885–1962—Knowledge—Africa. 3. Women
and literature—Africa—History—20th century. 4. Authors,
South African—20th century—Biography. 5. Authors, Danish
—20th century—Biography. 6. Africa—Intellectual life—20th
century. 7. White women—Africa—Biography. 8. Africa—
In literature. I. Title.
PR9369.2.S37Z7 2003
820.9'326—dc21   2003054065

The University Press of Florida is the scholarly publishing
agency for the State University System of Florida, comprising
Florida A&M University, Florida Atlantic University, Florida
Gulf Coast University, Florida International University, Florida
State University, University of Central Florida, University
of Florida, University of North Florida, University of South
Florida, and University of West Florida.

University Press of Florida
15 Northwest 15th Street
Gainesville, FL 32611-2079
http://www.upf.com

Contents

Preface and Acknowledgments

This book, which started out as a doctoral dissertation at the University of Florida, is an analysis of the writings of white women writers in Africa, particularly Olive Schreiner and Karen Blixen. These two writers offer fascinatingly multiple perspectives on the relationship between Europe and Africa from the heyday of European imperialism through the dismantling of colonialism and up to the present. In meditating on Schreiner's and Blixen's representations of themselves and those around them, on their representations of landscapes, and on their broader understanding of Africa geographically and historically, it becomes possible to see how ideas of race, class, gender, and nationality inflect the variety of literary modes the two writers worked in, and to see how cultural limits on behavior and self-invention coincide with literary limits not just on how one might write but also on what one might write about. Focusing on white women writers, whose apparent racial privilege is offset by apparent gender disadvantage, reveals the fluidity of racial and gender categories in colonial and postcolonial situations. As a result, the book should be of interest to a wide range of readers of nineteenth-century, modernist, colonial, and postcolonial (especially anglophone African) literature, as well to theorists of race, gender, and culture.

I owe huge debts of gratitude to all those teachers, colleagues, and friends who have informed, advised, adroitly needled, encouraged, and otherwise supported me, notably in recent years Elizabeth Langland and Laura Chrisman. I am grateful to the University of Florida and to the College of Charleston for institutional support in the form of a dissertation fellowship, research and development grants, and conference travel. I am also grateful to the editors and staff of the University Press of Florida, whose handling of this manuscript was expeditious, efficient, and courteous and whose anonymous readers proffered extremely valuable criticism. This book would not have been possible at all, however, without the support provided by my parents, Keith and Olive Lewis, my wife, Janet Watts, and my children, Megan, Zoë, and Oliver.

Certain portions of this book have appeared in earlier versions in scholarly publications. I am grateful to Indiana University Press for permission to reprint chapter 5, a version of which appeared as "Culture, Cultivation, and Colonialism in *Out of Africa* and Beyond" in *Research in African Literatures* 31.1 (Spring 2000): 63–79. I am grateful to Professor Wieslaw Krajka for permission to reprint chapter 7, a version of which appeared as "The Violence of the Canons: A Comparison between Olive Schreiner's *Trooper Peter Halket of Mashonaland* and Conrad's *Heart of Darkness*" in *Conrad in/and Africa*, volume 11 of the series Conrad: Eastern and Western Perspectives, published by Maria Curie-Sklodowska University Press. I am grateful to the Board of Governors, University of Calgary, for permission to reprint chapter 8, a version of which appeared as "Graves with a View: Atavism and the European History of Africa" in *ARIEL* 27.1 (January 1996): 41–62.

Quotations from *Winter's Tales* by Isak Dinesen, copyright 1942 by Random House, Inc., and renewed in 1970 by Johan Philip Thomas Ingerslev, c/o the Rungstedlund Foundation, are used by permission of Random House, Inc., and the Rungstedlund Foundation. Quotations from *Letters from Africa, 1914–1931* by Karen Blixen, copyright 1981 by the University of Chicago, are used by permission of the University of Chicago and the Rungstedlund Foundation. Quotations from *Out of Africa* by Isak Dinesen, copyright 1937 by Random House, Inc., and renewed in 1965 by Rungstedlundfonden are used by permission of Random House, Inc., and the Rungstedlund Foundation. Quotations from *The Grass Is Singing* by Doris Lessing, copyright 1950 by Doris Lessing and renewed 1978 by Doris Lessing, are reprinted by permission of HarperCollins Publishers, Inc. Quotations from "Small Passing," from *Familiar Ground*, Ravan Press 1988, copyright Ingrid de Kok, are used by kind permission of the author.

Introduction

White Women Writers and Their African Invention analyzes the cultural roles played by white women writing on or about farms in South and East Africa, focusing on Olive Schreiner and Karen Blixen and situating their work in the context of some of their contemporaries and successors, white and black, female and male. Schreiner's career as a published writer spans the years 1883 (when *The Story of an African Farm* first appeared) to the 1920s (when her widower edited and published *Undine* and *From Man to Man*). This period may be seen as encompassing both the high point of Victorian imperialism (the Golden and Diamond Jubilees of 1887 and 1897), as well as its gory demise in the First World War, a demise in some ways prefigured by the Anglo-Boer War (1899–1902). Living and writing in that postwar world marked by imperial decline, Blixen's writing career began in the 1930s with the publication of *Seven Gothic Tales* (1935) and *Out of Africa* (1937), and extended to her death in 1962. By decoding the apparent simplicity of Karen Blixen's famous opening to *Out of Africa*—"I had a farm in Africa"—this book probes the political complexity of writing, especially as a white woman, under colonialism and imperialism and of responding to the fragmentation of modernism and the struggles toward democratization and nationalism, both in Europe and Africa.

The book's three sections explore the manner and effect of the various inventions—of "I," "farm," and "Africa"—in the writers' work. The first section addresses the ambiguous position of the colonial woman, simultaneously subject to Victorian and colonial patriarchy yet participating in the subjugation of a local black population, simultaneously at home and not at home in Africa. The second section traces how a tradition of the English pastoral influences and shapes representations of African landscapes. Playing on the dual meaning of the word *occupation,* this section shows how Schreiner's and Blixen's literary farms at times and in part facilitated the occupation of the land by creating an occupation called farming, while at times and in part suggesting novel ways of representation more or less usable by nationalist authors interested in reclaiming the land. Finally, the third section addresses the broad historical invention of "Africa" by European discursive practices, situating Blixen's and Schreiner's work in relation to the European memory bank of literary and historical tradition that has tended to ignore, forget, or erase indigenous African experience. All three sections pick away at questions of difference and the violent psychic, physical, and environmental consequences that various discourses of difference—imperialist, nationalist, apartheid—have trailed in their wake. Blixen emerges from these investigations as someone working in the elegiac mode, mourning lost wholeness.[1] Schreiner, by contrast, despite closer attention to the political and material reality of her circumstances, emerges as a future-oriented idealist whose imagination tried to devise new routes toward understanding the common humanity of all.[2]

Although much of this book deals with enduring, successful, even powerful inventions, much is also about mutation and failure—the loss of Blixen's farm and of her lover Denys Finch Hatton, for example, or the failure of Schreiner to avert the Anglo-Boer War or to see Cecil Rhodes's policies officially abjured. The book also addresses the acute sense of instability Blixen and Schreiner experienced, both complicit with and occasionally critical of British colonialism and European cultural and literary conventions, frequently but inconsistently resisting hierarchical structures of race, gender, class, and nationality that they could never quite avoid. Likewise bound by the conventions of literary criticism but attempting to nudge against those boundaries, and similarly compromised by my own positionality as a white male British/American academic, I have thought of the nonlinear structure and method of this book as partly mimetic, imitating some of the formal and generic experimentation of Schreiner and Blixen. I have thus thought of this study less as a comprehensive and definitive linear argument than as a three-part meditation about inventions of self through time and space, specifically about white female selves in colonial Africa. To enable that mediation from as many significant angles as possible, I treated the phrase "I had a farm in Africa" as a heuristic device, allowing it to provide structure and to generate material. As a result, the book starts with the invention of the white woman writer's "I," goes on to discuss the invention of the "farm" in Africa, and finally addresses European inventions of "Africa" itself. The three sections are intended to serve as openings for further discussion rather than as scholarly last words, leaving room for discontinuities and contradictions that a more traditional argument might not have accommodated. In this way, I have tried to follow my own principle of the omphalos (see chapter 3), circling round and round my subject in the spirit of experimentation rather than definition, and avowing the connectedness of people, things, the things that people produce, and the people produced by things.

The appearance of linearity, however, foregrounds awkward questions of priority and selection that tend to lie shadowed in the text. Despite my claim to omphalogocentrism, despite the fact that lines run both ways, the structure of this text, no less than its selectivity, thus appears to have given priority once more to the white subject. What are the consequences of that? Can I, for instance, claim that my project is congruent with Toni Morrison's examination of whiteness and the literary imagination in American literature? In many ways our aims do indeed match. Like Morrison, I am not interested in replacing one domination with another (*Playing in the Dark* 8); like Morrison, I am interested in the effect of white people's racism on themselves (11); like Morrison, I insist on the serviceability and availability of blacks for white invention of individual, racial, and national identity (25). Morrison's claim that "when matters of race are located and called attention to in American literature, critical response has tended to be on the order of a humanistic nostrum—or a dismissal mandated by the label 'political'" (12) resonates with my discussion of the canonical discrepancy between *Heart of Darkness* and *Trooper Peter Halket of Mashonaland*. When Morrison writes of Willa Cather's noncanonical *Sapphira and the Slave-Girl* that it represents Cather's "struggle to address an almost completely buried subject: the interdependent working of power, race, and sexuality in a white woman's battle for coherence" (20), her claim matches my efforts to read the presence of Africans in Karen Blixen's short stories as well as her memoirs. And so on.

However, the marking of our texts is necessarily different. When Morrison writes, "I am vulnerable to the inference that my inquiry has vested interests; that . . . I stand to benefit in ways not limited to intellectual fulfillment from this line of questioning," she does so as "an Afro-

American and a writer" (12). The nature of her self-interest, whatever its extent, is not the same as the self-interested inventions of the non-Afro-Americans she writes about. Thus, while I am, like Morrison, vulnerable to the inference that my inquiry has vested interests, unlike her I am vulnerable to the specific inference that in perpetuating and prioritizing the white subject I share those vested interests with the white writers I critique. However, as Morrison says, while "in a wholly racialized society, there is no escape from racially inflected language . . . the work writers do to unhobble the imagination from the demands of that language is complicated, interesting and definitive" (12–13).

Part of that unhobbling involves worrying away at the totalizing kind of identity politics implicit in such phrases as "the white subject." While remaining acutely conscious of power relations among racial, gender, and national groups, this book takes a broadly phenomenonological approach to race, gender, class, and nationality insisting on the ways in which whiteness or femaleness are constructed in particular times and specific places. How one acts out one's being varies over time and in response to location and audience, as Schreiner's and Blixen's writing amply illustrates.

Let me place my comments more precisely in terms of the history of literary criticism. In the past, critics have tended to look at the writers in this study separately, or in terms of their specific physical location, or in terms of their location within specific literary traditions. In the case of Schreiner, that has meant a split between the work of those critics who see her as primarily South African, the pioneer of a South African literary tradition, and the work of those critics, mainly outside South Africa, who place her writing and her politics in a British tradition whether in her feminism or in her fiction writing. The split is perhaps an inevitable one, reflecting the actual splitting of her life between physical residence in South Africa and physical residence in Britain as well as the intellectual ambivalence created by being an "English South African." In the case of Blixen, the tendency has been to view her work in the light of European traditions—of the Gothic, pastoral elegy, personal memoir, travel writing, and so on—and in relation to European movements such as Romanticism and Modernism. These splits are all the more vexatious in her case, as she figures in both Danish- and English-language traditions. In both cases, critics frequently deal exclusively and selectively with either the writers' fiction or the nonfiction.

Following the work of Homi Bhabha in particular, however, such splits in colonial and postcolonial writers have become of central importance, opening ways for critics to produce much more carefully nuanced analyses of their subjects' work.[3] In foregrounding the ambivalence in Schreiner and Blixen, I am also picking up on the earlier insights of Raymond Williams in his accounts of the many layers of any particular "culture," which at any given time displays residual and emergent traces, and includes alternative and oppositional practice within what looks like a hegemony. With respect to women, who in South Africa in particular have had a long history of resistance, what I am interested in is the way that, in Gay Wilentz's formulation, through both alternative and oppositional practice, the writers in this study offer residual histories as emergent culture. In this regard, my attempt resonates with Wilentz's *Binding Cultures: Black Women Writers in Africa and the Diaspora,* in which Wilentz additionally stresses the familial, mothering roles of black women as storytellers in an oral rather than literary mode. The contention that there is no essentialist racial difference between the black writers of Wilentz's study and the white writers of mine has animated my desire to read, however cautiously, the term *African* as not necessarily racially exclusive.[4] Such a reading is in line with other recent critics who have already begun to insist on the cultural hybridity of Schreiner and Blixen: Susan Horton's book *Difficult Women, Artful Lives* pays close attention to their European Africanness, while Judith Raiskin pushes even further, labeling Schreiner creole and fascinatingly putting her in company with the contemporary South African "Coloured" writer Zoë Wicomb and with Caribbean authors Jean Rhys and Michelle Cliff. More recently still, Laura Chrisman has discussed Olive Schreiner as a sort of mediator between British imperialist and African nationalist conceptions of race as exemplified by H. Rider Haggard and Sol Plaatje, while Carolyn Burdett insists on the specifically South African source of Schreiner's engagement with European evolutionary and racial thought.

Such approaches typify the effect current trends in postcolonial, cultural, and gender studies have already had on the discipline of English literature and subdisciplines such as anglophone African literature and Victorian studies.[5] Interest in the ways in which the domestic sphere influenced the imperial adventure has led, for instance, to studies like Anne McClintock's 1995 book, *Imperial Leather,* which looks at South African women writers from Schreiner on in terms of a reformist discourse of health and hygiene. Developing such trends, my work sets out not just to show how the apparent European/African split in fact holds Schreiner and Blixen together as individuals, but also how that common split integrity marks Schreiner and Blixen as examples of similar forces of colonialism. While I pay attention to the specificity of local histories in east and southern Africa, I am at pains to demonstrate how these writers' literary constructions of Africa, mainly for a European (or at least metropolitan) audience, contributed in similar ways to those histories. Among my arguments for linking the writers together as specifically *women* writers in colonial circumstances is the claim that narrow local focus on a specific area's politics tends to obscure the bigger picture of the ways in which patriarchy and capitalism work.

At the same time as approaches have changed, so have historical circumstances changed. Like Laurence Sterne's Tristram Shandy struggling to write a comprehensive account of his life, this work has had to struggle not just with the histories it describes but with contemporary history happening around it. Not just events, but other works, other ways of working, have overtaken it and prompted new visions and revisions. Many years ago, I first conceived of the project in terms of "frontier feminism" and dreamed of comparing Karen Blixen, Olive Schreiner, Willa Cather, and Miles Franklin as pioneering women among men. Had I attempted such a transcendent, transcontinental project, I suspect that I should have treated the four women in heroic vein as stoic and noble souls whose ideals were ahead of their times in challenging the male-gendered modernity they found around them—as indeed, in many ways, they were.[6] By 1994, when I finally started drafting this work, it was apparent that I could no longer discuss women among men without regard to race, class, and geographical and historical specificity. My focus altered accordingly.

Then, while I was writing, one of the key inventions of my study, apartheid—an apparently solid object of opposition, and something that had inevitably colored (I use the phrase deliberately) my thought—was written off the statute books and into the history books. The South African election of April 1994 brought the promise of one of the most enlightened constitutions ever, clouded with various fears: the possibility of renewed sectarianism, the potential of a newly tyrannous majority, and the burden of promises and hopes possibly too enormous to be fulfilled. Still, the politics of the continent have shifted almost unimaginably, and as subsequent events have shown, the freedom and uncertainty opened up by South Africa's transition to majority rule have profound implications for the whole of sub-Saharan Africa, especially the anglophone south and east. Much recent critical work from and about South Africa, for instance, highlights the way that the sense of South Africa's difference from the rest of the continent was exaggerated both by the material reality of apartheid and by antiapartheid resistance, even when the latter discourse formally disavowed racialism.[7] The removal of formal apartheid from the southern tip of the continent has allowed critics, historians, and cultural theorists to rethink the various "seams" in South African society in light of broader continental and global circumstances.[8] The sense that Africa as a whole is finally free from colonial rule coincides with a renewed sense of neocolonial dependency within a global hegemony dominated by the United States. The shift in South Africa from a "spectacular" literature of resistance to an "ordinary" literature of "rememory" is consequently balanced by warnings from writers, politicians, and critics of the continuing need to resist a normalization process that offers "atomized consumer subject[s]" as "a feeble substitute for the democratic ideal" (Bertelsen 241).[9] In the face of such continuing changes, therefore, although much of my work here is novel, it insists on its own contingency. It will not be possible again to address in the same way the questions raised by studying selected white women writers in Africa. This very contingency, however, demonstrates the writers' continuing significance. On the one hand, Olive Schreiner's serial disappointment in the human and political potential of South Africa should make us wary of seeing South African history in particular solely in terms of miraculous progression from repression to freedom; on the other hand, the redeployment and commodification of *Out of Africa* should make us wary of the continuing, and apparently continual, recycling of colonial nostalgia.

One of the final images of this book is of a disinterred skeleton of Olive Schreiner being deployed in an attempt to unite people violently separated by the legacy of racialized colonialism. Numerous other disinterred figures haunt these pages. Not only do I attempt to bring to attention the huge numbers of nameless dead Africans x-ed out by the European history of Africa, whose stories have been hidden by colonial writing and memorialization of the land, but in paying attention to relatively underrepresented texts such as *Trooper Peter Halket of Mashonaland,*

Mhudi, or *The Grass Is Singing,* I also attempt to show that at any given time alternative and oppositional practices were possible and that a one-dimensional linear history of any form of domination—imperialism, patriarchy, colonialism, apartheid—underestimates the significance of resistance and is likely to produce narratives involving misleadingly clear-cut binarisms of metropole/colony, male/female, settler/native, white/black, and so on.[10] With respect to my own work, I hope that it, too, might be seen as alternative, holding on to residues of previously oppositional practice (especially in the cases of Schreiner, Lessing, and Plaatje) in order to promote an emergent culture in postcolonial Africa that can live up to the nonracial and nonsexist ideals of South Africa's new constitution.[11]

By insisting on the Europeanness of these writers' claims on Africa, this study furthermore intervenes in current debates in various arenas of African studies, where questions of authority—who gets to write about whom?—have been fiercely contested. These debates have frequently involved distinctions between disciplinary purism and discourses that acknowledge their political nature and distinctions between insiders and outsiders. In the field of African literature, the ability and right of "outsiders" to critique the work of "insiders" has frequently been called into question. In 1996, for instance, the Dutch Africanist Mineke Schipper was criticized by Ama Ata Aidoo in the women's caucus of the African Literature Association for presenting what Aidoo considered an exaggeratedly misogynist impression of gender relations in Africa through publication of Schipper's book *Source of All Evil,* a collection of African proverbs associated with women. Subsequent e-mail discussion on this topic was lengthy and often vehement, but it rarely had much impact on mainstream academic work in European and American literature departments, where African literature remains marginalized.

Much more prominent has been the widely publicized debate over Afrocentrism sparked by Martin Bernal's massive undertaking in *Black Athena* (1989) and the concerted attack on that work led by Classical scholar Mary Lefkowitz. While many of Bernal's theories regarding ancient history have been debunked, his critique of historiography and the "fabrication of Ancient Greece" is still persuasive and informs my reading of the European writing of African history. As I see it, Bernal's massive project has two principal corrective aims: to revise the so-called Ancient Model of the origins of Greek civilization, including colonization by

Egyptians and Phoenicians, and to demonstrate the racist ideology that led to the Western European "fabrication of Ancient Greece" from the late eighteenth century onward by inventing an Aryan model for the origins of Greek civilization. Bernal demonstrates the self-serving nature of European knowledge about race and draws attention to the coincident rise of academic disciplines and of racism. With regard to the latter point, he argues that the denial of an African source for Greek, and hence Western, civilization not only legitimates imperialism but also ultimately feeds into Aryanism's last word, the anti-Semitism of the Nazis. Bernal's critics have poked numerous holes in his arguments, especially with regard to the belief central to his Revised Ancient Model that "there is a real basis to the stories of Egyptian and Phoenician colonization of Greece" (Bernal 2). Lefkowitz led the attack in 1996 with a particularly dismissive rebuttal in *Not Out of Africa: How Afrocentrism Led to the Teaching of Myth as History*,[12] and shortly thereafter with a more temperate and probably more damning collection, coedited with Guy MacLean Rogers, entitled *Black Athena Revisited*. Although it seems some of Bernal's historical theories fail to hold water, his historiographical critique remains harder to refute. While the Egyptologist Frank Yurco, for instance, disputes the colonization theory, he does agree that Bernal's account of the ideological basis for the replacing of the Ancient Model with the Aryan Model "accords with the early study of Egyptian antiquity as it is generally understood" (Yurco 65); and Edith Hall, a specialist on the eighteenth century, agrees with the argument that "modern racial prejudice has been one of the reasons why cultural contact between ancient Hellenophone communities and ancient Semitic and black peoples has been and is still being played down" (Hall 335). It is that aspect of Bernal's work that makes me eager to hang on to his insights in support of my own arguments regarding the selectivity of European memory in its invention of Africa.

African philosophy has similarly been split between inclusive and exclusive schools taking universalist and so-called ethnophilosophical approaches. The former category, which embraces the disciplinary purism of Paulin Hountondji and the avowedly political work of Congolese Wamba-dia-Wamba, allows for connections with European thought (the Greeks, Marx) and generally operates in accordance with European traditions of philosophy as a systematic discipline transmitted by writing.[13] Culture-specific ethnophilosophers, by contrast, infer local philosophies from the rituals and orature of particular peoples. Despite its pan-African breadth, Senghor's concept of négritude may be considered typical of ethnophilosophy in its insistence both on the essential difference of African experience of the world and in its rejection of systematic reason as the basis for understanding that experience.[14] Recently, the Eritrean scholar Tsenay Serequeberhan has attempted to reconfigure specifically African philosophy as a hermeneutic practice bound to a history that is both European *and* African, which cannot by an act of will erase or deny the European presence. Such a position does not represent passive acceptance of Europe in Africa. On the contrary, Serequeberhan insists on the necessarily political nature of the philosopher's critique—but for Serequeberhan, as earlier for Soyinka,[15] the search or desire for that which is authentically African uncontaminated by anything European is irrelevant in its idealism. Even though I am an outsider, then, writing about outsiders and in danger of complicity with the very practice I critique—of writing Africa for my gain rather than Africa's—Serequeberhan gives me some philosophical ground on which to stand; he got there by way of Eritrea, I by way of England.

Not that I'm not still self-conscious. The relative ease with which I have been able to move between England, South Africa, Tanzania, and the United States implicates me in "the insidious nature of neo-colonialism," which "internally replicates . . . what previously was imposed from the outside by violence" (Serequeberhan 21). Nor do I wish to play down the personal nature of my investment in this study, to pretend that it stems solely from disinterested, universalist academic impulses. In fact, a large part of my motivation depends on autobiography, as I share Schreiner's and Blixen's geographically and psychologically dislocating experience of having been a European in Africa. And since the affective nature of colonial writing is so relevant to this study, allow me to indulge in a little bit of memorial invention of my own.

To parody Blixen, I might claim that "I grew up on a farm in Africa," but the farm was hardly a farm, and the Western Cape from 1969 through 1977 scarcely felt African to a little English boy. (The Jeune Afrique atlas of Africa shows the Western Cape as inhabited by Europeans, for instance.)[16] My father was the manager of a poultry business that provided day-old chicks and point-of-lay pullets to other poultry enterprises that provided the supermarkets with their chickens and eggs. My family lived in a three-bedroom bungalow on the slopes of the

Paardeberg, some ten dirt-road miles from the local post office, sixteen miles from the nearest town, the wine-center Paarl, and some forty miles from Cape Town where my brother and sister and I attended boarding school.

When I was still at the junior school, my father was invited by the headmaster to come and talk to the boarders about chicken farming. He started his speech by asking, "What came first, the chicken or the egg?" I don't know whether he'd anticipated a riotous outbreak with half of the audience shouting "chicken," the other half "egg," but we were all too shy in the presence of someone's dad to offer much. So, rather undramatically, but very emphatically, Dad gave the answer that the chicken must have come first, the farmyard fowl being the descendant of some distant ur-chicken eons ago in Asia. He had a picture of this bird, and very colorful and tropical it was, too.

In the same talk, my father attempted to demonstrate the great strength of a hen's egg by summoning to the front of the room the biggest boy in the school. He gave this boy a fresh egg and told him to squeeze the egg as hard as he could at both ends to try to break it. The boy was somewhat reluctant to do so, and rightly so it seems, for when he grasped the egg, it smashed in his hand with yolk and albumen oozing stickily through his fingers. It had been supposed to stay intact; obviously the boy had been putting pressure in the wrong place, not exactly at the tips of the egg. Still, we knew that eggs were strong. Most of us had seen photos of men standing on ostrich eggs, and many had even been to the tourist ostrich farms around Oudtshoorn and seen for ourselves.

I have vaguer memories still of the chick sexers. They drove out from Somerset West for the day and had to have their lunch provided in their break from picking up chick after cheeping day-old chick, turning them over in their giant palms and lobbing them in the appropriate box, female or male, valuable or reject. Theirs was an unimaginable task. Anything that had the word *sex* in it was unimaginable to me at that age, so I never dared ask how they did it or what became of the males.

I offer these three images from my memories of farming in Africa—read, of the agribusiness in South Africa—as they illustrate by their very banality that same ideological opacity that my analysis of Blixen's opening clause from *Out of Africa* tries to illuminate. My father's determined quest for an originary narrative, the strength and fragility of the eggshell, the determining nature of gender—all find analogies in my analysis: of the European use of evolutionary theory and of history; of the simultaneous power and vulnerability of the oppressed; of gender politics.

A more personal memory informs my particular interest in that last-listed category. Throughout our nine years at Clearsprings, my mother was homesick. She hated her isolation on the farm and never really adjusted. However, my father, brother, sister, and I liked our lives in South Africa and had little cause to miss the dreariness of England. My mother was, therefore, even more isolated, as she had no ally among us children with whom to commiserate or conspire on joint plans of action for "going home." My mother's experience, as a woman whose ostensible racial privilege led to an inner misery that her position as a woman trapped her in, informs my sympathy for the stifling power of colonialist patriarchy expressed by both Olive Schreiner and Doris Lessing. Similarly, her longing for a "home" that was elsewhere informs my reading of Schreiner's and Blixen's complex attitudes toward "home."

Besides all this, I could deconstruct my own parodic claim to having grown up on a farm in Africa by pointing out that, as a boarding school pupil, my growing up was done away from the farm in an environment essentially English, at one of South Africa's elite private schools, a foundation with an invented Victorian tradition that in typical colonial style epitomized English educational principles. When we studied English, it was understood that the Leavisite canon *was* literature and that South African literature was secondary (hence really second-rate), a subsection of the real thing (and hence really substandard). Thus, although we heard about Olive Schreiner and knew of *The Story of an African Farm*, we didn't study her any more than we studied local, contemporary black authors. As you would expect of a white liberal institution, we did read *Cry, the Beloved Country* and short stories of some of the other white writers who at that time represented South African literature (as opposed to *black* South African literature, which was a separate category, even subber than the sub), but none of them quite measured up to the standards of Matthew Arnold's touchstones or Leavis's top-rankers.

Some of our teachers were more enlightened than this account gives them credit for. Certainly they never explicitly declared the relative lack of value of South African or black South African writing or African writing generally. But the syllabuses they were required to teach were posited on that assumption. So I have some idea of the politics of canons. In fact, having grown up in South Africa, even as a highly privileged white child, Fredric Jameson's conclusion that all writing is, in the last analysis, political was axiomatic. What one *does* as a writer and person, given such an axiom, is by no means predetermined, and I am aware of the potential inconsistency between my political quietism (or whatever the opposite of "activism" is) and some of the more radical tendencies of my writing. I am also aware of the weakness of my continued liberalism,[17] in the face of forces of local reaction and global capital.

Whatever the limits on that liberalism's effectiveness, my background seems inevitably to have led to my strongly privileging a socially conscious humanistic ethic that assumes the permeability and artificiality of boundaries between literature, politics, economics, history, sociology, and so on. Such an attitude means that I treat Blixen's and Schreiner's generically different autobiographical "inventions" in similar ways, finding it impossible to untangle the literary from the testimonial. It also means that I treat Schreiner's and Blixen's lifeworks, with their public appearances and their published work in fictional and nonfictional modes, as if they were more or less of a piece—not, of course, as transparent representations of some extraliterary fact, nor of some transcendent metaphysical truth, but as part of a complex, historically specific textuality of which this decoding is one more recoding. Above all, I remain convinced that, despite the apparent marginality of white women writers in Africa, the questions of personal identity, appropriation of space, and the very notion of Africa are vital to our understanding of the interrelationship between Europeans and Africans, women and men, historically, in the present, and for the future.

1

"I"

Je est un autre.
[I is someone else.]
Arthur Rimbaud

This I, what is it? We try to look in upon
ourself, and ourself beats back upon oneself. Then we get up in great fear and run
home as hard as we can.
Olive Schreiner

Ke motho ka ba bangoe.
[Through others I am somebody.]
Tswana proverb

1

The Invention of the "I"

Olive Schreiner and Karen Blixen had very different experiences and understandings of the African farms they have written into European culture, and any comparison between the two writers runs the risk of blurring significant differences between the colonial histories of Kenya and South Africa and significant differences between Schreiner's and Blixen's specific roles in those histories. However, as white women striving to find space for themselves, especially as speaking and writing subjects, they share a history of resistance to the Victorian patriarchy, which strove to reduce them to objects. Out of this resistance, the pressure to find ways to speak, write, and be themselves led to a high degree of originality in their work. Not only is *The Story of an African Farm* (published in 1883) the first novel of any merit by a South African–born writer, but its breaching of stylistic and generic conventions also makes it a precursor of modernism. Blixen's *Out of Africa* (published in 1937) still defies generic categorization, and the consistently metafictional quality of her stories produces a weird blend of deconstruction and the Gothic. With both writers, the struggle to find means of expression accompanies the struggle to live and be in the world, specifically as women and as artists: Schreiner's feminist heroine Lyndall strives to overcome the dual standard that says to men, "Work!" and says to women, "Seem!" (*African Farm* 188) while Blixen declares in her letters that the "greatest [art] of all is the art of living" (*Letters from Africa* 95). They were pioneering women and frontier feminists in more ways than one.

When I use the term *invention*, therefore, I am recognizing the way in which Schreiner and Blixen produced something new out of their African experience. However, from its etymology, *invention* retains not just the sense of made-up-ness that characterizes constructionist models of gender but also some sense of finding or discovering something that was already there. This balance seems valuable to me in looking at Schreiner's and Blixen's representations of themselves and others for two reasons: First, it stresses the materiality of the situations they wrote about, in which, among other things, European discourses exerted material power over actual African space and actual African bodies; and second, Schreiner and Blixen employ both essentialist and constructionist approaches to the question of gender and race difference.

Invention also has the sense of an event, of the moment of creation of something usable (whether a Spinning Jenny or a Sony Walkman), and it seems crucial to me to place Schreiner's and Blixen's various inventions in their historical moments. Yes, they were highly original writers and women, but they were original in relation to particular sets of social circumstances and necessarily constrained by contemporary mind-sets with regard to race, class, gender, and so on. Their best-known works produced inventions of themselves in an apparently private, though legally bounded, space—the farm—in an apparently boundless and available landscape—Africa. They did so over a crucial period when the African continent was being demarcated as European both in terms of political possession and in terms of political and economic systems. The publication of *The Story of an African Farm* predates by one year the Congress of Berlin at which the European powers formalized their scramble for Africa, while *Out of Africa* appeared one year after Mussolini's invasion of Abyssinia. Furthermore, the historical span of the textual content of the two books—from about 1860 to 1930—embraces the rise of scientific racism, social Darwinism, and eugenics. All of these, as we shall see, leave their mark on Schreiner's and Blixen's work and make their inventions of themselves as specifically white women potentially very awkward to contemporary readers.

The role played by class further confuses the issue of Schreiner's and Blixen's historical invention; the vicissitudes of Schreiner's early life, as daughter of an impoverished missionary, rendered her oddly déclassée and left her dreaming of a utopian future, while the aristocratic Baroness von Blixen-Finecke, anachronistically adrift in twentieth-century Europe, projects a nostalgic, even elegiac feudal past. However, although the complexities of these issues of gender, race, and class prompt further caution in dealing with Schreiner-and-Blixen in the same breath, similarities can be found even in the distinctions between them.

For instance, if we look at the respective genres of *The Story of an*

African Farm and *Out of Africa*—novel and memoir—we find at first glance a central distinction between Schreiner's and Blixen's literary inventions and indeed in their attitudes toward the idea of invention. However, the apparent distinction between invention as the telling of stories and invention as the uncovering of the truth dissolves rapidly. Although *The Story of an African Farm* is ostensibly fictional, it is quite plainly autobiographical with the struggles of Lyndall and Waldo readily mappable onto the struggles of the young Olive Schreiner. In addition, in the preface to the second edition of the novel, Schreiner set out her methods and aims in a kind of manifesto, explaining that her work countered conventional false fictions set in Africa, and instead of painting in the brilliant colors of the "stage method," she has squeezed the pigment from her brush in order to paint "the life we all lead" (*African Farm* 27). "The facts creep in upon" her (28).

By apparent contrast, Blixen's true-life story of her eighteen years on her coffee farm in Kenya depends on a narrative characterization that is stronger on image and feeling than on fact. At the same time, however, *Out of Africa*, too, in its epigraph lays claim to telling the truth— "equitare, arcum tendere, veritatem dicere."[1] Like the Africans of her invention, Blixen might be thought of as unreliable but ultimately "in a grand way sincere" (*Out of Africa* 27). As she makes plain in *On Modern Marriage*, she believes that truth is a great deal more than the absence of lies (72); thus, even though her "facts" might be invented, she could still think of the invention as true. With both writers, therefore, but not in the same ways, we find a simultaneous grounding and ungrounding of truth in lived experience, a paradoxical process that the term *invention* attempts to capture.

Despite the apparent differences, then, we might go on to ask three related questions concerning Schreiner's and Blixen's self-inventions as women (and not just in *African Farm* and *Out of Africa*, but more generally): To what extent was the experience on which they grounded their work understood by them as gendered female; how does one cope with or write such experience in a male-dominated world and among a set of discourses in which the male is the norm; and how might one strategically deploy one's female experience and its representation in ways that effectively resist or transform the status quo? These are questions that continue to trouble contemporary cultural theorists, especially those feminists who wish to retain some sense of agency in the face of the supposed death of the subject. Elspeth Probyn, for instance, goes back to Raymond Williams to "retrieve some of the ways in which experience has been made to function," finding that his "concept of the structure of feeling expresses the richness of what it means to work from within the felt facticity of material being" (Probyn 5). While Probyn's response is to a contemporary crisis of representation, roughly a century earlier Schreiner too was concerned with a similar crisis: how to represent *her* self, how to represent her female self (in opposition to current definitions of woman), and ultimately how to bring about the representation of women through legal and parliamentary change. Like Probyn, Schreiner's crisis involved asking "the questions of 'who am I?' and 'who is she?' in ways that neither privilege 'me' nor discount how 'I' and 'she' are positioned in relation to each other" (Probyn 6). For Schreiner, as we shall see, it was a deeply conflictual crisis.

Born female into a colonialist patriarchy (in 1855), Schreiner resisted being made into a particular type of woman by power structures that saw her sex as determining her role. Such resistance put her in conflict not just with the male power structures but frequently also with the passive women made by those power structures. In fact, insofar as women, unlike men, had highly limited power to effect direct political change, and insofar as Schreiner saw herself as desiring change and potentially able to effect change, she frequently saw herself as someone not quite a woman (although female) speaking on behalf of women. While all her work stands as a model indictment of Victorian and colonialist patriarchy and inspired a later generation of feminists (for whom *Woman and Labour* was, in Vera Brittain's words, "the Bible"), Schreiner frequently railed at womanhood in general and the specific restrictions placed on her as a woman. To Havelock Ellis, for instance, who played the Waldo to her Lyndall as "other self," she wrote: "Oh, please see that they bury me in a place where there are no women. I have not been a woman really, though I've seemed like one" (*Letters* 142).

Susan Horton, whose *Difficult Women, Artful Lives* is the first full-length comparative study of the two women, points out that Schreiner's "closest companions" in her youth were the male writers she read: "Her fictional heroines are often taken to be instances of self-portraiture, and what both she and these heroines read most were writers who espoused various kinds of willed self-reliance: Emerson, Schopenhauer, Herbert Spencer" (81). Horton points out that even in her feminist writings

Schreiner can present herself as distinct from the women on whose be-half she writes: "Being a woman I can reach other women, where no man could reach *them*. A growing tenderness is in my heart for *them*" (cited in Horton 90; emphasis added). This same distancing limits the possibili-ties for female solidarity in Schreiner's fiction. As Tess Cosslett in her study of female friendship in Victorian fiction says of *African Farm*, "The need to emphasize Lyndall's isolation and independence, and her differ-ence from a conventional woman like Em leads to the friendship being underplayed, and indeed undermined by Lyndall's behavior. . . . Lyndall's scorn for the conventional woman's lot drives a wedge between herself and her devoted female admirer" (150–51).

The problem of identification/nonidentification is intensified in Schreiner's fiction by the way her New Woman heroines are as ham-pered by other women as by men, before receiving their final come-uppance. Tant' Sannie in *African Farm*, Mrs. Snappercaps in *Undine*, Mrs. Drummond and Veronica Grey in *From Man to Man*, for instance, op-press Lyndall, Undine, and Bertie quite as effectively as any men, and the gossipy Mrs. Goodman and Miss Mell (in *Undine*) are the very models of self-righteous hypocrites one would expect from stereotypical misogy-nist writing.[2] Lyndall's last landlady, too, treats Lyndall as the source of "a little innocent piece of gossip" (269), has "no time to be sitting always in a sick room" (268), and generally seems keener to get her hands on Lyndall's fifty pounds than to see her get well. Although Schreiner ideal-ized motherhood in *Woman and Labour*, her fiction suggests that actual motherhood is anything but the source of sisterly solidarity. Neither Undine nor Lyndall has much chance to love and nurture her baby. When the babies are born, and when they die, their mothers experience more suspicion than sympathy from the women around them. Rebekah, Schreiner's only picture of a mother successfully rearing her children, finds her maternal duties constantly infringing on her other relation-ships and limiting her ambitions.

Schreiner's heroines are thus doubly isolated—from male-deter-mined convention and from women made by such convention. Lyndall and Undine can have no existence and duly waste away, while the docile Em and the arrogant Mrs. Blair survive. The novels thus illustrate a point many critics have pointed out—that despite their frequently feminist aspirations New Woman novels of the late nineteenth century seemed unable to imagine positive ends for their rebellious heroines. Tess

Cosslett, for example, comments that "the New Woman writer's stronger awareness of the injustices done to women often caused her to give a much bleaker picture of women's chances and potential than earlier women writers had done" (162), and Gail Cunningham writes that "the common pattern of the New Woman novel is to show the heroine arriving at her ideals of freedom and equality from observation of her society, but then being brought through the miserable experience of trying to put them into practice to a position of weary disillusion" (49–50).

This latter formulation exactly describes the disillusionment of Lyndall in *The Story of an African Farm* who, speaking in the first person plural, for women, sketches out a pattern of "a little bitterness, a little longing when we are young, a little futile searching for work, a little passionate striving for room for the exercise of our powers,—and then we go with the drove. A woman must march with her regiment. In the end she must be trodden down or go with it; and if she is wise she goes" (189). Speaking in the first person singular, however, aware of "that solitary land of the individual experience, in which no fellow-footfall is ever heard" (196), Lyndall announces, "Women bore me, and men" (199).

In other words, while Schreiner/Lyndall/the New Woman is essentially the same as all other (white) women, equally bound by the patriarchal conventions of the time, she is simultaneously different from other women in her rebellion, her reluctance to march with the regiment. One way to write one's way out of this conundrum was to find what Gerd Bjorhovde calls "rebellious structures" to match the rebellious content. The most extreme form of this in narrative terms would mean ditching plot realism as Schreiner does later in her short allegorical fictions or as, to all intents and purposes, Blixen does in her metafictional Gothic tales.[3] The eccentric construction of *The Story of an African Farm,* and, to a lesser extent, *Undine,* represents a move in that direction, but as we have already seen, Schreiner was unwilling to do away with the appeal to authenticity of experience. Thus, although Rachel Blau du Plessis in *Writing beyond the Ending* takes *The Story of an African Farm* as the germinal text of female modernism and stresses the rebelliousness of its "critique of narrative" (30)—Schreiner's refusal to paint life according to the "stage method" described in her preface to the second edition—nonetheless the insistent appeal to the "life we all lead" determines that Lyndall must ultimately fail while the docile Em lives on.

What is more, Schreiner appears to have been unable to find a way to present Lyndall's death positively, as a glorious failure or moral victory, as her quiet slipping away occurs virtually removed from the world, in company only of the unsympathetic landlady and of the travesty-woman, Gregory Rose. In one of the cruelest moments of a frequently cruel narrative, Waldo, the one character really receptive to Lyndall's views, learns of her death only after he has completed a long letter to her. The sense of futility conveyed in that moment sets the seal on the book's pessimism—particularly, though not exclusively, about women: Life is a series of abortions, "a striving, and a striving, and an ending in nothing" (135). Even Em, left with the prospect of marrying Gregory Rose, contemplates the sadness of how "at last, too late, just when we don't want them any more, when all the sweetness is taken out of them, then [the things we long for] come" (296). So women—even the survivors—are presented as powerless to bring about positive change in their individual lives and unable to work together on each other's behalf.

Schreiner's own life was blighted by this pair of inabilities. Ruth First and Ann Scott, and more recently Karel Schoeman, have shown how much of an outsider the young, freethinking Olive Schreiner was in the Eastern Cape society in which she grew up. Her father was a failed and bankrupt missionary, already perhaps an oddity, like Otto in *African Farm*, by virtue of his German birth and "dreamy silent nature" (Hobman, *Olive Schreiner* 17), while her mother clung so strongly to her Englishness that she once beat Olive for uttering the Afrikaans "Ach." Effectively orphaned at the age of twelve by her father's insolvency (First and Scott 49), Schreiner was passed around among siblings, friends, and families who employed her as a governess; in this last position she was placed at what First and Scott call "an ambiguous point in the social structure: she became a 'higher servant,' socially subservient but culturally superior" (71).

She had no home of her own (references to "home" in her letters frequently mean England, a country she had not even visited), and her free-thinking atheism did not just defy conventional belief but was "triply stigmatized: she was adolescent, she was a girl, and she had had almost no formal education" (First and Scott 56). She was so intellectually isolated that it has been possible to identify the one person—a civil servant named Willie Bertram—with whom she felt able to discuss her ideas, and his presence in her life was no less fleeting than the Stranger's presence in Waldo's life. Similarly, she had little chance for mutual emotional involvement,[4] and her first sexual encounter (with one Julius Gau of Grahamstown) ended not just in tears but quite possibly in tuberculosis. She remained friends with the Cawoods of Ganna Hoek, but otherwise seems to have been thoroughly estranged from her employers and even from her prudish and puritanical brother and sister, Theo and Ettie. Given this sort of background, it is scarcely surprising that her first fictional heroine should bear the name Undine, an orphaned water nymph lost among mortals who gains her soul—and hence the capacity to suffer— through the love of a man, only to lose the soul but not the suffering when he rejects her.

During this stage of isolation—that is, before Schreiner's 1881 departure for England—writing was one possibility for positive individual change, as was her dream of becoming a doctor. The medical dream rapidly dissolved (First and Scott 112–15), but with the eventual publication of *The Story of an African Farm* in 1883, Schreiner found herself—reinvented?—among literary and intellectual equals sharing broadly sympathetic views. However, she still had no home as such, nor was she sufficiently at home among women to be able to invent a stable self as a woman. In the Men and Women's Club of which she rapidly became a forceful member she seems to have formed far stronger bonds with men—especially Havelock Ellis, Bryan Donkin, and Karl Pearson[5] (to whom she wrote of herself as his "man-friend")—than with the women, who, more conventionally brought up in Britain, both more class-conscious and more class-secure, viewed her with some suspicion. First and Scott talk of how Schreiner's "spontaneous expression, unfettered by Victorian notions of decorum" and her distance both "from the middle-class conventions of London society" and "during her adolescence and after, from family constraints" made her not just "a rebel against convention" but an "outsider" in England (161).

Schreiner's membership in the club terminated in a tangled row with Elizabeth Cobb and Karl Pearson stemming, as far as can be determined, from Schreiner's attraction to Pearson and her perception of Mrs Cobb's meddling to check their intimacy.[6] First and Scott suggest that Schreiner's bout of illness subsequent to this row was partly due to "the conflict between her intuitive, even unconscious mistrust of women and the sense of sisterhood she found obligatory" (171). A rather different but no less vexed conflict informed her much later decision (1908) to resign from the Women's Enfranchisement League when it became clear that the Cape League, of which she was vice president, would follow the lead of the Transvaal and Natal societies to push for votes for white women only, rather than go with the more radical Cape society's struggle for votes for *all* women.

This latter resignation shows the difficulty in talking about Schreiner's "mistrust of women" and "sense of sisterhood," as those phrases beg the very questions of women and sisters that Schreiner was struggling to come to terms with. As I have suggested, Schreiner's own position was closer to the radically questioning position of Elspeth Probyn, trying to work out who "I" is, who "she" is, and "how 'I' and 'she' are positioned in relation to each other" (Probyn 6). While it is clear that an impatience with *some* women led to her removing herself from organizations such as the Enfranchisement League, her commitment to the advancement of *all* women remained firm. First and Scott are probably on safer ground to talk about Schreiner's dissatisfaction with individuals and their organizations: "Her constituency was no single movement, but an imperative, a presence, a set of beliefs that gathered momentum from place to place" (264).

In fact, over time she became her own one-woman pressure group, unattached to any particular association, with a few influential women contacts (Emily Hobhouse and Constance Lytton, among others),[7] and an impressive array of male correspondents both in England and in South Africa. This quasi-assimilationist effect does not so much suggest "mistrust of women" as confirm the difficulties Schreiner confronted as an activist woman in a Victorian colonial society. While her younger brother, Will, could follow a career that led from the law to the highest of offices as attorney-general to Rhodes and later as prime minister of the Cape Colony, Olive Schreiner's gender denied her formal education, denied her a profession, denied her access to the political process, and thwarted her sense of achievement. Female networks of power simply were not available to her, especially in rural South Africa, so in wishing to exert power to change society she necessarily had to operate among males. To be sure, this analysis depends on a limited notion of power and the political—what we might more scrupulously refer to as the geopolitical—and overlooks the fact that the example of Schreiner's personal politics did have powerful effects. Nonetheless, her own perception seems to have been one of despair at the lack of immediate and tangible results of her work.[8] For instance, after the publication of *Trooper Peter Halket of*

Mashonaland, a harrowing account of the results of Cecil Rhodes's policies, and one which cost her enormous mental anguish in the writing and
publishing, she wrote to her brother Will: "In spite of its immense circulation I do not believe it has saved the life of one nigger,[9] it had not the
slightest effect in forcing on the parliamentary examination into the conduct of affairs in Rhodesia, and it cost me everything" (Rive 333). As a
woman she could not oppose Rhodes in parliament, and her intervention
in the geopolitics of the day was necessarily oblique, although apparently
public, and likely to be frustrating, limited by the existing structures of
power to the dismissible sphere of literature or to behind-the-scenes letter writing.

Possibly her most direct intervention in local geopolitics took the form
of the pamphlet entitled *An English South African's View of the Situation,* published in 1899, in which she argued passionately that the looming war between the British and the Boers was being fomented by the
agents of big capital quite against the interests of the "English South
Africans" and quite against the various principles of justice and democracy invoked by the warmongers.[10] Here we see very clearly the effects of
the restriction that Olive Schreiner felt she was under as a woman;
throughout the pamphlet, the "I" of the text is consistently identified as
a male. She offers her readers "the voice of the African-born Englishman
who loves England, the man, who, born in South Africa, and loving it as
all men, who are men, love their birthland" (6). This "manly," almost
jingoistic voice strives to make itself heard in the cacophony of male
voices prophesying war,[11] while women, far from being potential sources
of fuller identity (as in *Woman and Labour*) or of conscience (as in
Trooper Peter Halket), are reduced to being the potential bearers of a renewed and vengeful breed of South Africans (111).

This belligerent antiwar pamphlet, like *Trooper Peter Halket,* failed in
its public purpose: to dissuade the British people from tolerating further
military occupation of Africa by Rhodes and other forces of big capital. In
private, Schreiner was simultaneously working behind the scenes trying
to act as some sort of go-between for Jan Smuts, state attorney in
Kruger's South African Republic, and Sir Alfred (later Lord) Milner, recently appointed as governor of the Cape Colony and quite plainly looking for a justification to take over the gold mines of the Transvaal. In
letters to her brother Will, then premier of the Cape Colony, and to
Smuts and his wife, Isie, Schreiner agonizes about whether or not she

should attempt to see Milner to explain to him why war would be such a bad thing. She wrote directly to Milner, too, sending him a printer's draft copy of *An English South African's View of the Situation*. Even in the letter she reproduced her male-identified "I," writing rather plaintively, "I do not ask you to forgive my writing to you because there are times when a man has a right to do almost anything" (354).[12] As with her letters a decade earlier to Karl Pearson, this attempt to speak as man to man seems to represent more than just the sexism of current language use. Even in her apparent abjuring of womanness, there is perhaps a poignant sense that it is her woman's envious perception of a man's entitlements that prompts the line of approach.

Astute, and even cynical, as she could be about the origins of the war, the apparent naïveté and futility of her attempts to avert it once more highlight the difficulties of being an activist, especially an activist woman, in South Africa, not just in Schreiner's time but in our own when British colonial rule was succeeded by apartheid and, arguably, the demise of apartheid has made way for a new form of neocolonial dependency on multinational capital. Under each of these circumstances, and despite the best intentions of the drafters of South Africa's new constitution, what remain constant are capitalism and patriarchy. When, at the nadir of apartheid, Nadine Gordimer, in an influential review of First and Scott's biography, wrote critically of Olive Schreiner that her interest in feminist issues was "bizarre," since the "actual problem" of South Africa was one of race,[13] she may well have been revealing how effective both capitalism and patriarchy are at hiding their workings. *They* can still look like natural states long after racism has been exposed. In fact, capitalist patriarchy has been tremendously successful in dividing activist dissidence, so that in South Africa, for instance, one wouldn't automatically recognize Winnie Mandela, Helen Suzman, Lilian Ngoyi, Ellen Kuzwayo, Nadine Gordimer, and Mamphele Ramphele as belonging to the common category of woman, cutting across race and class.[14]

Thus confronted by questions of "representation,"[15] it may be useful to refer to Gayatri Spivak's elaborate dissection of the term—using Marx's distinction between *Vertretung* and *Darstellung* (roughly equivalent to the distinction between representation and re-presentation)—in "Can the Subaltern Speak?" In my list above of unrepresentative women('s) representatives, Marx's distinction is perhaps rather blurred as a result of the specific circumstances of political representation and lack thereof in colonial and apartheid South Africa. Elected representatives not only stood proxy for others (Marx's *Vertretung*) but also set out representations of themselves and others (Marx's *Darstellung*). In fact, Helen Suzman's justification for participating in the apartheid era whites-only parliament was always that South Africa's legal system allowed and required her representations of others to be represented in the official records of that parliament.[16] By contrast, Schreiner's resignation from the Cape Women's Enfranchisement League highlights the extent to which she was limited *both* in representing *and* in being a representative.

But in the same way that British colonial administrations in India managed to establish a version of history "in which the Brahmins were shown to have the same intentions as (thus providing legitimation for) the codifying British" (Spivak 282), so in colonial South Africa the codifying British had managed to establish a version of history in which their representation of the divisions among people was seen to be shared by the peoples thus represented. This explains, at least in part, the enduring difficulty in South Africa of recognizing that women as a category—however divided they may be made to appear—may share as much as, or more than, categories defined by race, ethnicity, class, or language.

First and Scott suggest that Schreiner was at least partly, perhaps intermittently, aware of the ways in which difference was invented and exploited in colonial South Africa, and they credit her with being unusual in recognizing "Rhodes and the international capital he commanded as the principal instrument" of the profound changes occurring in South Africa following the discovery of the Rand gold. They credit her, for instance, with being alone in recognizing "that the color question was really the labor question, and that labor, both black and white, could not be free unless it was united" (338). However, though she might have intermittently redrawn these categories, she could scarcely represent them either through claiming a shared, representative experience (as, say, however problematically, Winnie Mandela represented black women oppressed by apartheid) or by acting as a formal, elected representative (as, say, however problematically, Helen Suzman represented black political prisoners under apartheid). Thus, as First and Scott emphasize, Schreiner remained isolated, a fact which manifests itself in a "protective, patronizing attitude" to Africans (339).

It is fascinating, nonetheless, to speculate as to how Schreiner's politics might have developed had she not been embroiled in the 1890s in the male geopolitics of British expansion in South Africa but remained in England or at least remained in touch with a more thorough, systematic, and theoretical approach to politics. For instance, had she still been in England during the 1890s, that Janus-faced decade of decadence and novelty that identified the New Woman, she would have almost certainly come into contact with the African American feminist Ida B. Wells and the short-lived antilynching campaign she inspired in Britain. Vron Ware's discussion of this campaign and the various tensions it revealed in feminist movements in Britain and the United States highlights the way Wells and her English champion Catherine Impey offered a challenge to the role of English women in imperialism. The significance of the movement, says Ware, was that "it showed the possibility of an alliance between black and white women in which white women went beyond sisterly support for black women; by confronting the racist ideology that justified lynching, these white women also began to develop a radical analysis of gender relations that intersected with class and race" (220). Schreiner was never fully able to do that. "African mass organization [in which the women's section of the ANC was prominent] was beginning only as Olive died," write First and Scott, "and her perceptions of the special relationship between class and colour had yet to be theorized by a much later generation of analysts" (340). In fact, it seems to me that had Schreiner met Wells, that special relationship might well have been theorized earlier rather than later.[17]

Gordimer's and Schreiner's positions are perhaps a good deal closer than Gordimer acknowledges, and it is interesting how giving priority to race over gender both serves Gordimer's own purposes and suggests something about the way Schreiner has been (mis)read, with the "feminism" of her most famous work occluding her anticapitalist and antiracist fulminations elsewhere. Gordimer's refusal to identify herself as a feminist in apartheid South Africa is in some ways equivalent to Schreiner's male-identified "I" in *An English South African's View of the Situation;* it makes sure that she is to be taken seriously in the somehow realer world of male geopolitics with its "actual problem" of race. The very same urgency of national politics where men exclusively set the agenda kept Schreiner in the 1890s and Gordimer in the 1980s focused on local issues—on effects rather than causes—and left them both adrift, like Gordimer's postapartheid heroine Vera Stark with "none to accompany me," without a constituency to represent.[18]

Vera Stark is a white lawyer whose role as a champion of the oppressed alters radically as the oppressing force—apartheid—is dismantled. Her "success" in opposing apartheid in some ways removes a core of certainty in her life. It is as if one has been pushing and pushing against a door, and someone suddenly opens it from inside, sending one tumbling headlong into vacant space. Gordimer's heroine, previously working on behalf of the dispossessed, now finds herself dispossessed of that work. She might be seen as a self-conscious image of the committed writer—specifically in Gordimer's case, the committed *white* writer—for whom success will necessarily mean the loneliness of self-effacement. Like the model Roman dictator Cincinnatus, who retired to his farm once his task of saving Rome was complete, both Vera Stark and Nadine Gordimer must make the final surrender of the privilege of importance, so as not to impede the new order for which they have worked. While Schreiner's lonely strugglers are likewise figures of commitment, they are figures of her commitment as a *woman* writer. Thus, in Schreiner's case, given that (some) British women won the right to vote only in 1919, the loneliness is due to *non*achievement (or, at best, deferred success); hers is the spectacular isolation of the pioneer, of a Moses figure whose vision of the Promised Land is both fleeting and singular. Such a vision is, in a way, dispiriting. Schreiner expresses that sense through Lyndall: "'To see the good and the beautiful,' she said, 'and to have no strength to live it, is only to be Moses on the mountain of Nebo, with the land at your feet and no power to enter. It would be better not to see it'" (196).

If the aptness of the Moses image is conceded, it is fitting that where Schreiner comes closest to transvaluating nonachievement into deferred triumph is in the allegory "Three Dreams in a Desert." Here, in the second of the three dreams, a character identified only as "woman" has to cross a previously uncrossed river in order to reach the land of Freedom. She has to divest herself of "the mantle of Ancient-received-opinions" (77) and wear only Truth, a single "white garment that clung close to her" (78). Just as she is about to start her crossing, Reason, her guide, notices that there is something at her breast, drinking there cherubically. When Reason orders the woman to put this creature down, she is initially reluctant to do so, insisting that she can carry him and thus get them both across. When she does put him down, convinced by Reason that he is in fact powerful and perfectly able to fly to the Land of Freedom on his own, "he bit her, so that the blood ran down to the ground" (81). Immediately she becomes old and is filled with a sense of doubt and loneliness. "And she said, 'For what do I go to this far land which no one has ever reached? *Oh, I am alone! I am utterly alone!*' And Reason, that old man, said to her, 'Silence! what do you hear?' And she listened intently, and she said, 'I hear a sound of feet, a thousand times ten thousand and thousands of thousands, and they beat this way'" (*Dream Life and Real Life* 81/82). Like locusts crossing a stream, the woman and those thousands of women following her may be swept away, but "at last with their bodies piled up a bridge is built and the rest pass over" (82). The woman asks who will cross over that bridge of bodies, and when the answer comes—"The entire human race"—she "turn[s] down that dark path to the river" (83).

This short allegory graphically captures the way Olive Schreiner appears to have thought of herself vis-à-vis women and men. She is the pioneer, totally isolated, occasionally disheartened, whose labor for others is masochistic, involving physical suffering, ingratitude, and the renunciation of what she holds most dear. Her work is for women, certainly, and strives to educate women to care for themselves alone, but is also for men—or perhaps for a new order of male-female relations—and the entire human race who will benefit from the purging of the codependency of Passion (the cherubic figure at woman's breast) and its replacement by mutual Love. Gordimer's criticism that Schreiner was "bizarre" in concentrating on "women's issues" actually misses how radically Schreiner conceived of her work in transforming the whole of society through transforming the conditions that women lived under. As Schreiner stresses in *Woman and Labour,* there is no point producing New Women without New Men to accompany them in a future where "woman shall eat of the tree of knowledge together with man" creating "an Eden nobler than any the Chaldean dreamed of; an Eden created by their own labour and made beautiful by their own fellowship" (*Woman and Labour* 296).

And there—paradoxically enough, in her nonfiction—we can see Olive Schreiner's most radical invention: a Utopian promised land or promised time of closer union[19] where sexual relations are not "dominated by the sex purchasing power of the male" (252). Karen Blixen's Utopia, by contrast, is not located in the future but in the past, and while Schreiner's work is prophetic in nature and tone, Blixen's writing has an oddly post-humous feel to it. Although the two women's inventions—specifically their inventions of women and their relation to men in an African context—are comparable, this positioning of Eden, in the future or in the past, marks a very significant distinction regarding who they thought they were and what they thought they were doing. In short, it marks the difference between the politically active writer and the aloof, modernist artist. In both cases, being a woman made the achievement of those roles difficult and, very different though their personal circumstances may have been, the forces of gender-conventions shaping Karen Blixen and Olive Schreiner can be presented as strikingly similar. For instance, the young Karen Blixen, no less than Olive Schreiner, felt herself to be intel-lectually apart from her family and, in particular, apart from the "wom-anly" nature that her mother and her maternal relatives expected her to conform to. As with Schreiner, Blixen read mainly male writers in her youth, and as with Schreiner she courted the general disapprobation of conventional Christian society by latching on to one particular "free-thinker." In Blixen's case, this was Georg Brandes,[20] a Jewish philosopher who had first introduced the work of Nietzsche to Denmark and who had had a notorious row with 1880s Danish feminists like Blixen's Aunt Bess, who held chastity to be of greater importance than equal erotic freedom for men and women (Thurman 63). Instead of Schreiner's "dreamy" fa-ther, Blixen had the figure of Wilhelm Dinesen—romantic writer, trav-eler, hunter—to set against the conventionality of her mother and aunts. Instead of being removed from him by insolvency, Karen Blixen was separated from her father by his suicide shortly before her tenth birth-day. Severely restricted and isolated by these and other forces, both writ-ers as young women turned to male philosophers to ground their inven-tions of themselves. For Schreiner, the philosopher was Schopenhauer, for Dinesen, Nietzsche; both stressed the value of will and self-reliance.

However, whereas Schreiner's sense of self-reliance feeds that image of herself as isolated pioneer that we have already discussed, leading the mass of humanity to an ideal future, Blixen's use of Nietzsche depends on a more complicated idea of the real and the ideal, allowing her to adopt very self-consciously the "mask" of the artist and to create an ideal self and past that transcend present reality. Blixen's self is at once more di-vided and more deliberately invented than Schreiner's, and although both rely on imagination to resist the world around them, Blixen tends to use art as a defense against vulgarity, perfecting her own world in a retreat from the quotidian, while Schreiner is more openly rebellious, using art as a lever to move the world on toward a real state of social perfection. Eden for Schreiner is a state of human relations yet to be formed; for Blixen, the Fall is irreversible, and Eden can only be recalled once remote from it in time and space.

Moreover, although both women are painfully aware of the Fall, Schreiner's response is to attempt a moral and social regeneration, while Blixen's is to attempt an aesthetic and personal reconstruction. In fact, "The Deluge at Norderney," one of Blixen's most frequently discussed stories, suggests that since the Fall moral regeneration is no longer possible or relevant because it was not so much humanity that has fallen but divinity (*Seven Gothic Tales* 240). The Cardinal, who makes this claim (and who in fact turns out to be his valet, Kasparson, an ex-actor who has murdered his master and taken his place), tells a story, "The Wine of the Tetrarch," in which Barabbas, the thief pardoned by Pontius Pilate, finds his pleasure in life annulled by the Crucifixion. Barabbas's experience does not lead to moral self-awareness, however, still less repentance; the point of the story is drawn later by the Cardinal/actor, who says that he has "lived long enough to have learned, when the devil grins at me, to grin back. And what now if this—to grin back when the devil grins at you—be in reality the highest, the only true fun in all the world? And what if everything else, which people have named fun, be only a presentiment, a foreshadowing, of it? It is an art worth learning, then" (*Seven Gothic Tales* 267). In a fallen world, the morality of art is irrelevant, and for the Cardinal/actor the accuracy of illusion is more important than the truth. In a vein of thoroughly Wildean decadence, Blixen has the Cardinal/actor twice strike the keynote "Not by the face shall the man be known, but by the mask" (264). It is difficult to imagine a social program being devised from such an axiom, and indeed Blixen, unlike the morally earnest Schreiner, seems little interested in taking any practical steps toward the future improvement of society.

In her conclusion to *Difficult Women, Artful Lives*, Susan Horton suggests that both writers "conflat[ed] retrospection and anticipation into a pregnant present moment in which they *became* themselves in the act of 'remembering' and communicating a past that was a construction in and of the moment of writing" (244). Although this analysis of the

self-invention of Schreiner and Blixen is intriguing, in her own collaps-
ing of conventional linear notions of time Horton misses a fundamental
distinction between the two women that the temporal location of Eden—
in the future or in the past—indicates. *Out of Africa* recalls, from a distance of some thousands of miles, the period of Karen Blixen's stay in
Kenya, 1914–31, a period stretching back well over twenty years from
the time of writing to a time when European settlement of the country
was very recent, before colonial infrastructure and administration had
sedimented into regularized bureaucracy. Judith Thurman sums up the
arrogant sense of freedom white settlers enjoyed at that time by quoting
a letter from an early settler declaring, "We have in East Africa the rare
experience of dealing with a *tabula rasa,* an almost untouched . . . country
where we can do as we will" (cited in Thurman 121). Blixen explicitly
deplored such views, but in her elegiac reconstruction of her life, although she may not *quite* mourn the kind of license expressed by the
letter writer, she does appear to mourn a related kind of existential freedom to transcend the social, to create oneself in one's own image, as it
were.

In other words, in overstressing the similarity between Schreiner's
and Blixen's inventions of self and other with regard to time, Horton
risks losing the distinction between Schreiner's altruism (patronizing
though it may be) and Blixen's narcissism (generously intentioned
though *it* may be), between Schreiner's aim to produce an ideal world in
a real future and Blixen's desire to transform a real past into an ideal
picture. More bluntly, Blixen's response to European-determined social
conditions, which were no less stultifying than those confronting Olive
Schreiner, was to use Africa/Eden as a means to create a life for *herself:* In
reality (by escaping from her family in Denmark), in her autobiography
(by mythologizing—removing all "psychological or narrative ambivalence" (Thurman 282) from *Out of Africa*), and in her fiction (by driving/
allowing her to be a writer). In all three cases, this mythical Africa
prompts Blixen, like Schreiner, to distance herself from women: She
claimed that living in Africa allowed her to avoid the "fatal influence"
(*Letters* 245) of a paralyzing, annihilating home life dominated by female relatives; her memoirs present her in the "male" roles of, among
others, farmer, doctor, hunter, chief; the pseudonym Isak Dinesen is not
only male but a recall of the patronymic, too. As such, Blixen's self-production seems to validate Horton's claim, which she makes with regard to

both Blixen and Schreiner, that the attempt "to make woman their cross-cultural other" was "made possible partly because as white women in Africa each was able to operate to some extent as an honorary male" (5). The difference is in the "Africa" in which they found themselves and the Africans on whose "unwitting collaboration" (Horton 5) their self-production depended.

Such differences provide material more appropriate to part 3 of this study, but for now I need to stress that Blixen's Edenic Africa, which would, had it existed, have already been an anachronistic reconstruction of feudal Europe when she arrived in Kenya in 1913, was by 1937 rendered doubly nostalgic by her removal from it in time and space. Schreiner's Africa, if anything an anti-Eden, is always in a state of flux—of becoming, not having been. What it means, therefore, for Karen Blixen to write of the "I"—self-created and thoroughly idealized—who *had* a farm in Africa is significantly different from what it means for Olive Schreiner whose "I" is almost always a creation of immediate circumstance.

Of Masquerades and Masks

Miming and Alterity

Although they represent the clearest attempt at re-creating and lamenting a Paradise lost, Blixen's memoirs are not the only works that reveal her imaginative flight from the here and now. One of the most striking features of her fiction is its fictionality. At the most overt level, that includes the regularity of her use of stories within stories and such folk and fairy-tale devices as the transformations of the Lapp witch in "The Sailor-Boy's Tale." It also includes, however, more realistic mutations, frequently involving, as with Kasparson/the Cardinal, dressing up and assuming roles. Multiplicity of identity and the creation and more or less voluntary assumption of identity (posthumous or otherwise) feature prominently in Blixen's stories, with numerous characters, women particularly, restaging themselves in crucial "fictional" ways. One such character, Mizzi from "The Invincible Slave-Owners," is described by the narrator as a "partisan of an ideal, ever in flight from a blunt reality" (*Winter's Tales* 150). The phrase could equally be applied to Blixen herself. Commenting on Blixen's "spectacular" public readings in the United States in 1959, for instance, Susan Hardy Aiken writes: "There she fashioned herself as a radical icon, like a design by Beardsley: dressed all in black, the large dark eyes reinscribed through the added emphasis of kohl, the parchment-like face chalk-white. Both literally and figuratively, she *made herself up*, putting into practice the paradox by which she had lived and written: 'By their masks ye shall know them'" (18). By contrasting the elaborate and deliberate fictiveness of Blixen's inventions—both of characters in stories and of herself as a character—with Schreiner's attempted candor in fiction and in life, we can draw further distinctions between the invented "I"s of the two writers. Furthermore, analysis of moments from biography and fiction where bodies are dressed and undressed raises further questions concerning the nature of femininity and the body as well as femininity and its relation to categories of class and race. To address these questions we can consider two celebrated psychological theories: Joan Riviere's theory of politically active women who "masquerade" an exaggerated femininity in order to deflect male aggression for their encroachment into conventionally male spheres of activity, and Frantz Fanon's theories of the psychology of race set out in *Black Skin, White Masks*.

There is ample evidence in the two women's biographies (some already sketched out) to justify seeing both Schreiner and Blixen as performing a masquerade in Joan Riviere's terms, putting on a protective mask of femininity to allow them to work and compete with men in apparently nonthreatening ways. Aware of encroaching into conventionally male areas, like Riviere's intellectual, politically active patients, they (especially Blixen) would then seek the reassurance or other complimentary notice from a man. In very broad terms, we can read *Out of Africa* as showing how the hunter/farmer/chief Blixen plays the seductress/hostess to Denys Finch Hatton, while Schreiner's references to herself in letters as "little" and her marriage to Samuel Cronwright—he of the big forearms—fit a similar pattern of finding a suitably conventional male ego to flatter.[1]

However, in her essay, "Re-Placing Race in (White) Psychoanalytic Discourse: Founding Narratives of Feminism," Jean Walton pushes the idea of masquerade beyond gender and asks to what extent in psychoanalytic discourse "womanliness as a masquerade is simultaneously a masquerade of whiteness" (792). Thus linking gender and race, Walton's essay has profound implications for Blixen's and Schreiner's inventions of themselves as white women. Reexamining Riviere's 1929 essay "Womanliness as Masquerade," Walton points out that the alleged father-figure in the dream of one of her "masquerading" patients is black. While Riviere had concentrated on the man's gender to confirm her point that intellectual women, or "women who wish for masculinity," felt a need to "propitiate" a potentially retaliatory father-figure, Walton stresses the man's race and notes, "By fantasizing a black man, Riviere's patient is calling upon a figure whose relation to the phallus, as signifier of white male privilege in a racialized, patriarchal society, is as tenuous as her own" (784). The article proceeds to discuss the relation of femininity and race not just in psychoanalytic discourse but also in western art in which "More than any other subject, the female nude connotes 'Art.' The framed image of a female body, hung on the wall of an art gallery, is shorthand for art more generally" (796). Moreover, whereas it is tempting to read the masquerade of womanliness as similar, possibly even equivalent to Fanon's idea that "not only must the black man be black; he must be black in relation to the white man" (Fanon 110), and whereas there does seem to be some overlap between women and black people as Others in relation to the unmarked norm of white men, both Walton's rereading of black men in dreams cited by Riviere and Fanon's rereading of black men in dreams cited by Mannoni[2] insist that we do not privilege or universalize the psychological at the expense of historical and sociological specificity. Thus, when Blixen, with some justification, rails at the constraints of womanhood—"I find it intolerable to be an object" (*Letters* 321)—and when she writes to her Aunt Bess that what feminists desire is "to be human beings with a direct relationship with life in the same way as men" (*Letters* 259), her specific situation as a white person in an African colonial situation prevents us from reading her as an object of Otherness in the same way that we might read her various black servants, squatters, and so on. Subject and object positions are not prescribed once and for all by gender or race, which are inventions dependent on specific historical circumstances and affected by biological gender and by skin color. Crude though this may sound, there can still be hierarchies of objectification.

Susan Horton recognizes all this when she writes that "the African fellow workers [Blixen's] writings produced enabled her in turn to produce a particular identity for herself" (212). That identity—the innocent "I" who had a farm—is the identity of Mizzi, the good-natured slave owner, the impoverished aristo no less hopelessly trapped by her role than her servants are trapped by theirs. In the process, Blixen's self-portrayal gives us a heroine whose femaleness is both visible and invisible— visible in her dazzling masquerade to white men (Finch Hatton) and white readers (the audience of her 1959 U.S. tour), but invisible when it comes to her dealing with the black men with whom between 1914 and 1931 she was almost daily in intimate contact.

This paradoxical process is similar to the process described by Sander Gilman in his analysis of race and femininity in the iconography of European oil painting. In Manet's *Olympia*, for instance, Gilman suggests that, just as in Walton's article, the woman who masquerades woman as her most (apparently) natural self—that is, naked—conjures up an image of herself as art and simultaneously co-opts the image of a black person. Gilman sees Manet's *Olympia* as fitting into an iconographic tradition traceable back to at least the eighteenth century, whereby the "overt sexuality" of the black figures sometimes "indicates the covert sexuality of the white woman" (Gilman 231).

With *Olympia*, Manet presents a classic and very classical striptease in which, to quote Barthes, "Woman is desexualized at the very moment when she is stripped naked" (84). What looks like overt sexuality actually remains covert in the blinding dazzle of whiteness. Through the term *candor*—meaning frankness, but having its origin in the Latin for whiteness—it is possible to see the full extent of the paradox: The white woman becomes most white and most a woman in a womanly masquerade of candor, a candid display of what isn't.

Blixen presents a similarly radical subversion of reality/unreality involving bodies, dressing up and undressing, gender, race, nature, and art in "The Invincible Slave-Owners," a key story in *Winter's Tales*. This story, set in 1875, five years after the Franco-Prussian War, among spa-hopping aristocrats of varied European origins, is told largely from the viewpoint of a young single male, the Dane Axel Leth. Axel is presented as the character who comes closest to understanding the literal masquerade of the central female character. In fact, he understands it so well that he plays along with it. The woman in question, known as Mizzi, is apparently the impoverished daughter of a gambling father who maintains the pose of a splendidly wealthy and unattainable young woman, attended by her unfailingly loyal female servant, Miss Rabe. In this pair of performances, the two women are so compellingly convincing that Axel, along with everyone else in the spa, is taken in. Early in the story, he even feels shamed by his own "pretence and falsity," which he thinks have been shown up by Mizzi's "ruthless respect for the truth" (*Winter's Tales* 135).

However, through a chance eavesdropping, Axel learns the "truth" that the two women actually have no money and are thus playing a role.

Far from being outraged by his discovery of their deception, as he feels other men of his acquaintance would have been, Axel actively assists the women, because of his "good sense of art" (142), saving face for them by re-creating himself as their loyal and aged servant Frantz. His doing so, without Mizzi's foreknowledge or assent, indicates to the two women that the secret is out. Mizzi is furious at the humiliation but powerless to do anything about it, because to blow Frantz's cover would also mean blowing their own. Recognizing that powerlessness, Axel concludes that "the slave-owner's dependency on the slave is strong as death and cruel as the grave" (147), and he completely exonerates the two women for being "so honest as to give life the lie . . . partisans of an ideal, ever in flight from a blunt reality" (150).

Just the bare bones of "The Invincible Slave-Owners" illustrate the way this story, like so much of Blixen's work generally, confounds notions of the ideal and real, fake and original, truth and fiction. Its connection with Riviere's idea of the masquerade and Walton's racial reading of that becomes apparent in a number of details. The opening description of Mizzi portrays her as "a very young beauty of such freshness, that it was as if she was sweeping with her, into the closely furnished, velvet-hung room, a sea-breeze or a summer shower" (129). All eyes are on her, and Axel thinks of her in terms of a reviewer's description of a German actress. Her audience in the salon, however, becomes aware of an incongruity: "The astonishment and admiration which her loveliness aroused were, at the next moment, accompanied by a little smile of wonder or mockery, because her slender, forceful, abundant figure was dressed up, two or three years behind her age, in the short skirt of a schoolgirl, and she wore her hair down her back" (129). This paradoxical image—fairly standard in striptease—of the eroticized innocent, the young woman bursting out of her schoolgirl's uniform, is developed further in even more voyeuristic and tactile ways:

Indeed it looked as if she had, at the moment when her Maker was holding her up for contemplation, slid through His mighty hand, and in this movement had all her young forms gently pushed upwards. The slight calves of her delicate legs—in white stockings and neat little shoes—were set high up, so was the immature fullness of the hips, while the knees and thighs, which, in her quick walk, showed through the flounces of her frock, were narrow and straight.

Her young bosom strutted just below the armpits, high above a slim waist. Her milk-white throat was long and round, strangely dignified and monumental in one so young. (129–30)

When the description finally reaches Mizzi's face, the blend of innocence and eroticism continues; with no makeup, her "fair, smooth, rosy face had not a lie in it. . . . But by far the most striking feature in the face was the mouth, a thick, sullen, flaming mouth, like a red rose" (130).

I have quoted this description at such length because as a piece of literary portraiture it is no less spectacular—dependent on being seen—than Manet's portraits of Olympia and of Nana, or of the eighteenth-century nudes discussed by Sander Gilman, or even of Blixen's own 1959 persona. Again, although we appear to be dealing only with white women in Mizzi and her attendant, Miss Rabe, there are, in fact, significant points of comparison between Blixen's painting and the tradition Gilman describes that suggest we should look at the whiteness of Mizzi's candor as in part at least keeping her sexuality covert and displacing it elsewhere onto a black other.

It comes, for instance, as no surprise that Mizzi is dressed "with precise neatness in a white muslin frock, while the attendant Miss Rabe appears in "black silk." Furthermore, like Olympia, whose naked whiteness is offset not just by her black attendant but by a thin ribbon around her neck, Mizzi is adorned by "a black velvet ribbon round her throat, but no ornament whatever" (130). In addition to the complex play of the black/white, innocent/erotic associations, there are all sorts of hints of bondage in these descriptions, perhaps picked up in "The Invincible Slave-Owners" by the General, who imagines Miss Rabe as a "female Jesuit . . . jailer" and asks Axel, "What do you think, my friend, does she birch her?" (131). These hints are perhaps peripheral to the main point of the story, but they do suggest a peculiar confusion of female sexuality with the bondage of slave to slave owner, itself charged with racial associations,[3] and all further undercut by the idea that nothing is what it seems, anyway; all is masquerade.

In love with Mizzi in a very self-conscious way, and aware from his eavesdropping that she could love him but "would rather die" than have him know the truth of her situation, Axel, blessed with his good sense of art and dressed up as her servant, accompanies her from Baden-Baden to Stuttgart. His masquerade of subservience is a declaration of love, virtually a way of *making* love, and the tension—of extreme intimacy coupled with absolute distance—between the masquerading aristo and masquerading servant is highly erotic. Permitted to walk the length of the platform with Mizzi, a "walk of perhaps a hundred steps, the relation between Axel and Mizzi ripened and set" (147). At that point Axel experiences the story's central epiphany: "Axel realized and understood, the umbrella in his hand—with reverence, since he was now in livery—that the slave-owner's dependency upon the slave is strong as death and cruel as the grave. The slave holds his master's life in his hand, as he holds his umbrella. Axel Leth, with whom she was in love, might betray Mizzi; it would anger her, it might sadden her, but she was still, in her anger and melancholy, the same person. But her existence itself rested upon the loyalty of Frantz, her servant, and on his devotion, assent, and support. His treachery would break the integrity of her being" (147).

At the end of the story, Axel Leth, once more dressed as himself, is seen reflecting amid mountain scenery. He is watching a waterfall and musing on the contrast between the unceasingly moving cataract and the "small projecting cascade, where the tumbling water struck a rock" which "stood out immutable, like a fresh crack in the marble of the cataract" (151). This blend of flux and stasis, expressed in images suggestive both of female and of male, makes him wonder if there is in life a "corresponding, paradoxal mode of existing, a poised, classic, static flight and run" (151). Blixen suggests that the musical form of the Fuga offers such a mode, but that seems to be a diversion back into art. In lived experience, Axel (and, by implication, Blixen) confronts the paradox of *acting* a part in the world. Out of all of this ontological confusion Blixen's answer to the problem of *being* (a woman, a white woman, an aristocratic white woman) is to assume the role, to open her text with "I," where "I" is simply (apparently) someone who "had" something, not someone who is or was something.

All these paradoxical binarisms—black/white, slave/slave owner, male/female, art/nature, integrity/duality, intimacy/distance, etc.—stand as a composite emblem of the confusion of Blixen's own identity just as emphatically as the spectacular self-presentations Aiken describes. Axel's conclusions regarding slaves and slave owners seem clearly to be explanations and exonerations of Blixen's own behavior in regard to her African servants (especially Farah) and later to her secretary, Clara Svendsen, whose devotion to Blixen involved a complex abandonment and adoption of roles. Frequently in *Out of Africa* and *Shadows on the Grass,* Blixen presents herself as the slave owner humbly at the mercy of her slaves, simultaneously affirming and denying the voluntarism of that apparently symbiotic relationship, much as Orwell presents himself as given no option but to shoot his famous elephant.[4]

To put it as clearly as possible, "The Invincible Slave-Owners" suggests that, for Blixen, being a woman depends as much on performance of class and race as it does on performance of gender and sexuality and that those categories are inextricably interwoven. It is possible to take Joan Riviere's idea of the *sub*consciously motivated masquerade literally, with Blixen's various performances as woman, as white woman, and as aristocratic white woman all resting very self-consciously on illusions which she, like Mizzi, deliberately maintains and which she is able to maintain through the collaboration of her servants. As Jean Walton argues, however, the "masquerade" of femininity is more complex in its relation to blackness than Riviere's original analysis of it as propitiatory to masculinity claimed, because the real black men on whom the illusion depended occupied a position in colonial Kenyan society much more tenuous than her own. Her servants Farah and Kamante were not just "men who took her seriously as a person and worker. . . . They had to. Their livelihood and that of their families required it" (Horton 210). On a farm that was never economically viable—as Blixen admits at the opening of the section "Hard Times," it "was a little too high up for growing coffee" (*Out of Africa* 275)—it might be argued that Blixen's playing the role of farmer was just as economically desperate as Farah's and Kamante's, but, however reluctantly, she always had somewhere else to go back to.

While I believe it is true that Blixen and Schreiner would fit Riviere's pattern of women who, at least intermittently, masqueraded as women, their attitudes toward masks, role-playing, seeming, and being are radically different. There was, for Blixen, a moral and practical imperative to seem what she was; for Schreiner, there was a moral and practical imperative to be what she seemed. In a famous exchange in 1889 between Schreiner and Oscar Wilde, Schreiner claimed that she was living in the East End of London "because that is the only place where people do not wear masks upon their faces." Wilde, whose love of paradox matched Blixen's, retorted, "I live in the West End because nothing in life interests me except the mask" (cited in First and Scott 186).

The contrast between Schreiner's earnest drive for perfect integrity and candor and Blixen's homage to the willed integrity dependent on a good sense of art can best be illustrated by comparing the role-playing of Mizzi, Miss Rabe, and Axel in "The Invincible Slave-Owners" with the transvestism of Gregory Rose in *The Story of an African Farm.* Those who play roles in Blixen's fiction achieve the heroic stoicism of grand tragedy; in Schreiner's fiction, role players are figures of comedy or contempt (in addition to Rose, there is the con man Bonaparte Blenkins, the socially aspirant Mrs. Snappercaps in *Undine,* and the superficially demure and sweet Veronica Grey in *From Man to Man*).

However, it is the very nature of paradox to collapse opposite terms into each other, and in the same way that the truth about Dorian Gray's picture—justly illustrating his moral turpitude—undercuts Wilde's subversive claims for the truth of masks and even for his dismissal of morality as a criterion for judging art, so Gregory Rose's assumption of femininity actually seems to tell the inner truth about him, thus undercutting Schreiner's apparent faith in personal integrity. What would it mean in gender terms, for instance, for Gregory Rose to be himself? For a start, the "English rose" should be a girl—fair of face, speech, and demeanor. Schreiner depicts the Englishman Rose as living up to his name, and repeatedly feminizes him in *African Farm* even before she has him experience "womanhood" when he masquerades as a nurse to the dying Lyndall. The apparel all too aptly proclaims the (wo)man; the performed gender is truer than the real.

To set him in context, though, Rose first appears as a fresh-faced young English emigrant employed slightly grudgingly on Tant' Sannie's farm, rather like the young Englishman Tony Marston in *The Grass Is Singing.*[5] When we first encounter him, he is unaccountably depressed. Although there is a "rack for a gun" on the wall of his little dwelling, he is clearly no man of action, and he relieves his depression through writing—on pink paper—a letter to his sister. The house is "scrupulously neat and clean, for Gregory kept a little duster folded in the corner of his table-drawer, just as he had seen his mother do, and every morning before he went out he said his prayers, and made his bed, and dusted" (174). The reference to Rose's mother bears interesting similarities with Schreiner's strategic idealization of mothers elsewhere in her work, notably in *Trooper Peter Halket of Mashonaland,* where Peter's mother is associated with Christ and Peter's conscience (32, 36, 47), and *An English South African's View of the Situation,* where Victoria—queen and em-press—is invoked as a kind of great white Mother whose hand would strike no child (102).[6]

For the moment, however, I would like to examine another "feminine" presence in the room, "a little hanging looking-glass." Gregory's depression is linked through the word *reflection* with introspection, "female" vanity, and narcissism. As he begins to put pen to paper "he looked up into the little glass opposite. It was a youthful face reflected there, with curling brown beard and hair; but in the dark blue eyes there was a look of languid longing that touched him" (175). The "but" is significant in that last sentence as it presents the brown beard, a token of masculinity, as being in contrast to languor and longing. In other words, there is something "feminine" in Gregory that his "masculine" beard cannot mask. Indeed, he is acutely conscious of notions of manliness and unmanliness, rejecting his first attempt at writing to his sister and cutting a reference to himself looking at himself. He does so, "reflecting" that it might seem "conceited or unmanly to be looking at his own face" (175).

Gregory's narcissism is intriguing for at least two reasons: It seems to anticipate a familiar trope and marker of the Decadents/Decadence, and it also exposes the peculiarly complex affinities created by homosocially defined English notions of "manliness." On the wall of his little house Gregory has pasted prints from the *Illustrated London News* "in which there was a noticeable preponderance of female faces and figures" (174). Like a boarding school boy, in his study Gregory Rose gazes alternately at images of women and of his bearded but "feminine" self. Olive Schreiner entitles the chapter in which this occurs "Gregory Rose Finds His Affinity," where the "affinity" superficially refers to Rose's "courtship" of Em. However, it seems to me that we should see the affinity as being a recognition that the images of the women on his wall, the image of Em, and the image of his own face are not alternatives but samenesses. They are his own true but shaming mask.

Rose's apparent shame at this unmanly affinity reveals itself in his comments on his fellow-male, Waldo. Waldo's being kissed by Em brings out all of Gregory's snobberies as well as his jealousy of Waldo's easy masculinity: "He's only a servant of the Boer-woman's," Rose writes to his sister, "and a low, vulgar, uneducated thing, that's never been to boarding-school in his life" (176). Later, when Gregory has transferred his affections to Lyndall, he is further jealous of Waldo because of the place Waldo holds in *her* heart. He attempts to denigrate Waldo to

Lyndall by calling him a "soft" (230), a phrase that recalls an earlier state-ment that "If a man lets a woman do what he doesn't like, *he's a muff*" (207).

However, it is the boarding school–educated Gregory whom Lyndall has *always* considered feminized, describing him as a "true woman—one born for the sphere that some women have to fill without being born for it" (197). To Em, Lyndall suggests Gregory has never come to full man-hood, claiming he's one of the category of men "you never see without thinking how very nice they must have looked when they wore socks and pink sashes" (183). Since Lyndall seems to be such a clear mouthpiece for Schreiner's own rebellious feminism, Lyndall's contempt for Rose tends to override the rebellious potential of his breach of gender boundaries. The female clothing helps him to no new affinity with other women nor to a gender fluidity that could continue to work to destabilize the status quo. He is not the New Man destined to accompany the New Woman into the utopian future Schreiner posits at the end of *Woman and Labour*. Rather, as a woman, finally—specifically as a serving woman, and a serv-ing woman serving another woman—Gregory achieves only some sort of self-stabilizing answer to his agonized narcissistic question, "Am I, am I Gregory Nazianzen Rose?" (270).

The narcissism of Rose's dressing-up can be stressed by comparing its private nature, surreptitiousness, and secrecy with the public nature of Axel Leth's performance. As with Leth, it would be possible to see Rose's transformation as an act driven by love. It is not, however, possible to see it as love*making*, and the only person privy to it as a declaration is him-self. Whereas the tension of Axel's walk of a hundred paces gains its erotic tension from the fact that Mizzi *knows* Frantz must really be Axel, through having Lyndall assume Rose is exactly who he says he is (that is, a woman!), Schreiner removes virtually all eroticism from his ministra-tions, intimate though they are. In one extraordinary instance, for ex-ample, "She made Gregory turn open the bosom of her nightdress that the dog might put his black muzzle between her breasts." When he has done so, Gregory simply "left them lying there together" (274) without, apparently, another thought in the world.

In addition to this, while Axel employs an old tailor and theater dresser to help him in his disguise (even if he hides his true motivation for it), and while the success of the disguise depends on his being under public scrutiny *together with* Mizzi, Rose performs his transformation alone and is scared of being seen at all. Rose makes sure that he is "out of sight of the waggons [sic]" before heading across the open veld to "a deep gully which the rain torrents had washed out, but which was now dry. Gregory sprang down into its red bed. It was a safe place, and quiet" (270). When he has safely effected his change, he looks around "like a sinner hiding his deed of sin." In line with the contempt displayed by Lyndall for him, he appears to find something at least potentially shameful in his actions.

Ultimately, while Axel's experience allows him to return to reality with an artistic ideal of his "paradoxal mode of existing, a poised, classic, static flight and run," Rose appears to gain nothing at all from his experience. Despite the potential promise of marriage to Em, he is simply emasculated. We last see him back at the farm "with his dead pipe lying on the bench beside him, and his blue eyes gazing out far across the flat, like one who sits on the sea-shore watching that which is fading, fading from him" (294). He should be what he seems, a woman, but as he cannot be that, he is nothing.

We can extend these contrasts with their reversed and self-reversing paradoxes to Schreiner and Blixen themselves and their self-inventions: Schreiner wanting the candor of masklessness to allow herself and others an "impersonal" existence, Blixen preferring the mask of art. Against the artful image of Blixen's various pictorial (self)-representations, we might pose Havelock Ellis's apparently artless memorial image of Olive Schreiner "coming suddenly and quite naked out of the bathroom in the house where I was staying into the sitting-room where I was waiting for her, to expound to me at once some idea which had just occurred to her, apparently unconscious of all else" (cited in First and Scott 136).[7]

That display of candor fits what Horton calls "Schreiner's need to confess—to be *exposed*" (48), but what truth is exposed—of selfhood, of womanhood, of whiteness—is, to cite Wilde again, never plain and rarely simple. The camera is never quite candid, the "I" never quite one.

The Whites of Their "I"s: Miming Alterity
from Positions of Racial Power

While Schreiner's and Blixen's fiction tends to render whiteness invisible, their nonfiction, in having to respond to the presence of actual black people, makes it visible. Closer analysis of their inventions of themselves as women in the specific context of their contemporary racial situations shows how illusory the idea of any singular subject-position actually is. When they pronounce their "I"s, they cannot do so simply as women but must inevitably speak as white women. Ultimately, I would argue, they owed their ability to speak as "I," both of and for themselves and others, to their whiteness. Indeed, the almost exclusively European audience of both writers attests that their self-inventions are as white as the whitest "I."

We must probe further, therefore, what it meant to be a white woman in colonial Africa and how limited the range of any such meaning might have been. In her book *Beyond the Pale,* Vron Ware attempts "to unravel the different meanings of white womanhood ... searching for significant moments in the past which would explain how this category was produced" (xii); Ware's search takes her East from the colonial center to India, and West to the United States, rather than South to Kenya and South Africa, but her focus on nineteenth-century racism and imperialism and their effects on the present makes her work apposite to the present study. In her analysis of the career of Annette Ackroyd as a schoolteacher in India and of Catherine Impey as an antilynching activist in Britain, for instance, Ware shows the conflicting pressures on white women that made it difficult for them to find a coherent feminist position that might embrace women of color without either imposing a Eurocentric set of values or facilitating racially prejudicial attacks on their culture.

Ware's concentration on the last quarter of the nineteenth century—when Schreiner was active and Blixen was growing up—highlights a period in English history when the very notions of "Englishness," of race, nation, and the connections between them were hugely problematical. Robert Young's book *Colonial Desire: Hybridity in Theory, Culture, and Race* starts from the premise that "Fixity of identity is only sought in situations of instability and disruption, of conflict and change" (4), and argues that what we now tend to see as the fixity of late Victorian Englishness was, in fact, anything but fixed.[8] Thus, Young and Ware are interested in the way in which a dominant imperialist ideology, anxious about its own entropic effects,[9] could create a stabilizing idea of Englishness, specifically bringing it about that white women were "seen as the 'conduits of the essence of the race'" (Ware 37). Both writers recognize that, in the same way that women were frequently put on a pedestal as "purer" than men, sexually speaking, so they also came to be seen as "purer" racially. The English woman (understood as white) thus becomes a figure of intense anxiety, a hyper-vulnerable category to be protected at all costs from black crime and desire, and whose putative purity—both sexually and racially speaking—creates tremendous difficulties for coherent feminist and antiracist practice.

Of course, neither Blixen nor Schreiner is coherently and consistently feminist and antiracist, and their mainly critical positions regarding mainstream British imperialist ideology are complicated by the fact that Blixen is Danish and Schreiner, with her German father, is not quite English, so that any national-cum-racial inventions of themselves should question the very nature of nation and of race. We have already seen some of the effects of this in Schreiner's invention of the all-white "English South African" (rhetorically figured as male). Looking at Schreiner's and Blixen's references to black characters (real and fictional) sheds further light on the extent to which these rebellious women were able to transcend the racial anxieties of their times. In particular, it allows us to see how the desexualization of the racial contact zone works not just to create a viable subject position but also to sidestep the very possibility of interracial desire and hybridization.

Black characters in *The Story of an African Farm* are presented as peripheral. In *Out of Africa* they play a larger role but almost exclusively as loyal servants to Europeans or within their own separate communities. To the extent that nothing in either work suggests the apparently separate racial spheres are under threat sexually, it appears that mainstream ideology of total racial difference was so deeply embedded in the two writers as to make the idea of miscegenation virtually unthinkable. The absence of the stereotypical figures of sexually threatening black men and sexually vulnerable white women might suggest that Schreiner and Blixen are less racist than mainstream imperialist ideology. On the other hand, any apparent difference between their attitudes and those of mainstream imperialism is perhaps allied to Horton's claim that being in Africa allowed Schreiner and Blixen to claim "honorary male" status, a status heightened by the two women's resistance to conventional family and married life. Part of it, too, might be the result of the relative novelty of specifically English colonization of South and East Africa at the time of Schreiner's and Blixen's experience there, as well as that intraracial sense of alterity that they felt as daughter of a German father among Boers and as a Dane among the British. Then again, in Blixen's case in particular, the sense of class superiority seems to have overridden any assumption of special vulnerability arising from the fact of being a "white woman." In fact, it is easier to show the mainstream racist attitude Ware describes in more canonical works of fiction—from *Heart of Darkness* where Conrad's Marlow insists on "the women" being "out of it" (84) or *A Passage to India* where Adela's accusations against Aziz lead to the British all rallying around to "the banner of race" when the Collector, almost choking with emotion, refers to her as "an English girl fresh from England" (Forster 165). Later, we shall see the apogee of this attitude in *The Grass Is Singing*, where Mary Turner, whom the entire white community has ostracized as a "poor white," is "furious" that a black farm laborer she has just struck with a whip "had the right to complain against the behavior of a white woman" (Lessing 136). All of these "white women" are presented as being far more dependent on men than any of Schreiner's heroines or Blixen's autonomous "I" of *Out of Africa.*

If not exactly in the mainstream, though, there is no denying the racial attitudes of Schreiner and Blixen. While *Woman and Labour* nods in the direction of recognizing the global exploitation of women—as tea-pickers, for example (208)—the "we" of whom Schreiner writes as a representative are highly racialized as women not just of European origin but specifically of pre-Christian Teutonic origin, "women who were never bought and never sold; that wore no veil, and had no foot bound" and whose "racial ideal was no Helen of Troy . . . but that Brynhild whom Segurd found . . . the warrior maid" (147).[10] As Robert Young shows, this location of a Germanic source of the essence of Englishness was fairly prevalent in England, at least from Thomas Arnold on (Young 67), but Schreiner's formulation of womanhood is particularly noteworthy in that she too talks about a *racial* ideal, suggesting that for her, too, women were the "conduits of the essence of the race," never merely female.

In addition, it should be noted that "Europe" for Karen Blixen generally means Northern Europe. Mediterranean Europe is associated with "the South." She sets this distinction up very early in *Out of Africa*: "Those old milords who figure in the history and fiction of the eighteenth century, as constantly traveling in Italy, Greece, and Spain, had not a single southern trait in their nature, but were drawn and held by the fascination of things wholly different from themselves" (24).[11] Furthermore, that fascination is set up as analogous to sexual desire: "The love of woman and womanliness is a masculine characteristic, and the love of man and manliness a feminine characteristic, and there is a susceptibility to the southern countries and races that is a Nordic quality. . . . As it is almost impossible for a woman to irritate a real man, and as to the women, a man is never quite contemptible, never altogether rejectable, as long as he remains a man, so were the hasty red-haired northern people infinitely long-suffering with the tropical countries and races" (24). In both women we thus find a near equation of "race" and "nation." We also find that near equation couched in the language of reproduction and heterosexual desire.

The desire of North for South, however, remains only analogous to heterosexual desire and—explicitly at least—does not trouble the assumption in both writers of the greater determinedness of racial boundaries than of gender boundaries. In some of her earliest letters from Africa, Blixen blithely remarks that the absence of "social problems" (*Letters* 5, 8) in British East Africa results from the absence of intermarriage, which in turn depends on the various "races differ[ing] too much for any intermixture to take place" (5).[12] Thus, although Blixen never states that the races should remain as clearly delimited as she assumed they were, she comes perilously close, and there is certainly no positive recommendation for the meeting of the twain. In her writing about the future of marriage (whether in letters or in *On Modern Marriage*), Blixen is somewhat ambivalent about the benefits that birth control will bring to modern women. There is no ambivalence, however, in her repeatedly returning to the idea that what will take the place of "love" as a basis for marriage is some form of eugenics.[13] Similarly, as First and Scott point out, Schreiner's elevation of the role of motherhood did not in itself put her at odds with the eugenic theories of contemporary imperialists (including Schreiner's friend Karl Pearson), who, confronted with a declining birthrate in late nineteenth-century England, were concerned "for the next generation of soldiers and workers" (First and Scott 277), and saw the health of that generation as dependent on its "true" Englishness.

Likewise, in Schreiner's fiction one can find ample examples that implicitly or explicitly support notions of racial "purity." In *Undine*, for instance, there is one particularly obnoxious description of a "swell nigger," a servant of Albert Blair, who speaks "in very good English and in a very leisurely and self-possessed manner" (350). This servant affects disdain for Undine—at this point in the story working as an ironing woman in New Rush (Kimberley)—but the affectation is exposed by his rapid pocketing of the five shilling payment she refuses, and it is while he is out spending that five shillings that Albert Blair, the object of Undine's unrequited love, dies. This episode is highly racist in its apparently paradoxical suggestions that the assumption of English dress and speech are corrupting and yet at the same time unable to hide an essential shiftlessness. Here is the quintessential "cheeky" native all too familiar in racist discourse, damned for being different, damned for attempting to be the same.

For Blixen, difference is usually more positively rendered; indeed, the Masai she idealizes thoroughly, declaring them to be "unswervingly true to their own nature, and to an immanent ideal" (*Shadows* 17), and the Somali, similarly, are rendered as ever the same: "a chivalrous nation" (*Out of Africa* 155), "a fighting race," "wiry people, hardened in deserts and on the sea" (158), and so on. Judith Thurman writes that the Masai attracted Blixen because of their "Nietzschean allure" (120), and there is clearly a huge amount of projection in her description, not only of the Masai but of almost all the Africans in her memoirs. The section entitled "The Somali Women" not only contains such projection but is also the most female-identified portion of *Out of Africa*, and thus sheds light on Blixen's complex self-invention as a white woman in Africa.

Admitting that generally "In my life at the farm I saw few women" (158), Blixen records that she frequently spent time with the Somali women in quiet conversation; in other words, this was one situation in which she was not openly in a position of mastery.[14] Artfully using *style indirect libre* to reproduce the tenor of those conversations, Blixen expounds on the huge respect for women implied by the Somali custom of bride-price and compares it unfavorably with European customs of marriage in which nations "gave away their maidens to their husbands for nothing" and where "there was one tribe so depraved as to pay the bridegroom to marry the bride" (157). She goes on to mythologize "the mother" of the Somali women—never blessed with a name and whom she initially compares to a "female elephant" (158)—as the symbol of a "great ideal . . . the idea of a Millennium when women were to reign supreme in the world. The old mother at such times would take on a new shape, and sit enthroned as a massive dark symbol of that mighty female deity who had existed in old ages" (159). Here she comes close to Schreiner's theoretical apotheosis of the mother figure both in *African*

Farm—"We bear the world and we make it," says Lyndall (193)—and in *Woman and Labour*, where, reproducing that idea of womanhood as the conduit of the essence of the race, she declares that "with each generation the entire race passes through the body of its womanhood as through a mold" (131).

Blixen, however, is less interested ultimately in the worship of women as mothers than she is in the worship of women as lovers. In a paragraph that ostensibly deals with Somali warriors' respect for "their" women, Blixen clearly projects her understanding of her own relationship with Denys Finch Hatton, whom she repeatedly holds up—as she holds up the Somali—as a model of the chivalric code. The Somali husband, she says, is

> abstinent by nature, indifferent to food and drink and to personal comfort, hard and spare as the country he comes from: woman is his luxury. For her he is insatiably covetous, she is to him the supreme good of life: horses, camels, and stock may come in and be desirable too, but they can never outweigh the wives. The Somali women encourage their men in both inclinations of their nature. They scorn any softness in a man with much cruelty; and with great personal sacrifices they hold up their own price. (159)

In a sentence echoing the complex slave/slave owner rhetoric we examined earlier, Blixen goes on to describe "the young girls who had no men to squeeze, in their little tent-like house . . . making the most of their pretty hair and looking forward to the time when they should be conquering the conqueror, and extorting from the extortioner" (160). Blixen's own pride in her household as a suitably feminized place for the lean and hungry wanderer Finch Hatton to return to after his safaris, and her comparison of herself to Scheherazade telling tales to the Sultan Denys spring to mind here.

Unusually, however, the self-identification with the Somali women is made explicit (or very nearly so) when Blixen says that at the great religious celebrations the Somali women

> so reminded me of the ladies of a former generation of my own country, that in my mind I saw them in bustles and long narrow trains. Not otherwise did the Scandinavian women of the days of my mother and grandmothers—the civilized slaves of good-na-

tured barbarians—do the honours at those tremendous sacred masculine festivals: the pheasant-shoots and great *battues* of the autumn season. (161)

That phrase, "the civilized slaves of good-natured barbarians," is redolent
of so much. It confuses boundaries of race, nation, and gender in a way
unusual to *Out of Africa*, it prompts questions of legitimacy of control,
and it introduces ideas of invasion and occupation. Technically the
"slaves" are women—Somali and Scandinavian—while the "barbarians"
are their men, so the comparison is apparently between two distinct and
discrete cultures the structure of whose male-female relationships is
similar. So far, so clear. But reading the sentence as a projection confuses
the issue. Karen Blixen's being a woman leads one to read the sentence as
a projection of her *own* ideal of male-female relationships based on a no
less distinct and discrete set of gender differences. However, given that
barbarian slave owners would normally be invaders, one cannot help but
also associate Blixen the white colonist with the barbarians, or invaders.
Her idealization of various Africans contrasted with the barbarous bureaucracy of colonial Kenya certainly supports such an identification.[15]
In other words, we might conclude that as a white colonist Blixen thinks
of herself as both male (or involved in a male practice at least) and barbarian (though good-natured), whereas as a woman she thinks of herself as
female and consequently civilized but enslaved. As usual in *Out of Africa*, there is a good deal of self-exoneration in this apparent paradox—
not least in the addition of the adjective *good-natured*—but, more impor-
tantly, it shows how issues of race and gender overlap in the invention of
Karen Blixen's "I."

Such overlaps are only intermittently apparent. Most of the time,
Blixen works to keep gender and race as explicitly separate categories. For
instance, in a brief section of *Out of Africa* entitled "Of the two races,"
she again declares that the relation between male and female is analogous
to the relation between white and black, as if all four terms were wholly
adequate, distinct, and discrete. The point she attempts to make is that
men and women always overestimate their psychological importance in
the lives, respectively, of women and men, in exactly the same way that
blacks and whites overestimate their psychological importance in the
lives, respectively, of whites and blacks. This is a neat comparison and
certainly serves an antiracist, debunking purpose of deflating white folks'

sense of self-importance, but it doesn't begin to deal with the question of *power* relations as such, nor does it allow for the actual complexity of Blixen's own position as a white female employer of black men, a position, as we shall see in analysis of *The Grass Is Singing*, where the actual workings of heterosexual desire can upset any notions of the parallel distinctnesses of black/white male/female, and instead set them at odds with each other.

Unlike in Blixen's real-life masquerade of femininity, her writerly "playing the white" seems to mean "playing the white *man*,"[16] and in these instances she uses a masculine self-identification as another line of defense against any sexualization of the contact zone between black and white. Susan Horton shows how clearly Blixen lived and spoke different gender views according to racial and gender circumstance. In a speech written for an audience of African women, for instance, she could propound a conventional view of female passivity, declaring that a woman's value "lies with the opposite sex," and that while man is the "being who acts," the woman "has her center of gravity in what she is" (Horton 100). All her behavior, and her letters home to Denmark, however, reveal her operating according to a very different standard, presenting herself to her brother Thomas as someone deserving "the V.C. for my work here" (*Letters* 194; cited in Horton 101) no less than he deserved his V.C. during the war. Then again, in her relationship with Denys Finch Hatton—whose sexual availability is marked, among other things, by his nonfamily, non-African status—she plays a "hyperfeminine persona," using "feminine wiles aimed at keeping Denys attending to her" (Horton 101). She can masquerade as Scheherazade, the seductive Oriental woman, only among white men; at other times, the mask of masculinity preserves her status as a working rather than a sexual being.[17]

Schreiner's *Woman and Labour*, as its very title might suggest, attempts to reintegrate this splitting of the subject, but in her work, too, there is little suggestion that cross-racial desire could disrupt the separateness of the power structures of black/white female/male relations. *Woman and Labour*, in fact, contains a passage which suggests that such a situation was virtually unthinkable for Schreiner. Arguing that races and classes are in "totally distinct stages of evolution," she declares that "the lowest form of sex attraction can hardly cross" the evolutionary gap. She then goes on to imagine what would happen were one "to place a company of the most highly evolved human females—George Sands,

Sophia Kovalevskys, or even the average cultured females of a highly evolved race—on an island where the only males were savages of the Fuegan type," and concludes that "it is an undoubted fact that, so great would be the horror felt by the females towards them, that not only would the race become extinct, but if it depended for its continuance on any approach to sex affection on the part of the women, death would certainly be accepted by all, as the lesser of two evils" (261–62). Likewise, "A Darwin, a Schiller, a Keats . . . would probably be untouched by any emotion but horror, cast into the company of a circle of Bushmen females" (262).

Blixen uses an almost identical argument in one of her longest and most impassioned letters to her brother Tommy. It is the letter in which she aligns herself with Lucifer and talks about true piety as "loving one's destiny unconditionally," and it is profoundly bound up with her attempt to make sense of who she is in light of professional pressure arising from her *shauries* (troubles) on the farm and personal pressure concerning her presumed miscarriage earlier in the year (1926). Part of the argument hinges on the way in which certain circumstances actually make it impossible to "be oneself"—for instance, if one were an actor without a stage, a violinist without hands, or a mathematics professor "among savages on a desert island" (*Letters* 283). This last image was originally Tommy's, but it clearly struck a chord with Blixen, as she comes back to it in a letter, also concerned with the question of being oneself, to her mother two years later. "One must be in contact with one's surroundings," she writes, "so that a professor of mathematics on a desert island or among the Hottentots or la belle Otero among Russian Dukhobors with the best will in the world *cannot* manage to be themselves, or to be anything at all" (*Letters* 375).

Blixen's and Schreiner's use of Hottentots and Bushmen as representatives of the very bottom rung of human evolution, furthest removed from the fine arts and pure science, is indicative of the pervasiveness of racialized science in the late nineteenth and early twentieth centuries. Schreiner's use of the Fuegans and of Charles Darwin is particularly rich (in the slang as well as conventional sense) because Darwin had actually come into contact with Fuegans in his voyage on the Beagle, and at the very time Schreiner was writing *Woman and Labour* the Fuegans were indeed dying out, not as the result of any sexual and reproductive failure but through their being hunted and poisoned by not very good-natured white barbarians. The Bushmen and Hottentots, too, had been victims of white genocide, even at times having been hunted as "vermin."

As figures of fascinating horror to "civilized" Europeans, the alleged sexual repulsiveness of the Fuegans, Bushmen, and Hottentots clearly figures largely as a justification for their destruction; they cannot even be left on their own once colonial contact has been made.[18] To be sure, Schreiner emphasizes that there are intraracial hiatuses just as wide as the pair she uses as extreme examples. But it seems that in indicating cultural difference the leap is more or less automatically to racial difference. For the dominant Victorian sensibility, transcultural sexuality becomes more horrifying when it is recognizably transracial. And when the very possibility of transracial sexuality appears, the response of nineteenth-century white colonists was generally to repress it as completely as possible, not just by denying that it happened but by policies of genocide, apartheid, or any combination of the two.

In her analysis of Blixen's and Schreiner's gender identification, Susan Horton picks up Fanon's idea of the mime, of the black person wanting "not to be white but to be 'black' as white imagines black to be," and she suggests that Blixen and Schreiner "mimed" being women in this way:

> Dinesen in her exaggerated femininity and Schreiner in the woman persona constructed for European male correspondents are instances of woman *miming* "woman" in the way Michael Taussig describes in *Mimesis and Alterity*, each producing "a 'nature' that culture uses to create second nature." (104)

Horton's reference to Taussig establishes a general point, but Taussig's specific interest in the mutual observation and mimicry of Fuegan Indians and the crew of the *Beagle* allows us to look closer at Schreiner's representation of transracial sexual repulsion and Blixen's representation of cultural differences.

Taussig presents the encounters between Darwin and the Fuegans in 1832 as a paradigmatic scene of "First Contact" between the European medical-scientific objective observer and his supposed non-European antithesis. Taussig's account is a complex component of his argument that we should see the mimetic as "curiously baseless, so dependent on alterity that it lies neither with the primitive nor with the civilized, but in the windswept and all too close, all too distant, mysterious-sounding space of First Contact" (72). Even if we accept the baselessness and apparent mutuality of the contact, of mimesis and alterity, certain material differences—whether between Darwin and the Fuegans or Schreiner and Blixen and colonized Africans—mean that *power* relations are necessarily asymmetrical. First, we should note that the observing gaze is male or male-aligned. Second, we should note that while mimicry might appear to be confusingly mutual, physical objects and ownership cannot be so easily swapped. Taussig implies this in his section entitled "The Spirit of the Gift, the Spirit of the Mime" when he writes, "You can imitate a sailor pulling faces, but you can't so easily or convincingly imitate his buttons or knife of steel" (93). However, his explicit aim is to establish that in a world of perfect equality, "there is indeed an intimate bond between the spirit of the gift and the spirit of the mime" (93).

The first point highlights the extent to which as a recorder of her life on the farm at Ngong, Blixen is in a tradition of travel writing generally assumed to be documentary and objective (however subjective her work may actually be), a tradition that generally depends on the gaze of a male subject. Furthermore, that male subject is aloof from his own desire and never represents himself as desired, even though he is both desirable and capable of acting on his desires. The second point confirms my earlier claim that although Blixen's comparison of the relations between the races and the sexes may from time to time appear to reverse that gaze, in its very claim to reciprocity it misses the material point that power relations between the sexes and between the races she represents are not equal.

In other words, Blixen is able to mime woman successfully, precisely because she is in Africa where European colonization has left "swell niggers" only two choices: to fail at miming whiteness, or to "succeed" in miming the blackness of a nature before culture, without civilization. However sympathetic Blixen or Schreiner may be toward Africans, then, their tendency to use Africans as foils facilitating their own self-invention ultimately results in patronizing reifications ("the Masai," or, in Schreiner, "my black people") which confirm that their subject position is still "the familiar one of the privileged possessor of the masculine gaze" (Horton 214). As with Axel Leth, who dons the clothes of a servant in order to learn the apparent truth that slave owners are dependent on their slaves, only to return to his former self and former privilege, so Blixen and Schreiner, although they may occasionally subvert conventional notions of hierarchy and the fixity of gender and racial identity, can only ever mime alterity from a position of power.

The Childless Mother and Motherless Child, or the Orphanhood of the White Woman Writer in Africa

> To be unhomed is not to be homeless, nor can the "unhomely" be easily accommodated in that familiar division of social life into private and the public spheres. . . . The unhomely is the shock of recognition of the world-in-the-home, the home-in-the-world.
>
> **Homi Bhabha**

In 1959 Nadine Gordimer posed a question—"Where do whites fit in?"—that might be seen as central not only to her work but also to the questions I have been raising about Schreiner and Blixen. Gordimer's answer to her own question depends on the understanding that the idea of home is an invention, that it depends on "the emotional decision that home is not necessarily where you belong ethnogenetically, but rather the place you were born to" (*Essential Gesture* 34). So far I have attempted to set Schreiner's and Blixen's self-inventions in the very broad contexts of race, class, and gender, looking at their oscillating sense of identification and alterity in relation to the world at large. Now I want to turn to the apparently narrower context of the family and examine their sense of self in the homes to which they were born. And, predictably enough given my use of Bhabha in the epigraph above, I point to the ultimate inextricability of world and home.[1] Indeed, this chapter indicates how Schreiner's and Blixen's struggles with normative, gendered roles within the family cannot totally free them from charges of complicity with European master-narratives that are also, in their specific historical and geographical locations,[2] narratives of the master. In particular, Blixen's and Schreiner's struggles against such roles within the (white) family need to be set against the struggles of African women whose family structures, already different from those of Europeans, were terribly disrupted by racialized colonial rule. In order to demonstrate the continuing urgency of these issues, this chapter goes on to describe similar struggles in contemporary South Africa, among writers who have attempted to counter the violence of race-based politics by moving toward a more inclusive, woman-centered humanism. Among the plethora of stories emerging from the Truth and Reconciliation Commission (TRC) and from formal autobiographies in the 1990s, the voices of women have emerged strongly—so strongly, in fact, that Susanne Klausen comments in her review of the award-winning TRC documentary *Long Night's Journey into Day* that "African mothers emerge as the moral centre of the TRC process. Perhaps, . . . these women are the moral centre of South Africa as a whole." As in the "rememory" project of Toni Morrison's *Beloved*,[3] so in anti-apartheid and post-apartheid South African writing, women writers like Nadine Gordimer and Ingrid de Kok, for instance, have used potent familial images of motherhood to draw attention to the way in which reconceiving the self in the white family and remembering the splintered black family might help to reintegrate or reconcile the nation.[4]

In addition to the oscillations of identification and alterity that we have already looked at, we might add a further pair of split senses: of Schreiner and Blixen as mothers/not-mothers and orphans/not-orphans. Put another way, they appear to oscillate between inventions of themselves as beings whose roles are defined respectively by a sense of connectedness and by a sense of detachment. "Mothers qua mothers," writes Nancy Huston, "must be 'other-oriented'; they embody connectedness and attachment. Novelists qua novelists must be selfish; they demand for themselves disconnectedness and detachment" (711). Thus, the woman writer experiences a particular gender-specific struggle when she decides to be a writer, a role which conflicts with socially constructed expectations of motherhood, homemaking, and family life.

As we saw at the end of chapter 2, the feminist motivations behind Schreiner's and Blixen's thinking on motherhood and marriage led to texts (*Woman and Labour* and *On Modern Marriage*) that could be read as quite the opposite of emancipatory, instead feeding an imperialist and eugenicist anxiety about racial purity, about degeneration and/or the sterility that was believed to result from hybridity. Furthermore, the attempted rebelliousness of Schreiner's feminist elevation of the status of motherhood could appear ironically to support conformist movements such as the Church of England Mothers' Union, dedicated as they were to a no less elevated ideal of motherhood which could restore a "high tone in the homes and people of this country" (cited in First and Scott 277). Motherhood, therefore, in producing future English soldiers and workers, and the ideal English home for them to grow up in, might be construed more as an imperialist practice than the emancipatory, feminist one Schreiner imagined.

But women are necessarily daughters before they are mothers, and we need to keep in play both directions of the parent-child relationship if we are to find how Schreiner and Blixen came to invent an "I" not just as white women in Africa but as white women *writers*. By assessing Blixen's and Schreiner's nonexperience/avoidance of those relationships through separation from a family home and actual childlessness, and by examining their fictional use of parentlessness, I hope to show that in the same way that actual loss of parents (or widowhood) allowed Victorian women writers, particularly travel writers, the autonomy to write (and travel), so orphanhood has consistently acted as a useful enabling metaphor for white women writers in Africa, whether native or not, from Schreiner, through Blixen, to Nadine Gordimer.[5]

Let us start, however, with biography. Olive Schreiner may have produced an idealized theoretical image of motherhood, but her actual reproductive history is bleak indeed. She had at least four miscarriages, and the only baby she carried to full term died the night after it was born. Schreiner was deeply attached to this dead baby and had it carried with her when she moved and reinterred with her in her tomb on Buffelskop. As with so much else, her fiction is uncannily prophetic in regard to her own childbearing; the deaths of Lyndall's and Undine's babies seems to foretell her own child's fate, while the five-year-old Rebekah's sleeping with Bertie's stillborn twin in *From Man to Man* matches Schreiner's keeping of the dead baby with her.

Blixen appears to have been (or to have thought she was) pregnant only twice, both pregnancies apparently ending in miscarriages (Thurman 174; 208–9). The second occasion, when Blixen was forty-one, prompted a terse exchange of telegrams in which the ever-chivalrous Denys Finch Hatton urged Blixen to "cancel Daniel's visit" ("Daniel" being their codeword for the pregnancy).[6] Blixen's disappointment, both in the pregnancy and in her lover, resulted in a long and openly feminist letter to her Aunt Bess (*Letters* 258–65) in which she expresses the fundamental desire to be judged according to universal standards of human decency. Feminism, she says, had already revolutionized European society (rightly so in her judgment), but continued attention to women's sexual morality indicated "to what a great extent women are regarded as sexual beings, to what a small extent as human beings" (*Letters* 263). Rather like Schreiner wishing to be considered Karl Pearson's "man-friend," she claims that modern women are more "gentlemanly" and that love between modern men and women might be described as "homosexual" in that it represents a human ideal of "sincere friendship, understanding, delight shared by two equal, 'parallel moving' beings" (264). To balance this praise of a parallel, "homosexual" relationship—an idealized version of her actual relationship with Finch Hatton?—a letter to her recently married brother Thomas reveals a rather different desire: "You know that I have said that I would like to be a Catholic priest, and I still maintain this—and I am not far from being one—but he would have to be more than human if he did not sometimes heave a deep sigh on seeing the lights lit in the windows and the family circles gathered together" (*Letters* 281–82). The images of the parallel line and the family circle perfectly catch the oscillations within Blixen between desires for detachment and attachment. Lacking the generational attachment that children of their own would have brought, both Blixen and Schreiner at times played the role of mother with others who could be their children only in fantasy: Blixen being talked of, according to her servant Kamau, as the mother of the children on the farm, and Schreiner talking about her mother as if she were her own child.[7]

Furthermore, if we extend the idea of motherhood to include things one has brought into the world, both women's African farms become their children. In Blixen's letters from Africa, there is a notable progression from the first few years of assuming and fervently longing for a child, especially a male heir to take back the family estate of Dallund (*Letters* 16, 47, 55, 61), to considering the various children on the farm her own and writing that the farm itself was "a kind of child for me" (*Letters* 131). The similarly childless Schreiner, whose *African Farm* she once thought of as being appropriately titled "A Series of Abortions," is, perhaps paradoxically, the mother-novelist. Frequently in her letters she refers to the physiological strain of writing in terms that suggest a similarity between writing and giving birth. To Havelock Ellis, for instance, she writes that "artistic work takes the life-blood out of one" (*Letters* 50), and to Betty Molteno she reverses the analogy, writing that childbearing is "like writing a book—it may be a great labour and half kill you, but if you don't feel it's a great joy and bliss to suffer the agony of writing it, and a reward in itself, you're not fit to write it!!" (Rive 291). More than this, Schreiner is the mother-novelist because of her insistence on her work's mutual connectedness not just to her but to the world. Despite the motherless status of Undine and Lyndall, the novels themselves, having been written according to "the method of the life we all lead" (*African Farm* 27), might be said to have navels, their "severed umbilical cord[s] . . . evidence of a process that connects this being's present with its past" (Huston 713); they do not live in some other-worldly palace of art.

Without the capacity to be mothers, men are not confronted with quite the same choice between producing novels and reproducing navels. At a very obvious level, therefore, this issue seems to concern gender difference and the oscillatory gendering of Schreiner's and Blixen's "I," the woman who writes. Indeed, according to Frans Lasson, editor of Blixen's letters, the key to Blixen's becoming a writer and what "must have seemed to her to finally seal her fate as a woman: to be one who was unable to hold on to another person" (Letters xxiii), was her loss not just of the farm but also of Denys Finch Hatton and, with him, the possibility of a family. In Lasson's view, Blixen's agonized achievement of a writer's autonomy coincides with and even depends on her failure to be a woman who could "hold on to another person." Lasson's terms seem to exemplify the widely held gender distinction that women tend to be socialized into a sense of connectedness to others, and to confirm Regenia Gagnier's insight that the autonomous subjectivity of the nineteenth-century writer was gendered male, however "feminized" the sphere of writing may have become.[8] Most male writers would have felt neither the same sort of pressure to succeed both "as a man" and as a writer nor the same sort of conflict between those roles.

Likewise, Judith Lee uses terms highly reminiscent of Dinnerstein and Chodorow when *she* spells out the dilemma facing the woman artist. In her essay "The Mask of Form in *Out of Africa*," she presents Blixen as believing that "since [woman] has always existed in a world in which there is someone else, she can only be herself in relationship to an other, specifically to a man; at the same time, she can fulfill her nature as an autonomous being only by acting out an identity that is not available to her and which she must imagine" (Lee 268) That identity which must be imagined into existence combines the detached autonomy of the writer/ orphan with the connectedness of the woman/mother; it is what puts navels in novels.

In these terms, then, we might raise the question as to how much Schreiner's and Blixen's work is phallogocentric and how much it obeys, rather, the law of the mother. Balancing the linear male law of the phallus might be the circular female principle of the omphalos.[9] In this light, the two women's choice of pseudonyms and other self-naming is fascinating. Retaining the patronymic, as Blixen did in her pseudonym, Isak Dinesen, and as Schreiner did in keeping her "own" surname when married, makes it possible to make a case for pen- and penis-envy, arguing that in their literal use of the name-of-the-father they are reinscribing a phallogocentric order.[10] And Schreiner's pseudonym, Ralph Iron, with its homage to Emerson (supported by the naming of the characters Em and Waldo in *African Farm*) and its rigidly inflexible metal, emphasizes the male line of descent. However, Gerald Monsman suggests that Schreiner's "Iron" hints at "irony," and Blixen chooses "Isak" because it means "one who laughs," thus iron-izing the surname in her case, too. The irony is all the more apparent when we consider that it is the previously barren Sarah who names her son Isaac, and that the birth of Isaac means the displacement of Hagar and her son Ishmael. "To Sara it has been a divine joke, a postmenopausal miracle," writes Else Cederborg, "and so it was to Karen Blixen, who came home as the prodigal daughter, broke, ill, disillusioned, but who all the same could 'give birth' to a book and a new identity" (*On Modern Marriage* 14). That sense of irony might be linked to resistance to authority is an idea of long standing. For instance, Regenia Gagnier (citing Aristotle, Bergson, Eco, and Cixous) describes humor in general as occurring "when one sympathizes with a breaker of a rule or convention because one sees the contradiction between her and the frame she cannot comply with . . . humor reminds us of the presence of a law that we no longer have reason to obey" (*Subjectivities* 197).

In fact, insofar as both writers' work resists the linear law of the Father and produces instead the circularity and antilogos associated with écriture féminine, Susan Hardy Aiken argues that *Out of Africa*, in "elud[ing] all unitary generic classifications . . . forces a radical reorientation of traditional perspectives by calling into question conventions of reading that depend on a notion of the book as a figure of solidity, unity, linearity, and integrity" (13). And if, further, one describes Blixen's habitual use of the mise-en-abîme in her fiction as producing concentric circles, and Schreiner's use of tangential events as producing eccentric ones, the new term I have suggested—the omphalogocentric or navel-centered law of the mother—seems appropriate.[11]

It is certainly easy to see Schreiner's work in this light both in her fiction—in the naming of her central characters in *African Farm* (Lyndall) and *From Man to Man* (Rebekah) after her mother—and in her nonfiction. *Woman and Labour* elaborates on parts of Lyndall's feminist monologue in *African Farm* where she declares, "We bear the world and we make it" with the no less memorable lines "With each generation the entire race passes through the body of its womanhood as through a mold" (131), and "No man ever yet entered life farther than the length of one navel-cord from the body of the woman who bore him" (109). The image of the circle is there not just in the omphalos but in the *os cervix*, too: "As the *os cervix* of woman, through which the head of the infant passes at birth, forms a ring, determining for ever the size at birth of the human head, a size which could only increase if in the course of ages the *os cervix* of woman should itself slowly expand; . . . so exactly the intellectual capacity, the physical vigor, the emotional depth of woman, forms also an untranscendable circle, circumscribing with each successive generation the limits of the expansion of the human race" (*Woman and Labour* 131). While this statement appears essentialist in drawing attention to what Schreiner sees as the key biological difference between men and women (elsewhere she is generally very clear as to the constructed nature of gender) and while it would appear to be a very risky essentialism, potentially reconfining women to the domestic, Schreiner hammers away at the point that what she wants is a totally new order, one so utopian that an awareness of our shared having-been-mothered-ness makes war, for instance, an anachronism.[12] She wants to replace the restrictions of the Garden of Eden on the navel-less Adam with the openness of a new Garden in which the navelled "woman shall eat of the tree of knowledge together with man" (*Woman and Labour* 298).

However, the future female solidarity hymned in *Woman and Labour* and its attitude to motherhood is only a theoretical presence. Back in "the life we all lead"—that is, in Schreiner's fiction—it is glaringly absent. We have already seen how Lyndall's experience of motherhood, the loss of her child, and the loss of her own life depend on the absence of female friendship and support. The "successful" mother of *African Farm* is the grotesque figure of Tant' Sannie. In an age when death in childbirth was a high risk, when syphilis was rife, and when double standards of sexual behavior were enshrined in law, marriage was more likely to be fatal to women than to men. However, in Tant' Sannie—a woman so fat, it is as if it were not so much consumption that killed her second husband but *her* consumption of him—Schreiner creates a monstrous black widow figure. She is presented in a remorselessly satirical vein as stupid, capricious, and hypocritical. Neither the status she has as a property owner nor her dominance of men appears as a positive example of female empowerment. Instead, in her disrespect for men ("As for a husband, it's very much the same who one has") and her acceptance first of the consumptive Englishman and then of the puny "Little Piet Vander Walt," she embodies mere appetite. When she is first introduced, she is dreaming not of either of her two husbands but of the sheep's trotters she had eaten earlier that evening. Similarly, when Piet Vander Walt arrives for his "upsitting" with her, she tells of another dream: "of a great beast like a sheep, with red eyes, and I killed it. Wasn't the white wool his hair, and the red eyes his weak eyes, and my killing him meant marriage?" (201). The successful mother, in short, bears an uncanny resemblance to misogynistic (male) fantasies of (female) sexual voraciousness.

Under the rule of this wicked stepmother, the two English girls, Em and Lyndall, are grudgingly brought up in almost total isolation from life outside the farm. Em, who has some claims to the farm as a potential inheritrix, seems happy enough to wait until she is seventeen when she will be able to marry. But her "little orphan cousin" Lyndall, perspicacious and thirsty for knowledge, chafes miserably. Schreiner therefore sets up in this highly "uncoordinated 'family'" (du Plessis 21) twin "scripts" of bildung and romance, twin scripts that are ultimately inseparable. As we have seen from chapter 1, although Schreiner's sympathies are with Lyndall, the heroine of the bildung script, her novel is able to reward her transgression of the romance script only with death. Em, on the other hand, gets her reward of marriage but realizes its emptiness. Schreiner's "writing beyond the ending" is thus even more radically subversive of possible narrative outcomes for female characters in Victorian novels than Rachel Blau du Plessis suggests, for marriage and death are effectively no different: Either you get the erotic attachment that causes your physical death, or you get the psychic death of an empty marriage.

Such outcomes, as du Plessis points out, cause a violent "rupture of story," quite unlike the ending of that other novel of a female orphan's bildung and romance, *Jane Eyre*. The connections and dissimilarities between Jane's orphan status in that novel and Lyndall's orphan status in *African Farm* are revealing. In the former, Jane's orphanhood plays up the essentially conservative romance ending. As du Plessis has it: "Access to a fulfillment that reiterates the status quo is always facilitated by having a character begin so marginalized . . . that if a plot simply provides such a character with access to what must usually be taken for granted, the atmosphere of gratitude will finally impede any criticism from occurring. The critique of social conditions that orphans symbolize (poverty, vulnerability, exclusion) will be muted by the achievement of the blessed state of normalcy, so thrillingly different from deprivation. Through the mechanism of orphans, novels can present standard family, kinship, and gender relations as if these were a utopian ideal" (9). The ending of *African Farm*, by contrast, with Lyndall's deadly motherhood and Em's deadening marriage, both overshadowed by Tant' Sannie's consumption of men, resists *all* notions of normalcy. The orphan is not the oddity to be brought into the normal fold, but rather the very figure of a normal state of deprivation and alienation. Through the mechanism of orphans, Schreiner shows that "standard family, kinship, and gender relations" are not so much utopian as mere fictions of the "stage method" of painting human life that her preface abjures. Schreiner's refusal of the romance ending signals even more than "a dissent from social norms as well as narrative forms" (du Plessis 20); it indicates how fully she was aware that the latter construct the former.

That awareness is perhaps even more explicit in the intertextuality of *Undine* where Schreiner names her orphan heroine after a figure from German mythology. Undine, in the version by Friedrich de la Motte Fouqué, is no Cinderella with a fairy godmother, Prince Charming, and happily-ever-after. Instead, she is a capricious water nymph who gains a mortal soul by marrying a mortal man. However, she can only finally be released from immortality if that mortal man remains true to her. He does not, of course, and she is left with the burden of a soul that can be tormented for all eternity. It is an obscure, odd, and disturbing tale, presumably told to Schreiner by her father, just as in *African Farm* on "Long winter nights . . . the old man [Otto] had told of the little German village, where, fifty years before, a little German boy had played at snowballs" (54). The appeal of such a tale, though, to the multiply marginalized Schreiner lies less in its sentimental associations with her father than in its heroine's separation not just from parents but from her own rightful world. Whether as a freethinking teenage girl in a rigidly Protestant colony, as a New Woman *avant la lettre*, or as an English pro-Boer, she continually found herself or placed herself in a category of one, "addict[ed] to marginality" as Rachel Blau du Plessis has it (30).

Karen Blixen's version of the immortal fairy orphan unromantically adrift in the world of mortality is Alkmene. In the story of that name from *Winter's Tales*, the orphan-girl adopted by an otherwise childless parson and his wife establishes "a deep, silent understanding, of which the others could not know" with the local landowner's son, Vilhelm. In his narration of their relationship Vilhelm records: "We seemed, both of us, to be aware that we were like one another, in a world different from us. Later on I have explained the matter to myself by the assumption that we were, amongst the people of our surroundings, the only two persons of noble blood, and that hers was possibly, even by far, the noblest. In this manner, too, our companionship was mainly of the woods and fields; it became suspended, or latent, when we were back in the house" (202).

Judith Thurman calls the story "one of the most purely tragic and transparently autobiographical stories she ever wrote," and discerns in Vilhelm's and Alkmene's sense of difference from the rest of the world—especially the domestic—the "aristocracy of two" made by Wilhelm Dinesen and the young Karen (Thurman 31, 26). What makes the story tragic is its refusal of romance, in particular its turning the romance of Shakespeare's *The Winter's Tale* into tragedy. Alkmene is introduced to the parson's family as someone "singularly and tragically situated in life, so that indeed she might be named Perdita after the heroine of Shakespeare's tragedy" (194). But whereas *The Winter's Tale,* as all of Shakespeare's late romances, both brings the father and lost daughter together again, and perpetuates the cycle of generation by cementing the romance between daughter and male lover, Alkmene's orphanhood means that she can neither be reunited with a father—Blixen's lost Wilhelm—nor matched with an appropriate male suitor—Vilhelm.

Furthermore, Alkmene is not only passively "situated in life" in singular and tragic separation. She actively seeks such separation, twice running away from her adoptive parents. On the second occasion, when Vilhelm, who has gone to find her and bring her back to the parsonage, asks her why she wants to run away from people who love her, she replies: "What about the children, Vilhelm, who do not want to be loved?" (205). Far from being downhearted, as the parson's wife had desperately feared, when the parson informs her that she is adopted, Alkmene is "changed" in a way Gertrud considers positive. "She has come back to me," she says, "and keeps to me as sweetly as when she was a small girl. I myself feel young with it. I happened to look into the mirror today. You may laugh, but it was the face of a young woman that I saw there" (207). Although Gertrud does not recognize it, the burden of *obligation* to love has been removed. Later, when it is apparent that, despite their kindredness of spirit, Vilhelm and Alkmene are not meant for each other, Alkmene again suggests that the loving attention of uncongenial people is more of a burden than a blessing: "I want to ask you a question," I said. "Have you not known that I loved you all the time?" "Love?" she said. "They all loved Alkmene. You did not help her. Did you not know, now, all the time, that they were all against her, all?" (220). Above all, then, the orphan resists the stifling nature of "normal" family love. What Thurman says of Blixen is, I think true of Schreiner, too, that there is in her work and thinking "a frontier—more of a fixed circle like an embroidery hoop—that separates the wild from the domestic. Within it there is firelight and women's voices, the steam of kettles, the clockwork of women's lives. Beyond it there are passions, spaces, grandeurs; there lie the wildernesses and battlefields" (25).

What the two women fought for in their chosen battlefields were rather different, but the desire for exclusivity—the category of one, or the aristocracy of two, frequently allied with a sense of noble suffering—was similar.[13] The orphan, in her radical isolation, makes living itself an act of great risk, and, as Thurman says, the greatest gestures in such a life "have to do with that 'exquisite *savoir-mourir*' that Isak Dinesen also admired so deeply" (28).[14] Certainly, in "Alkmene" the moment of greatest hope is when Alkmene thinks that Vilhelm's having been "turned out" of his father's house means that he, too, has no "home" and that they will be able to "go on the high roads together." In that case, she continues, "I shall do something so that we shall not have to beg. I shall learn to dance" (211). However, in the same way that Karen Blixen had somewhere to go back to—however unsatisfactory—when Karen Coffee failed, so Vilhelm's loss of his father's house results only in his going to his uncle. The tightness of the family circle closes in, closing out the occasion for art.

The autobiographical nature of "Alkmene" is evident here. It is only the orphan, free from the ties of home, who has the capability of the free expression of the artist. Judith Thurman detects Karen Blixen's uneasy attitude to "home" as early as 1900 when the teenage Tanne, having lived for a time at Folehave with her maternal grandmother, described her grandmother's house in a thank-you letter as the place "where to all of us are some of the most *hyggelige* things we have ever known." Thurman comments that the use of the word *hyggelig,* meaning something between "comfortable" and "homely," was "a clever little hypocrisy," likely to be taken as a compliment by Mrs. Westenholz, but "summ[ing] up what Tanne considered were the most mediocre and contemptible aspects of life at Folehave" (Thurman 47, 48). On her return "home" to Denmark in 1931, Blixen showed her complete disregard for the principles of *hygge* by leaving doors open in the middle of winter, thereby "fighting a second battle for the ground she had won in Africa: the recognition that she was other, unique, a *destinée* misplaced among them" (Thurman 258). In an intriguing note, Thurman links the Danish *hyggelig/ unhyggelig* with the German *heimlich/unheimlich* (48), which through Freud's theorizing suggests a further dimension to her rejection of the safe circle of home for the creative risk of the uncanny, the unknown wilderness.[15]

Blixen could thus most fully become an artist by inventing herself as an orphan, whose "home" on the farm had the appeal of the *unheimlich,* a place of sojourn or passage rather than of stasis. As such, it comes as no surprise that one of the sections that Blixen cut from the original manuscript of *Out of Africa* was about her mother. "The idea that the sovereign narrator is someone's little girl is somehow incongruous," Thurman comments (282). In fact, *Out of Africa* even in its very title denies its European parentage, unless one is to infer, as in horse-breeding parlance, a suppressed "By Europe" to indicate the text's sire. In addition, it ignores Blixen's actual European family in favor of her extended family of African "watoto" [children].

Making "Africa" her new home, or at least her temporary orphanage, puts Blixen in line with tendencies of earlier European women writers in and of Africa. In her comprehensive study of Victorian women travel writers in Africa, Catherine Barnes Stevenson writes that while male travel writers tend to produce quest-romances in which their rhetorical strategies present themselves as heroic explorers confronted by "a dangerous continent—often perceived as feminine—which must be dominated by the force of his will," women travelers "develop strategies of *accommodation*" (160, emphasis added). Women travel writers' heroism, Stevenson says, "rooted in fortitude and patience, achieves its triumphs through adaptation, not conquest" (161).[16]

One of the writers whom Stevenson takes as typifying such strategies is Mary Kingsley, whose impulsion to travel in Africa resulted from the death of her parents within six weeks of each other when she was thirty years old. Finding herself for the first time in her life with "five or six months which were not heavily forestalled" with service to family members, Kingsley was able to go to West Africa and, in writing up her account, to "gain an identity, a sense of personal value, that was otherwise unavailable to her" (Stevenson 99, 94). Her relationship to her perennially wandering father was not unlike Blixen's, and her choice of West Africa—at the time considered to be as fatal a place to white folk as any on earth—as a site to complete his work or compete with him, smacks of Blixen's "*savoir-mourir.*"

It seems, therefore, that being orphaned—whether through invention or actual event—offered Blixen, Kingsley, Schreiner, and others the radical autonomy that allowed them to be writers, by liberating them, to some degree at least, from family obligations. As I suggested earlier, the anxiety involved in this process concerning loss of "womanliness" (where that term is defined in terms of connection and other-centeredness) makes it look as if the issues involved are primarily issues of gender. However, in this final section I would like to return to race issues and to suggest that in seeking to establish a new "accommodation" in Africa, these writers are still writing as much about the condition of whiteness as about the condition of femaleness or, for that matter, the condition of the writer. In short, they are struggling with Gordimer's question, "Where do whites fit in?"

Being orphaned is not necessarily a disaster; in fact, as we have seen, in itself it can be the source of invigorating new identity. Furthermore, being orphaned does not necessarily mean loss of power over others. The cuckoo is also an orphan. And if white women in Africa are able to come in themselves to a new and invigorating identity, then they are enabled to do so because they are occupying someone else's nest and being fed not by the wicked stepmother of fairy-tale but simply by a weaker bird. Schreiner's and Blixen's presence as women *in Africa* means that, while the exclusively female experience of, or capacity for, physical mother-hood might be figured as a potentially utopian marker of radical sameness, transcending political, national, and racial difference,[17] it is probably more realistic to see the image of the orphan, the uprooted child who has *a* home that is not yet *home*, as that which marks the white woman as still alien, still extrafamilial in Africa.

The "accommodation" that Nadine Gordimer, for instance, has made in South Africa—where white settlement has the longest continuous his-tory in Africa and where white rule lasted longest—is to a situation in which whiteness should no longer afford one the privileges of the cuckoo. A great deal of her work has thus been aimed at showing the marginality of South Africa's racial elite, a racial elite that believed it was at the very center of a world of strangers, unaware of its own strangeness. Abdul R. JanMohamed links Nadine Gordimer's and Karen Blixen's work in his description of the Manichean aesthetics of colonialist literature,[18] and notes that their attempts at "genuine and thorough comprehension of Otherness . . . entails in practice the virtually impossible task of negating one's very being" ("Economy of Manichean Allegory" 84). Of Gordimer he goes on to add: "Unable and unwilling to turn away from the colonial situation, Gordimer makes a virtue of necessity by systematically scruti-nizing the social and psychological effects of the Manichean bifurcation on her white protagonists, even though she is acutely aware that the price she pays for this deliberately restricted focus is her inability, as a writer, to participate in the formation of a genuinely national litera-ture" ("Economy of Manichean Allegory" 102). Since the publication of JanMohamed's work Gordimer's participation in the formation of a na-tional literature through extraliterary means has become apparent, espe-cially in her work for and on bodies such as the Congress of South Afri-can Writers, founded in 1987.[19] Furthermore, the formal end of apartheid has allowed her finally to feel at home in her immediate world. In her moving peroration to *Writing and Being,* she writes: "I am a small mat-ter; but for myself there is something immediate, extraordinary, of strong personal meaning. That other world that was the world is no longer the world. My country is the world, whole, a synthesis. I am no longer a colonial. I may now speak of 'my people'" (134).

Of course, Gordimer is also acutely aware of the fact that she—like Schreiner and Blixen before her—is a major participant in the wider world of international literature. She knows full well that one of the consequences of her use of the English language and her description of essentially European culture is to make her work legible to a very wide readership and eligible for all sorts of international honors—to make Nadine Gordimer, in fact, into a big figure, however small she might wish her "I." This tension, between the desire for self-effacement and worldwide recognition, places (or has placed) her in a peculiar position at international conferences, where she scrupulously insists on her marginality as a white woman to the black people of South Africa of whom she is not representative and whom, largely, she has tended not to represent.[20]

For instance, in her 1982 William James Lecture entitled "Living in the Interregnum," she explores the uncertainties of whites who wish to live under majority rule (a segment within a segment already) as to how to offer their *selves* for and in a future South Africa. The essay covers a broad sweep of legislative and economic measures that might be taken in order to effect a "humanly" structured society, but its main focus, naturally, is on cultural measures and the role of the writer within society. As a preamble to this section Gordimer says, "I have already delineated my presence here on the scale of a minority within a minority. Now I shall reduce my claim to significance still further. A white; a dissident white; a white writer" (*Essential Gesture* 272), and she differentiates between the "black writer's consciousness of himself as a writer" and the "white writer's self-image" (274): "The black writer is 'in history,' and its values threaten to force out the transcendent ones of art. The white, as writer and South African, does not know his place 'in history' at this stage, in this time" (276).

The issue of the apparent opposition of history and politics to art is one that I have raised earlier and deal with more fully later; for the moment, I am interested in taking at face-value Gordimer's claim that the white South African writer is adrift in time, in much the same way as the orphans Undine, Lyndall, and Alkmene are adrift in their respective worlds. And in the same way that those heroines resist the various modes of romance (whether Victorian romance-plot, travel-writing as equivalent of medieval romance-quests, Shakespeare's late plays, or the popular understanding of romance as love) by actively seeking separation, so the metaphorical orphanhood of Vera Stark (her divesting of the baggage of family relationships) disrupts the romancing of the post-apartheid state in Gordimer's *None to Accompany Me*. The romance of Gordimer's novel, for instance, is closer kin to Shakespeare's late plays with their tragicomic cross-generational concerns of loss and gain than to *Jane Eyre;* the brave new world of post-apartheid South Africa confronts a younger generation, while Vera Stark, Gordimer's newly marginalized orphan/tenant, can only, like Prospero, look on from the sidelines without the benefit any longer of her white magic. That image—of Vera Stark's accommodation to marginality—provides a metaphor for the way in which someone defining her "I" as white and African can take her place in the world, as an orphan in *a* home in Africa that is yet not quite *home*.[21] In short, Gordimer's first post-apartheid novel continues the trend in her work to resist romanticizing race relations in South Africa by insisting, in JanMohamed's words, "that syncretism is impossible within the power relations of colonial society" ("Economy of Manichean Allegory" 85).

The most obvious symbol of syncretism for Gordimer to explore is interracial romance[22] and the "hybrid" products of such romances. In "Where Do Whites Fit In?" she wonders whether interracial marriage will be useful in breaking down color consciousness, but, rather like Blixen earlier, she downplays the likelihood of its becoming widespread: "Personally I don't believe it will happen on a large scale in Africa" (*Essential Gesture* 36). Thus her work has been more concerned with replacing black and white in relation to each other than with replacing those terms. Although this obviously involves ambiguities that might lead to eventual hybridization or syncretism, her work is still acutely, necessarily, color conscious. In *July's People,* for instance, we might see July's urbanization or the Smales children's easy mixing with the village children as symptoms of a present or future hybrid state, but the book's chief purpose—as in Blixen's "Invincible Slave-Owners"—is, as Jan-Mohamed states, "to examine the dependence of whites on their African servants" ("Economy of Manichean Allegory" 101). The ambivalence of the book's very title also suggests that categories of "people" are never as cut and dried as Victorian racism and the apartheid state would have had them. Who are "July's people"? Are they the members of the immediate blood family to which July belongs, or are they the white madam and master who, in the text's postrevolutionary situation, effectively belong to him? In either case, however, July takes precedence in the re-placing of black vis-à-vis white, and the novel ultimately shows the adult Smaleses unable to adapt to the reversal of roles; unlike the blacks who had "had to understand and accommodate themselves to white laws and customs," the Smaleses fail to learn "the intricacies of the African world" (*Manichean Aesthetics* 142).

In JanMohamed's reading of Maureen Smales's final dash toward a descending helicopter that will decide her fate one way or the other, according to the race of its occupants, "Gordimer stresses the drastic and appalling nature of the master's self-recognition: Maureen is so horrified by her own perverse involvement with her servant and by her identity as master that she wishes to abandon it at any cost" (*Manichean Aesthetics* 143). This willed annihilation might thus be read as a highly dramatic metaphor for his description of the white writer's virtually impossible task of self-negation involved in her attempt to know the Other.

In keeping with the evolutionary rather than revolutionary changes that occurred in South Africa from 1990 on,[23] the representation of white self-negation of *None to Accompany Me* (1994) is less dramatic. On the other hand, although it may lack drama, it is nonetheless a grand gesture in its own way and a successful one to boot. Deeply concerned, like Shakespearean romance, with family relations across the generations and with the connections between self-governance, family, and government of the state, and with the same sense of ripeness we find in Shakespeare's romances that the brave new world is for a new generation, Gordimer's book nonetheless resists the "romance" plot at every turn, with divorce, marital deceit, maternal indifference, abortion, and separation. To keep up the Shakespearean romance connections, it is as if Paulina at the end of *The Winter's Tale* really did walk off alone to some forgotten bough, there to mourn the love that's lost, or as if Prospero went back to Milan where every third thought would be his grave, without demanding the audience's notice and applause.

The Paulina figure of *None to Accompany Me* is Vera Stark, a lawyer and mother of two children, who lives up to her name by learning to live without her "people" and "find[ing] out about my life. The truth" (313). The end of the novel finds her on a crisp highveld winter's night (filled with the luminescence of Schreiner's opening to *African Farm*) in a state of exalted solitude with her feet planted on the "axis of the earth;" rooted, apparently, but alone; belonging but no longer owning.

We know nothing of Vera's parents, but her home for forty-plus years—from World War Two up until the end of the novel (c. 1993)—is the house she acquired as part of the divorce settlement with her first husband. This house, provided by "people who did not know what they themselves were, part of Europe or part of Africa" (293), she feels a fraudulent acquisition, as it was her infidelity that led to the divorce. Nevertheless, it is the house in which her two children are brought up, the house in which her father-in-law (father of her second husband) dies, and the house to which her grandson comes. Not the house of an orphan like Alkmene or Undine or Lyndall by any stretch of the imagination; but from Vera's sense that the house does not really belong to her, nor she to it, stems her sense, if not of orphanhood, at least of cuckoodom. And in her selling it, we can see both Alkmene's desire to escape the stifling circle of family and the white cuckoo's desire to escape its history. Thus, in the images of orphan and home, Gordimer unites the personal and the political, private and public in a way that extends Schreiner's or Blixen's use.

Furthermore, Vera's "escape from history" differs from that of Gordimer's earlier creation, Rosa Burger in *Burger's Daughter* (1979). In that novel, Rosa escapes physically to the South of France, only to find it ultimately unable to accommodate her. Vera's escape is not to a new geographical location at all but to a new arrangement within the old geography. Gordimer's use of the house to link the domestic and the national seems to build on a motif also used in *My Son's Story* (1990), where, according to Homi Bhabha, "each of the houses . . . is invested with a specific secret or a conspiracy" but also "marks a deeper historical displacement . . . the condition of being Colored in South Africa" (147).[24] This connection between specific houses and deeper historical (dis)placement and/or racial (re)accommodation "requires a shift of attention from the political as a theory to politics as the activity of everyday life" (Bhabha 149). Vera Stark's work for the Legal Foundation, an organization fighting for black Africans' claims to their land, is itself political in this latter way. What is more, it ultimately brings the political right back home by changing Vera's own accommodation. While she may have spent a lifetime trying to get rid of the cuckoo's privileges, Vera's own purging of privilege does not come until the novel's end when, separated from her family (her husband is living with the son of whom he is not the father in London; her daughter is living with her female partner in Cape Town) she moves into the maid's quarters of a house now owned by her black friend Zeph Rapulana. Rapulana has himself moved very considerably in the accommodations of the new South Africa, from his position as spokesperson for a small rural community to board member of a number of banks and institutions.

Annick, Vera's lesbian daughter, is suspicious of her mother's relationship with Zeph, but Gordimer is at pains to establish that the new orphan/tenant will not enjoy closer union with her newly arrived landlord. Early in their relationship Gordimer gives us Vera's assessment: She "had never before felt—it was more than drawn to—involved in the being of a man to whom she knew no sexual pull" (123), and in her self-defense to Annick, Vera insists that her new home is "an annexe. Quite separate, own entrance and so on. There's no question of intrusion, either way" (311). If this is a model for racial cohabitation, it is one that seems to accept and respect (or assume *but* respect) racial difference, while ceding priority of rights of ownership to South Africa's blacks. Vera gives up her house, but she can't evade history by giving up her whiteness, a whiteness that has enabled, among other things, the invention of the white writer's "I" as the speaking subject of African history.

Granted the inescapability of that whiteness, my judgment on these particular texts in this particular academic study, my very selection of them, reveals my own writer's "I" as white, too. And it might be argued that in my emphasizing the "orphanhood" of white women writers, I am still underplaying the material existence of black family life in colonial Africa generally and South Africa in particular, a family life that was so comprehensively brutalized by white rule that the trade unionist Emma Mashinini, for instance, recalls in her autobiography that in prison "I could see my youngest daughter's face and I wanted to call her by her name. I struggled to call out the name, the name I always called her, and I just could not recall what the name was. I would fall down and actually weep with the effort of remembering the name of my daughter" (86).[25]

Even Nelson Mandela, for instance, in *Long Walk to Freedom* finds space for an apologia in which he defends his prioritizing of national rather than familial needs, expressing "regret that I had been unable to be with her [his mother] when she died, remorse that I had not been able to look after her properly during her life, and a longing for what might have been had I chosen to live my life differently" (506).[26] The prohibition on his daughter Zindzi to touch him when she was finally allowed to visit him in prison has acquired iconic status.[27]

In comparison with these experiences, the "orphanhood" of Schreiner,

Blixen, and Gordimer still has the trappings of white luxury. However, in the attempt by Gordimer in particular to divest herself of those trappings lies the hope that eventually people will not be able to describe either luxury or suffering in terms of color. Indeed, in their survey of recent South African autobiography considered as a cultural activity, Sarah Nuttall and Cheryl-Ann Michael cite the case of Emma Mashinini to show how South African women autobiographers have "negotiate[d] personal trauma by equating it with the struggle for human rights" (303). While Mashinini's late-apartheid autobiography sees those human rights in community terms (that is, black South Africans need to be accorded their rights), Nuttall and Michael argue that more recent autobiographers have, like Schreiner and Blixen earlier, aimed to mark their own distinctiveness and rebelliousness by separating their personal stories from the communal, so that Mamphele Ramphele, for instance, "adopts less the representative voice of community than claims a space of transgressive individuality" (311). However, although Schreiner and Blixen may resist the master-narrative of the family romance, their lack of acknowledgment of that narrative's tacit racial norm means that they are unable significantly to undermine the narrative of the master. Where Gordimer opens the door to a critical and self-critical white consciousness, the generation of Gordimer's daughters has had to accommodate itself to a new racially conscious sense of shared human identity in South Africa.

Such moves toward a "transgressively" universal discourse of human rights, based on the rejection of an essentialist understanding of racial community by white and black writers, had already been tentatively urged in Ingrid de Kok's "Small Passing" (in *Familiar Ground*). Here, as with the testimonies from the Truth and Reconciliation Commission, and as with the "rememory" of U.S. slavery in Morrison's *Beloved*, de Kok posits suffering as the factor common to all human experience. Such suffering needs to be addressed in equalizing, qualitative terms rather than accounted for in some sort of quasi-Utilitarian calculus of pain. As Nuttall and Michael have it, "Healing and freedom now mean a revisiting of the trauma of the apartheid past, in order to lay it to rest and in order to achieve forgiveness but not forgetting" (308). In de Kok's superb and moving poem written in the midst of one of the most violent and racially polarized periods of apartheid, de Kok attempts to come to terms with the comment of a man to a white woman who had just delivered a stillborn child that her suffering was insignificant in the face of the daily suffering of black women in South Africa. Recognizing the material basis for the man's comment, the poem offers support for his point of view insofar as it graphically represents that latter suffering:

> Child shot running,
> stones in his pocket,
> boy's swollen stomach
> full of hungry air.
> Girls carrying babies
> not much smaller than themselves. (*Familiar Ground* 62)

However, the final section repudiates the man's calculus of comparative racial misery and reasserts a nonquantitative faith in the irreducibility of suffering, whether great or "small." To do so, de Kok imagines an extraordinary solidarity of mothers. Black South African mothers will not tell the bereaved white mother "her suffering is white. . . . They will not compete for the ashes of infants." Rather, says de Kok:

> I think they may say to you:
> Come with us to the place of mothers.
> We will stroke your flat empty belly,
> let you weep with us in the dark,
> and arm you with one of our babies
> to carry home on your back. (*Familiar Ground* 62–63)

De Kok preempts accusations that her poem still appropriates black voices and uses them to validate white self-exoneration through her tentativeness ("I *think*" and "they *may*"), but more profoundly the poem suggests that the white woman is not merely comforted by a passive group of black victim-mothers. Instead, in the image of the black mothers *arming* the white woman with one of their babies, de Kok acknowledges the activism of black women and suggests that they can *use* the white woman and turn her back into "her" community primed to undermine familially and racially exclusive narratives of maternity

Similarly, the apparently barren white couple of Vera's daughter and her lover, like the bereaved mother in "Small Passing," are "armed" with an adopted black baby, thus becoming parents of a daughter of no kin to them, in the same way that Bennett has been father to the son Ivan who was no kin to him. In the shared home or orphanage of the new South

Africa, maybe finally the responsibilities of parents to children—especially Schreiner's and de Kok's connectedness of mothers—can begin to overcome not just racial apartheid but the fracturing of human relations that racialized beliefs engendered.[28] The constitution of the new South Africa—one of the most progressive of such documents in the world—still holds out hope that such an aspiration may be both humanly and legally binding, giving the protective force of law to an omphalogocentric order in which the individual's relatedness to others matters more than her autonomy. Remembering community through mothers, it seems as though South African feminist writers offer the last best hope of fusing the European-derived discourse of universal human rights with the frequently quoted African sense of *ubuntu* expressed in the proverb that serves as an epigraph to this section—"A person is a person because of other people."[29]

2

"Had a Farm"

Rus hoc vocari debet, an domus longe?
[Should this be called a farm, or a townhouse far
removed?]
Martial

Gicigo kia mugunda gitinyihaga.
[A piece of land is not a little thing.]
Gikuyu proverb

Stories of African Farms and
the Politics of Landscape

The previous section dealt mainly with biography and inventions of the self in rather abstract terms of race, class, and gender. In chapter 3, however, we began to see how the more material politics of location might influence how white and black writers perceived themselves as they moved toward a subject position where they could speak as "I." This section continues to explore that politics of location with closer attention to geography to see what role inventions of the farm play in establishing white landownership in Africa as natural in a site of apparently natural productivity. As in the previous section, it is again necessary to explore the works of Schreiner and Blixen as balanced between European narrative practices they in part repudiate and African practices that in part repudiate them. Showing the significance of Schreiner's and Blixen's stories of African farms necessitates comparing their work with later writers, white and black, whose need to claim, or claim back, the landscape differs from theirs. This section therefore compares Schreiner's and Blixen's work not just with colonialist and imperialist practices and European literary traditions but also with a whole range of nationalisms, including the competing forces of African and Afrikaner nationalism in South Africa and Ngugi wa Thiong'o's cultural and linguistic nationalism in Kenya.

Effectively orphaned from their immediate families, both Karen Blixen and Olive Schreiner are oddly homeless, too, in terms of national affiliation: Is Blixen a Danish writer or an English one?[1] In what ways, if at all, might she be considered Kenyan or African? Is Schreiner part of English literary tradition or prototype of a South African one? Such questions come to a head in both writers' use of the term *farm* to designate the particular tracts of African land represented in their work. But just how, if at all, does the English concept of the "farm," with aesthetic associations deriving from a particular history of landscape representation in European art and the pastoral tradition in European literature, transcend cultural and geographic difference? Do the social relationships between country and city dwellers, farmers and farmworkers in Britain get reproduced identically when capitalist farming arrives in Africa? How is it possible for someone of European origin to write of a farm that is *in* Africa but geared to European economic systems without at least some form of cultural imperialism? Do African writers necessarily have to repudiate European narratives in toto, or can they use them subversively? The case of Olive Schreiner suggests that even if the colonial writer or artist produces a landscape resistant to imperial eyes, that very representation may have complex, not necessarily emancipatory, nationalist consequences. At the same time, the case of Schreiner's African nationalist admirer Sol Plaatje suggests that European ways of seeing can be strategically subverted.

To set this discussion in context, let us start by briefly examining the English tradition of landscape representation and the place of the farm in that tradition. As Raymond Williams explains in *The Country and the City,* the life of the country and its representation in English literature have had a complex, mutually influential history. On the one hand, the pastoral tradition in literature has tended to privilege "the country" in the English consciousness as a site of "a natural way of life: of peace, innocence, and simple virtue" as opposed to the city's "noise, worldliness, and ambition." On the other hand, the country is also associated with "backwardness, ignorance, limitation," while the city is associated with "the idea of an achieved centre: of learning, communication, light" (Williams 1). Above all, Williams stresses that the idea of the country, hence of the countryside, landscape, and farm, is an ideological construction varying over time both in responding to social and economic change and in producing such changes. He locates specific terms as emerging at specific times: "Countryside," for instance, "is an eighteenth- to nineteenth-century development, in its modern sense," while the term *farm* was "originally a fixed payment, then from the sixteenth century, by extension, a holding of land on lease, and so to the modern meaning" (307).

Landscape art in England, likewise, has a fairly definable genealogy, connected to the nationalistic chorographic and cartographic projects of late Elizabethan England through which, in Richard Helgerson's words, "the land . . . emerge[d] . . . as a primary source of national identity" (75).[2] Developing out of topographical drawings of "prospects," landscape comes into its own as a distinct genre in the seventeenth century, reaching its apogee in the eighteenth and nineteenth centuries in the work of painters such as Gainsborough, Constable, and Turner.[3] In *The Idea of Landscape and the Sense of Place, 1730–1840*, John Barrell specifies that the word *landscape* comes into English from Dutch in the sixteenth century as a "painter's word." Even when the meaning became extended to cover the idea of land "considered with regard to its natural configuration," an educated person of the eighteenth century "would have found it very hard, not merely to describe land, but also to see it, and even to *think* of it as a visual phenomenon, except as mediated through particular notions of form" (Barrell 2). In the Dutch tradition, according to Svetlana Alpers, the distinction we now make between landscape art and cartography "would have puzzled the Dutch" (54) in the seventeenth century, for whom maps held an aura of knowledge "as a kind of image. Their making involved possession of a kind that must not be underestimated in considering the relationship of art to mapping" (66–67). From this bare summary it is apparent that Schreiner and Blixen, even were they to deal with European farms, would be representing sites bearing a very heavy, frequently contradictory, associational and ideological burden, including ideas about national identity and ownership.[4] If we add into the mix Williams's idea that the relationship of country to city corresponds to the relationship of colony to metropole, then the fact that Blixen and Schreiner, with their cultural inheritance from a metropolitan Europe, are dealing with farms in Africa at times of colonialist expansion makes it all the more difficult to unravel the assumptions and ideological effects of their work.

Recent critical opinion on landscape representation, especially the representation of "new" landscapes, insists that landscape's heavy ideological load results in a depiction of social conditions according to top-down ways of seeing.[5] Moreover, that way of seeing tends to render poverty as picturesque or to shift it outside the frame in an aesthetic move analogous to the actual removal of the rural poor from land previously considered common. Ann Bermingham, for instance, in *Landscape and Ideol-*

ogy, draws attention to the contemporaneous late eighteenth-century "emergence of rustic landscape as a major genre in England at the end of the eighteenth century" and "the accelerated enclosure of the English countryside" (1). In Williams's view, the dominance of the top-down way of seeing was so overwhelming that even such voices as John Clare's protesting the enclosure laws are muted by his inheritance of a structure of feeling that both displaces the source of dispossession and romanticizes what has been lost. Rather than attacking "visible and active landowners," Clare's verse targets "'low' and, as it would seem, alien 'tyrants'"; rather than specifying Clare's actual economic loss, *Helpstone,* for example, suggests that "what wealth is most visibly destroying is 'Nature': that complex of the land as it was, in the past and in childhood, which both ageing and alteration destroy" (Williams 137, 138).

The tendency to see "Nature" rather than human beings occurs away from the metropole, too, in colonial travel writing. In *Imperial Eyes,* Mary Louise Pratt stresses how the aesthetic transformations of the "naturalist's quest," whereby any social changes are not expressed as changes at all "but are naturalized as absences and lacks," come to "embody . . . an image of conquest and possession" by effectively emptying the landscape of its human population. Pratt's account of John Barrow's travel writing from South Africa claims that "the European improving eye produces subsistence habitats as 'empty' landscapes, meaningful only in terms of a capitalist future and of their potential for producing a marketable surplus" (*Imperial Eyes* 61). Pratt's account of travel writing accords with J. B. Harley's discussion of the hidden agenda of early modern European cartography in which he claims that "the scientific *episteme* serves to dehumanize the landscape" and allows space to become "a socially empty commodity, a geometrical landscape of cold, non-human facts" (Harley, "Silences and Secrecy" 66).[6] Harley urges caution in reaching for clear-cut conclusions regarding cartography as a discourse of power, but he insists that cartography needs to be questioned not for its objective accuracy or inaccuracy but in relation to the "subjectivity . . . inherent in its replication of the state's dominant ideology" (71); the "truth effects" are more significant than the facts. In looking at Schreiner's and Blixen's representation of African farms, therefore, we need to recognize their complicity with hegemonic discourse and the potential ambiguities of their work within that discourse. It is easy to demonstrate their complicity.

At the time Schreiner and Blixen were penning their representations of Karoo and Kenyan landscapes, the upheaval in those places in land distribution, occupation, ownership, and use was far more dramatic and socially disturbing than even the enclosure period in Britain. For example, Schreiner was writing *The Story of an African Farm* in the 1870s, at a time when the series of Cape-Xhosa wars was coming to an end. The defeat of the Xhosa finally cleared the way for the Glen Grey Act of 1894 under which land was parceled out among the Xhosa on a "one-man-one-lot principle" in order to "prevent the accumulation of capitalist land" (Switzer 67). In a move that has ironic resonance with the English Enclosure Laws, individual plots were allotted, but only on land seen as "commonage," which meant that those allotted the plots did not qualify for the vote.[7] The process of "land alienation" in Kenya, which began very hesitantly with the chartering of the Imperial British East Africa Company in 1888, gathered pace in the early twentieth century, culminating after the First World War in the British government's allocation of 3 million acres of highland farmland to a number of "soldier-settlers."[8] The provision of cheap labor was a consistent problem for the settlers, resulting in what Richard D. Wolff describes as a "proliferation of policies." He adds, "The authorities restricted African reserves, manipulated hut and poll taxes, structured indigenous leadership and tenure systems in the reserves, facilitated squatting, moved towards a South African type of pass system, and even utilized prison terms to give prisoners some minimal training in work discipline" (Wolff 107). For a brief period after the war, a policy of forced labor was even implemented for public works (Thurman 170–71). Blixen's own 6,000-acre farm was part of the 4.5 million acres of land that already by 1915 had been divvied out among 1,000 white farmers "as if it had been vacant" (Thurman 119).[9]

The literary presentation of Blixen's and Schreiner's farms, then, as if they were uncontested and uncontestable entities, as if they really were farms in a sense familiar to European readers, inevitably prompts questions of complicity with colonialist power. How can they possibly be separated from the "naturalist" tradition in which writing the landscape—whether in maps, pictorial art, or travel writing—embodies conquest and possession? And even if they disavow English conquest and possession, what are the local and national consequences of writing the African farm? What possible ambiguity might there be in the "truth-effects" of their work? Even if there is any, of what significance might it be, balanced against the more obvious complicity?

If we concentrate on Olive Schreiner's representation of the Karoo landscape in *The Story of an African Farm*, I would suggest that Schreiner herself was anxious about such questions (as in so many things, presciently so), and that we might reformulate the first question in her case, as follows: Given the ideological baggage of the English language, Victorian culture, and pastoral tradition, is it possible to write an African landscape that *resists* imperialist ideology?

The short answer is partly. As with all the various oscillations mentioned in part 1, so in Schreiner's handling of landscape there seems to be no claim that is not also disclaimed, with the claim and the counterclaim producing further possibilities in an endless dialectic. What most marks her handling of landscape is, in fact, a kind of literary-generic hybridity, a hybridity capable of producing new forms even while apparently legible to the old order.[10] However, I am already rather too far in advance of myself, and I need to go back to that overly monolithic notion "Victorian culture" before looking at Schreiner's colonialist/anticolonialist English/South African hybridity.

Asked to pick out three figures who represented the best of Victorian culture to Schreiner, we might light on the trio of Herbert Spencer, John Stuart Mill, and John Ruskin. What did each of those mean to Schreiner? Not only was Herbert Spencer the personal catalyst to Schreiner's free-thinking; he was also part of the general Darwinist assault on religious certainty. John Stuart Mill's vocal advocacy for women's rights, among other things, made Schreiner revere him as the "noblest of those whom the English-speaking race has produced in the last hundred years" (*Letters* 402). In John Ruskin, Schreiner saw "a curious antidote to this commercial, striving, self-seeking, individualistic world" (*Letters* 276). For all these men's various Victorian privileges and prejudices, they were hardly figures endorsing the status quo. Like Schreiner they considered themselves rebels—within the establishment, to be sure, but opposed to its norms, nonetheless.

Of these three, John Ruskin is clearly the most relevant to my thesis here because of his enormous influence on British art and art criticism.[11] His particular appeal to Schreiner appears to have lain in his insistence on the morality of aesthetic production and criticism and the consistency with which he extended that same Victorianly earnest morality to his social criticism. Although Schreiner lost her Christian faith early, and Ruskin lost his late, both writers were shaped by their youthful immersion in the Bible, and each was driven by a similar sense of mission. As Gerald Monsman says of Schreiner, she "absorbed ineradicably the central motif of the missionary's calling: one who is sent to carry on a work, to perform a worthy service" (7). Ruskin displayed a similarly evangelical attitude in preaching his gospel of the moral and spiritual effect of art.

The mission of both writers was, in short, to help the world see rightly. Schreiner's insistence on the "truth" of her narrative method conforms to Ruskin's attitude toward landscape painting. As Ann Bermingham explains, such painting for Ruskin "is treated as much more than a matter of representing scenery. It is, or ought to be, a means by which one discovers the 'truth of nature,' immanent with divine presence" (176). Ruskin draws a distinction between medieval and Gothic art,[12] when painters "either painted from nature things as they were, or from imagination things as they must have been," and the later, falsely sophisticated Renaissance images in which "finish of execution and beauty of form" take priority over the moral urgency of visionary intensity (*Works* 12:147).

However, Ruskin is of interest in this discussion not only because of his evangelical attitude to right seeing. He is also interesting because of a kind of intellectual hybridity in the ideological contradictions of his oscillation between opposite poles: On the one hand, "red" Ruskin could, like Marx, equate factory work with slavery and declare the chief blight of the times to be the "degradation of the operative into a machine" (*Stones* 192). On the other hand, Ruskin the paternalistic "Tory of the old school" (*Praeterita*) aired ideas of social justice involving the "upper classes . . . keep[ing] order among their inferiors, and rais[ing] them always to the nearest level with themselves of which those inferiors are capable" (quoted in Bermingham 177). As a proponent of imperialism, Ruskin urged the young men of his day to their "destiny" and "found colonies as fast and as far as she is able, formed of her most energetic and worthiest men" (Oxford inaugural lecture 1870).[13] Riven, red, Tory Ruskin, in short—surely the very figure of the Victorian sage—should remind us of the inadequacy of setting up either/or questions and expecting straight answers from them.

However, with the proviso that either/or questions are likely to break down or branch out into further such dilemmas, it is still useful to consider the complexities of Schreiner's landscape representation in terms of at least the following binarisms: colonialist/anticolonialist (or complicit/resistant); Victorian/avant-garde; European/African. Equally interesting is the divergence between local South African criticism of *The Story of an African Farm* (especially by white literary critics; criticism by black critics opens up a whole new line of inquiry) and Anglo-American criticism of it. Together, these sets of binarisms draw attention to the hybridity of the novel and the awkwardness of placing it in English and South African culture or the history of colonial and anticolonial writing.

To contemporary and even current critics of *The Story of an African Farm*, the novel often gives the impression of having sprung from nowhere, and it is frequently dealt with as if it were a prototype—whether of the New Woman novel, of female modernism, or of South African fiction—in ways that tend to blur the complexity of the geographical and temporal conditions under which it was produced. At two extremes we might perhaps locate Lloyd Fernando, whose *New Women in the Late Victorian Novel* (1977) places the novel almost entirely in terms of English literary tradition, and Karel Schoeman, whose 1991 biography of the young Schreiner insists on its local origins. Where Fernando dismisses the novel's South Africanness in an offhand reference to its having its source in a "simple environment" (130), Schoeman insists on the coincidence of the first twenty-five years of Schreiner's life with "what may well have been the most dramatic quarter-century in the earlier history" of South Africa (v). As Schoeman emphasizes, Schreiner's investment in the landscape is deeply personal, not to say solipsistic. Despite the bitterness of her childhood, she recalls with delight the "immense" distances of the Karoo and clings to the memories "of the places I lived at, they were so unutterably lovely" (*Letters* 266). However, it is not possible to utter that private vision of unutterably lovely landscape for the benefit of a reading public, specifically an English reading public, in ways that are purely private or purely aesthetic. According to Abdul R. JanMohamed, colonial literature in general is "an exploration and a representation of a world at the boundaries of 'civilization,' a world that has not (yet) been domesticated by European signification or codified in detail by its ideology. That world is therefore perceived as uncontrollable, chaotic, unattainable, and ultimately evil" ("Economy of Manichean Allegory" 64). And Schreiner's "immense" distances and the barrenness of significance of her landscape might easily be read as reproducing just such an "ultimately evil" world in need of domestication. No less than sixteenth-century European cartographers, eighteenth- and nineteenth-century English landscape artists, or the photographers for the Sierra Club, Schreiner might be read as staking claims. However, she is only in part a colonist. In part she is also—however problematically—a native, and the claims she makes are couched as counterclaims. We have already seen in her preface to the second edition of *African Farm* that Schreiner attacks novelists who use the "stage method" of writing, and she pours scorn on conventional colonialist depictions of Africa, "best written in Piccadilly or in the Strand," which feature "cattle driven into inaccessible krantzes by Bushmen . . . encounters with ravening lions, and hair-breadth escapes" (28). Her own understanding of realism demands that, "should one sit down to paint the scenes among which he has grown . . . sadly he must squeeze the colour from his brush, and dip it into the grey pigments around him." This is life painted according to "the method of the life we all lead" (27).[14]

Above all, the implication of the preface is that the writer has a deep *moral* imperative to this method. As for Ruskin, so for Schreiner, realism of representation was not just a question of style, of technical skill or accuracy of reproduction, but was fiercely tied to an ethics of "right seeing." That did not necessarily mean allegiance to a kind of photographic accuracy either, as both writers allow for visionary sensibility. As we have seen, Ruskin revered the medieval and Gothic artists for their accuracy not just in representing "things as they were" but also "things as they must have been." Such an attitude validated for Ruskin Gothic grotesquerie or literary creations such as Dante's centaur, but did not allow for the fanciful "sophistication" he saw characterizing the Renaissance. Similarly, Schreiner claims to represent "the life we all lead," while at the same time justifying her own use of dreams and allegories, and disqualifying both naturalism[15] and the "stage method" Piccadilly scribblers. Both Ruskin and Schreiner insist, no matter how inconsistent their logic, on correcting not only visual inaccuracy but misrepresentations of the truth itself.

With no novelistic precedent for Schreiner's landscape, even mundane descriptions are charged with this kind of literal and moral visionariness. In his Penguin introduction, Dan Jacobson makes this clear when he calls the opening sentence of *African Farm* "almost heroic" in describing the moon as bright enough to "fill the sky with a hard, blue radiance" (18), and Irene Gorak, in her article entitled "Olive Schreiner's Colonial Allegory," extends the paradox when she writes that in *African Farm* Schreiner "combines an interest in the visionary sensibility with a desire to illustrate the range of yet-unpainted types of an existing Cape community" (57).

Finding a language for these "unutterably lovely" scenes, these "yet-unpainted types" that the South African–born Olive Schreiner loved is necessarily bound up with the language of moral truth that the English-speaking Olive Schreiner had grown up with. Words like *measure, proportion,* and *perspective,* which all too easily slip from the technical to the metaphysical, are key here.[16] Technically, part of Schreiner's problem in depicting landscape is that the Karoo she was depicting, in its *immensity*—in JanMohamed's terms its resistance to the control of measurement—confounds classical European notions of proportion. At the same time, in a highly influential review of Schreiner's life and work, Virginia Woolf criticizes Schreiner's own lack of "measure": Woolf admires Schreiner "as a martyr" who has had to sacrifice not her life but, "perhaps more disastrously, humour and sweetness and sense of proportion" (Clayton 94). Although I am quoting Woolf rather out of context, it is almost as though the "evil" of the proportion-defying landscape Schreiner lived in has infected the writer. Loving such a landscape puts one beyond the pale and is evidence of having "gone native."

And it seems there is no way to represent the Karoo landscape and still retain a European sense of proportion. J. M. Coetzee's *White Writing,* the most extensive analysis of the aesthetics of landscape representation in South African literature, traces European attitudes to the picturesque, the sublime, and the pastoral as they affect colonial South Africa from 1652 onward. He shows that from the earliest white travel writers in South Africa, the landscape has resisted European models in each of those categories. William Burchell, for example, produces painterly descriptions of the Cape Peninsula area as if in the tradition of Claude, but as soon as he crosses the Hex River Mountains and reaches the Karoo, he finds it harder to describe the landscape within a familiar set of aesthetics; this leads him to consider the existence of "a species of beauty with which, possibly, [European painters] may not yet be sufficiently acquainted" (38). And it is in precisely this "unutterably beautiful" landscape with its "alien species of beauty" that *The Story of an African Farm* is set.

One of the chief aspects of the African landscape Schreiner sets against the "inaccessible krantzes" of Piccadillyan stereotype in *The Story of an African Farm* is its apparent emptiness and negativity. Like Roy Campbell, who saw in the veld not "a positive limitlessness but 'a gap in nature, time and space' to be apprehended only in terms of its 'vacuity'" (Coetzee 53), Schreiner frequently describes the landscape in terms of absence—whether of color, of feature, of activity, of variety, of life. The first daytime description sets the tone:

> The plain was a weary flat of loose red sand sparsely covered by karroo bushes, that cracked beneath the tread like tinder, and showed the red earth everywhere. Here and there a milk-bush lifted its pale-coloured rods, and in every direction the ants and beetles ran about in the blazing sand. The red walls of the farm-house, the zinc roofs of the outbuildings, the stone walls of the kraals, all reflected the fierce sunlight, till the eye ached and blenched. No tree or shrub was to be seen far or near. The two sunflowers that stood before the door, out-stared by the sun, drooped their brazen faces to the sand; and the little cicada-like insects cried aloud among the stones of the "kopje." (38)

Elsewhere, Otto rides home across the "still monotony" of the plain, Waldo rides for half an hour on the farm without recognizing it, and even when the relief of rainfall intervenes, the rain's very persistence makes it acquire a sense of monotony. Similarly, the little "kopje"—virtually the only salient feature—"was not itself an object conspicuous enough to relieve the dreary monotony of the landscape" (174).

Given Coetzee's suggestion that Schreiner's novel, for all its novelty, is "out of a literary tradition of [her] own, a tradition of the English novel of rural life" (63), it is interesting to contrast the "kopje" with Penistone Crag, the most salient geographical feature in *Wuthering Heights*. While the kopje remains resolutely antipathetic to humanity, apparently random in its *lack* of signification, the rocks around the Heights are sympathetic, expressive, and essential: Catherine Earnshaw claims that her "love for Heathcliff resembles the eternal rocks beneath—a source of little visible delight, but necessary" (Brontë 122). The final impression left by *Wuthering Heights* of the landscape retaining the continued *presence* of Catherine and Heathcliff is diametrically opposed to the overriding sense that Schreiner's veld is a "site of wholesale absence" (Coetzee 64).

In fact, the very monotony of the landscape that Coetzee so astutely describes is in itself opposed to the treatment of landscape in English novels of rural life, where one type of landscape tends to gain its significance through contrast with another. As two obvious examples, I might cite *Wuthering Heights*'s contrast of the landscape around the Heights with the gentler environs of Thrushcross Grange, or Hardy's contrast in *Tess of the D'Urbervilles* of the Frome valley around Talbothays Dairy with the barrenness of Flintcombe Ash.

But if monotony and absence of distinction make it impossible to produce a conventionally picturesque rendering of the scene,[17] might not the vastness of the Karoo make it capable of a Romantic representation, drawing on the tradition of the sublime? Not so, says Coetzee, arguing that the sublime in Romantic art tends to be vertical, not horizontal, sudden, not extended; mountains claim priority over endless plains in the Romantic imagination. The Karoo's vastness appears as "mere space, contemplated under the dome of heaven," which, according to E. L. Magoon in his 1852 *Home Book of the Picturesque*, "prostrates rather than sustains the mind" (cited in Coetzee 60).

That prostrating levelness raises another difficulty in representing the Karoo as a readable landscape. Like Mary Louise Pratt, Coetzee suggests that seeing physical landscape in terms of pictures frequently depends on implied "prospects,"[18] points from which the viewer can look out across landscape. *Out of Africa* makes glorious use of such a prospect, opening high up on the Ngong Hills, whose geographical position and elevation "combined to create a landscape that had not its like in all the world" and whose "immensely wide" views meant that "everything that you saw made for greatness and freedom" (13). With the flatness and "featurelessness" of the Karoo, by contrast, Schreiner has no prospect or vantage point *from* which to describe landscape. The "kopje" on the farm breaks the "solemn monotony" of the veld, but it is not a place one would want to climb to in order to get a better view. In fact, making allowance for the dazzle of the Karoo sun, one could see virtually as far from the level plain, and there would be nothing more, nothing different, at least, to see from the slight prominence of the "kopje." Nowhere on Schreiner's farm is there a viewpoint from which a framed, bounded landscape can be surveyed. Nowhere is there a viewpoint to offer the sense of proprietorial uplift that Blixen describes.[19]

Coetzee, citing Barrell, points out that the absence of a viewpoint

means that there is none of that "kind of phenomenological distance between viewer and landscape that exists between viewer and painting, creating a predisposition to see landscape as art" (Coetzee 46), or, as Mary
Louise Pratt might add, as prospect, or indeed as property; instead, the
Karoo landscape, apparently alienating, forbidding, and negative in its
vastness and lack of feature, ironically forces the characters moving on its
surface not to be separate from it (with an implied ability to exert control
over it), nor, like Catherine and Heathcliff, to give it some kind of ghostly
animation, but to be trapped in it as an inanimate part of it. In the final
scene of the novel, that is exactly what has happened to Waldo. He has
become so completely part of the landscape that "the chickens had
climbed about him, and were perching on him" (300).[20]

But while the landscape's resistance to European models of representation stresses the revisionary nature of Schreiner's African farm, and
while the specific absence of prospects may make it possible to read her
landscape as counter to the imperialist "Monarch-of-all-I-survey" mode
described by Mary Louise Pratt in *Imperial Eyes* (201–27), absence generally—as JanMohamed and Harley show—can still work to justify imperialist occupation of the land. After all, emptying the land of all features suggests either the physical removal of human population or an
intellectual incapacity to see, or see as human, the population that is
there. As with E. M. Forster's opening description of Chandrapore in
which the narrative voice finds "nothing extraordinary," and where the
colors have been so squeezed from his brush that "the very wood seems
made of mud, the inhabitants of mud moving" (*Passage* 7), so in Schreiner's novel indigenous Africans are reduced to mere traces of the landscape, passively accepting ill treatment by man and nature, and responding in grunts, laughter, or unintelligible sounds.[21] The land no more
belongs to them than it does to the ants, beetles, and spiders Schreiner so
frequently describes. And if it doesn't belong to "them" and "they"
haven't done anything with it anyway, then, so runs the imperialist logic,
"we" must be justified in making it into something, improving it, giving
it order, or in JanMohamed's terms, "domesticating" it.[22] In Forster's
Chandrapore, the "chaotic" Indian town is overseen—both literally and
figuratively—from the Civil Station laid out on a slight rise where the
bungaloid British bureaucrats had created a landscape with which they
could feel familiar: individual, demarcated houses and gardens, and
streets intersecting at right angles (*Passage* 8). *The Story of an African*

Farm is almost exclusively rural, but it should be clear that the idea of emptiness and lack of order, along with notions of lack of order and lack of significance, played a large part in British and Boer expansionism in South Africa and subsequently in the ideology of apartheid. Schreiner's novel, therefore, even in demonstrating the inapplicability of British aesthetico-political principles to her surroundings, may have, at least inadvertently, facilitated their geopolitical implementation.

On balance, however, as Coetzee acknowledges, the chief effect of Schreiner's landscape representation is anticolonial rather than ultimately imperialist. Although Coetzee, like Pratt, insists on the close connection between travelers' records and "the imperial eye," claiming that "landscape art is by and large a traveler's art, intended for the consumption of vicarious travelers" (174), he nonetheless concludes that Olive Schreiner's landscape consistently thwarts the vicarious traveler; as such, he claims, Schreiner's landscape is anticolonial in its "assertion of the alienness of European culture in Africa and in her attribution of unnaturalness to the life of her farm" (66).[23]

While such a claim remains difficult to decide conclusively, a contrast with *Out of Africa* supports it. In Blixen's rhapsodically affirmative opening vision of the Ngong Hills, where the difference from European norms makes for "greatness and freedom, and unequalled nobility" (13), the very air offers "a vital assurance and lightness of heart." Writes Blixen, "In the highlands you woke up and thought: Here I am, where I ought to be" (*Out of Africa* 14). Her slipping between first and second person seems to confirm Coetzee's definition of landscape art as "intended for the consumption of vicarious travelers." It invites the reader to share this buoyant, empty space. No such invitation emerges from Schreiner's opening descriptions. In the daylight description quoted above, the sun causes the human eye to ache, the sunflowers to droop, and the "cicada-like insects" to cry aloud. Waking up here, no metropolitan Victorian would think: Here I am where I belong.

Even in the novel's opening nighttime description that immediately precedes the passage quoted, and in which Schreiner depicts the "loving moonlight" as casting "a kind of dreamy beauty," that beauty is also described as "weird and . . . almost oppressive" (35). Gerald Monsman, in his account of the passage, draws attention to the way Schreiner's diction "suggests a surfeit that threatens to suffocate or drown the child. As [Lyndall] sleeps, the light 'poured down,' 'fell in a flood,' and when she awakes it 'was bathing her'" (Monsman 53). As Schreiner's focus moves from the moonlit girls to the utter darkness of Waldo's room, the sense of suffocation intensifies; Waldo can see nothing from his box under the window, and he imagines each inexorable tick of his father's hunting watch to represent someone dying. In the darkness Waldo has a vision of a kind of waterfall of death: "He saw before him a long stream of people, a great dark multitude, that moved in one direction; then they came to the dark edge of the world, and went over" (*African Farm* 35–37). While it might be argued that such a vision is too general to carry the argument I am making about Schreiner's use of a specific landscape, the tying of its sense of spiritual desolation to the descriptions of physical desolation that surround it textually—and in such a prominent position in the text—does support the contention that Schreiner's landscape asserts the "alienness of European culture in Africa."

Furthermore, unlike the best-selling "non-fictional quest romances" of Victorian travel writing which Patrick Brantlinger asserts "exerted incalculable influence on British culture and the course of modern history" (*Rule* 180), *The Story of an African Farm* radically breaks with any idea of the quest romance and suggests that there's really nothing new for Europeans to discover in "Africa." Instead of chronicling a journey, whether to enlightenment or to the heart of darkness, to find a goddess or to shoot elephants, Schreiner's novel is entirely static; it describes only travel *within* its defined area. There are no great falls to describe, no semimythical sources to discover, no controversial geographical claims to prove or disprove. The book opens and closes *on the farm,* with no metropolitan penetration of and withdrawal from colonial space, no confirmation of the traveler's preconceived notions of what s/he expected to be able to "discover" and classify.

Instead, characters drift across the landscape of the unnamed, virtually featureless, and hence unmappable "African farm," like the farm's own lost sheep and straying ostriches. Waldo and Lyndall's "strangers" remain entirely strange as to name, origin, and destination. Bonaparte Blenkins's origins are similarly obscure (47), and he finally drives off the page (295) with Tant' Sannie too fat to catch up with him. We know next to nothing of Lyndall's parents or of Em's, and the farm's black workers drift in from, or out into, the semidesert, either absconding or expelled by Tant' Sannie, to be left like Hagar in the wilderness.

The more deliberate journeys that characters do embark on are mundane and disillusioning. Lyndall goes off to boarding school hoping to "come back again . . . know[ing] everything that a human being can" (185). Instead, she comes back with opinions formed in reaction against the school's attempts to "finish" her. Waldo also sets out to enlarge his mind and "taste life," and like any conventional Victorian traveler, he records his travels in an extensive letter (252–62). However, his efforts as traveler and writer are futile; as in the earlier allegory of the Hunter's quest for Truth told *to* Waldo by his stranger, so Waldo's own quest is disappointing. His most profound realization is a negative one made in Grahamstown, where he learns to feel ashamed of himself "dressed in tancord" (260) and to realize that "he was not meant to live among people" (261). It is therefore his journey home that is "delightful" and that includes the one picturesque description—of a "deep little kloof" that also makes an appearance in *Undine*[24]—in the entire novel. Bursting to tell of his experience, as any good travel writer should, he writes it all down in a letter to Lyndall, only to have Em finally tell him that his writing is in vain. In one of the novel's characteristically jarring moments, he learns as we learn that "Lyndall is dead" (263). Actual journeys, it seems, are at best merely tiring, generally disappointing, and at worst cruelly sundering. They are not the physical counterparts of the Hunter's quest for Truth, nor are they even informative or beneficial in any way to those who would read about them.

Waldo's account does, however, make for illuminating comparisons and contrasts with those of earlier Victorian travel writers. At a key point in his letter to Lyndall, Waldo, like any conventional travel writer, describes how he worked his way to the top of a promontory from which he had a "prospect" of a "long, low, blue, monotonous mountain" (259). This "mountain" is the sea he had set out in search of, but the prospect is disappointing, at least initially. Waldo's disappointment, however, is different from the disappointment, both aesthetic and logistical, experienced by Speke on first viewing Victoria N'yanza. Speke, after all, was still able to claim that his "expedition had now performed its functions" (Pratt 206). For Waldo, the expedition performs a function quite different from his expectations: His vision suggested that "the ideal is always more beautiful than the real," that the idea of appropriation or appropriability is flawed ("It was not my sea"), and finally, after the first day of disappointment, that the sea is the one wanting questions answered and is not an object to be discovered at all (259). Waldo's refusal of mastery and

knowledge links his travel writing with what Mary Louise Pratt identifies as a nonmainstream tradition of women travel writers such as Mary
Kingsley and Mary Falconbridge in which she claims that "a comic and
self-ironic persona indelibly impresses itself on any reader" (213). Such
irony in Waldo's account is exaggerated by Schreiner's narrative technique. While Falconbridge and Kingsley are assured of an audience,
which, as Pratt emphasizes, to some degree ties them to the imperialist
project, Waldo's writing—of which Schreiner records only a fragment—
never reaches its intended audience, the already dead Lyndall.

Among other critics who discuss apparently gendered differences in
Victorian travel writing,[25] Susan L. Blake suggests that women travel
writers tend to resist the Linnaean, taxonomic, (male) scientific approach,
instead opting for a style that allows the people and landscape observed to
speak to them, a process that necessarily involves a degree of assimilation. Waldo's assimilation with the landscape—intellectualized in his
comments on the sea—is realized in his death when, having gone out to
sit and muse in the sunshine among the stones of the farm, he becomes
one of the stones, a perch for the chickens (300). Schreiner's presentation,
then, of Africa is novel both as fiction and as travel writing, resisting the
English taxonomic conventions not just of Piccadilly and the Strand but
of the Royal Geographic Society and the *Illustrated London News.*

Questions of audience and medium, however, lead to further issues
that are more local: If the landscape resists English expression and expro-
priation, does it similarly resist African and/or Afrikaner articulation?
Whom does Schreiner's landscape representation ultimately inform or
benefit? Given the absence of a literary market within 1880s South Africa, it would have been almost impossible for Schreiner to conceive a
target audience other than an English one. Even the book's title establishes that *The Story of an African Farm* was aimed out of Africa. To have
entitled it *Thornkloof* as she once thought of it when it was a work in
progress would have implied a familiarity with such names and the landscape to which they applied that Schreiner knew she would not find in
her readers. (Imagine, by contrast, what it would mean for *Wuthering
Heights* to have been called *The Story of a European Farm*—or English
or even Yorkshire.) Both Schreiner's preface to the second edition and her
insistence on the book's being published at the relatively low cost of one
shilling "because the book was published by me for working men" (Rive
111) confirm whom she expected as readers.[26] Despite all that, however,

and whatever her connection to prevailing English landscape ideology, nevertheless, in establishing the validity of a specifically African landscape for literary treatment in English, she does pioneer a way for African writers—black or white—to follow.

For black writers, finding ways to write about land is necessarily more materially political than it could be for even the most consistently anti-imperialist white writer. Founded in 1912, the fledgling South African Native National Congress's first defining issue was provided by the massive alienation of land and property rights embodied by the notorious 1913 Natives Land Act. This legislation "established the clear legal distinction between African Reserves and white farming areas, delineated the two categories of land on the map of South Africa, and ordained that no land could be shifted from one category to the other" (Ross 88). Eighty-seven percent of the total land mass came to be considered white, and with the act's disqualification of sharecropping, many formerly prosperous black families were evicted from land which they had farmed for years and which they had always considered theirs.

As secretary of the South African Native National Congress, Sol Plaatje traveled the length and breadth of the country chronicling the plight of these families in *Native Life in South Africa*—"some of the first, and still some of the finest, of South African campaigning journalism," according to Robert Ross (90). In this work Plaatje brilliantly sets out how devastating the act was to black South Africans, who found themselves "without a president, 'without a king,' and with a governor-general without constitutional functions, under taskmasters whose national traditions are to enslave the dark races" (76). The only avenues of recourse open to Plaatje and the SANNC were writing and sending a deputation to the king in London. As with Schreiner's efforts to avert the Anglo-Boer War in the 1890s, Plaatje's efforts as writer and lobbyist were in vain. However, for the purposes of this chapter, it is fascinating to explore further the connection between Schreiner and Plaatje, especially by looking at the differences between Plaatje's journalistic representation of the landscape and his fictional representations of it.

In *Native Life in South Africa,* as one might expect, Plaatje is scrupulously objective in his descriptions of his travels, listing place-names, arrival and departure times, and names of many people whom he meets. The land tends not to be invested with any particular emotional, metaphorical, or mystical meaning. Plaatje seems to be moving across the landscape like a European cartographer or chorographer, presenting his readers with a knowable and known geography across which roads and railways provide unexceptional networks of commerce and movement. The "native life" that he sketches out, therefore, bears no relation to the earlier descriptions of peoples and customs laid out by European travelers such as John Barrow. Similarly, it bears virtually no relation to the mysticism attached to the land in Haggard's imperial romances of the Zulus or to the mystical attachment Schreiner imagines the Boers to have. On the contrary, Plaatje's "natives" inhabit the same modern space as their white counterparts, and they have to deal with that space in the same ways. The crucial difference between "natives" and whites is not racial or cultural but political: Black South Africans have to negotiate their lives without access to effective representative bodies.

Some of this demystifying, commonsensical approach in *Native Life in South Africa* comes across in *Mhudi,* too, but in setting the novel historically, Plaatje plays off the literary modes available to him, partly reproducing the imperial romance mode familiar to English readers from the work of Rider Haggard and partly resisting that mode in ways prefigured by Schreiner's work. I do not wish to undermine the originality of *Mhudi,* which has enormous significance in South African literature as the first novel written and published in English by a black South African. However, even the most original of literary works has forebears. As in Schreiner's work, the accommodations Plaatje makes in his fiction with the discursive tradition of African landscape representation attests to the enormous political power of white representations, whether in maps, laws, or novels. In seeking to find a contestatory mode, familiar enough to render the unfamiliar in readable ways to a possibly reluctant audience, Plaatje seems to have learned something from Schreiner. He certainly knew and admired Schreiner's work—to the extent that he named his first daughter, Olive, after her—and set *Mhudi* in a similar landscape to that of *African Farm.* His biographer, Brian Willan, draws particular attention to his "finely drawn . . . descriptions of landscape and natural phenomena" (361). Without Olive Schreiner's example, Plaatje may have found such descriptions harder to produce. While that comment is necessarily speculative, what is certain is that Plaatje could have had no earlier locally produced literary model.[27]

Specific quotations suggest the debt that Plaatje owes to Schreiner's literary example. On one occasion, for instance, he describes the night sky as "purple" (75), recalling the opening scene of *African Farm*. Similarly, in describing Mhudi's response to the landscape of the Free State she travels across, Plaatje, like Schreiner, not only stresses the oppressive vastness, the barrenness and ugliness, but also focuses on insects—the ladybirds, butterflies, ants, and centipedes—as counterindications of life and beauty on a comprehensible scale (153–54). Such local similarities, however, are less significant than the general differences in the purposes to which the two writers put their landscape description. As we have seen, however, Plaatje's role as a representative of "natives" dispossessed of their land by the 1913 Natives Land Act means that his agenda differs significantly from Schreiner's. He is less interested in correcting Europeans' romanticized version of African geography than, like Achebe in *Things Fall Apart*, with providing an alternative to their versions of African history. His agenda is to people that previously unpeopled space of European cartography, art, and literature. Moreover, while Plaatje is unconcerned with giving lessons in landscape to his potential European audience, such lessons would be even less significant for his potential African audience. As Tim Couzens points out, the style of *Mhudi*, despite some overly ornate periphrasis, owes much to local oral traditions of storytelling (Plaatje 12–13), in which the landscape is, of course, familiar, rather than, in Schreiner's case, previously unpainted or romanticized out of all existence. As an ironic result of this difference in agenda—concentrating on the African subject, Mhudi, rather than the African object, the farm—Plaatje seems much more willing to pander to romanticized European norms of landscape, presumably in part as a deliberate strategy of familiarization. Not only does *Mhudi* involve no fewer than three hairbreadth escapes from lions,[28] but Plaatje also has Mhudi ascending to the tops of koppies (43, 156) from which to view the prospects before her, prospects that teem with game in quantities to match Blixen's descriptions of Edenic Kenya; the sense of spiritual elevation that accompanies the physical also reminds one of Blixen.

Furthermore, Plaatje sets a crucial scene in which Ra-Thaga (Mhudi's Rolong husband) and the good Boer de Villiers tend their wounds in a conventionally idyllic kloof. This is a crucial scene, as I say, because it links the alliance of Barolong and Boer with the image of desirable land. From where the two comrades sit, they can see the progress of a "trickling fountain" that winds its way down the escarpment to a "dell" before "spout[ing] and widen[ing] into a creek whose banks were *rich* with *ver-*

dant grass and other *luxurious* undergrowth" (156; emphasis added). Having described this scene, Plaatje then does exactly what Williams detects in John Clare's writing. He mutes his protest at the actual white appropriation of land by conquest and legislation by romanticizing what has been lost not in terms of the specific history and politics of South Africa but in terms of a generalized Nature: "Leafy trees with creepers round their stout stems stood on the fertile banks of the rustling creek, where their branches furnished many an aerial tryst for birds of every plume. Nature had spread a peaceful calm around the oasis, and it were gross sacrilege for man to rupture the sublimity of the wilderness with his everlasting squabbles" (156).

The question of audience raised earlier might explain Plaatje's strategy here (in the same way that questions of audience might explain Schreiner's male-identified "English South African"). Scenes such as the one just quoted pander to the educated white liberal's sensibility and present readable scenes with whose message s/he can empathize (roughly: This is a rich and beautiful land with resources ample enough for all of us), while at the same time establishing Plaatje's own credibility by demonstrating that he knows and can use the writerly conventions. And the educated white liberal reader might well have embraced the doubly euphoric ending of *Mhudi* (the two good Boers—Hannetjie van Zyl and de Villiers—and the two heroic Barolong—Mhudi and Ra-Thaga—head off into the sunset in marital bliss) not just for its romance but for the way in which Mhudi and Ra-Thaga's grateful acquisition of a wagon and a gun[29] from de Villiers endorses the idea that material progress is unambiguously beneficial and dependent on the passing of technological know-how from white to black.

However, Plaatje is nothing if not politically canny, and *Mhudi* also carries a much more radical message, in tune with the ideals of black nationalism.[30] Through the character of Mhudi he presents a perspective of the Boers more critical than Ra-Thaga's, and through the character of Mzilikazi (enemy of both the Barolong and the Boers for the bulk of the novel) he curses the naïveté of Barolong collaboration with the Boers. While Ra-Thaga allies himself with de Villiers, Mhudi finally associates herself with Mzilikazi's youngest and most favored wife, Umnandi. Even though she approves of Hannetjie van Zyl, Mhudi feels an "inexplicable dread" (115) in her dealings with the Boers, a dread which is confirmed by her witnessing Boer violence against first a Hottentot maid (116) and later a Hottentot ox driver (162). Even Ra-Thaga finds the Boer separation of eating and drinking utensils for Boer and non-Boer outrageous (118), but the demands of his collaboration with de Villiers override his need to be frank and honest with his wife, and the two men decide not to tell Mhudi this little detail. Here Ra-Thaga reproduces exactly the same kind of assimilationist position he had earlier taken with regard to the Matabele, when he had justified Mzilikazi's raid on Kunana because Mzilikazi had indisputable property rights and only bothered those subjects who failed to pay legitimate taxes. This passive position raises Mhudi's ire. In terms that radical black nationalists could apply after 1913 to South African whites, she insists that the Matabele are "interlopers and intruders" whose time will come: "Someday, somewhere, and somehow they [the scattered remnants of the Barolong] will turn up and teach Mzilikazi that the crime of one man killing two potential women-slayers is no excuse for massacring whole generations of innocent men, women, and children" (68).

The Matabele do indeed get their comeuppance, mown down by Boer rifles much as a later generation was to be mown down by British Maxim guns in the 1890s during the white settlement of Rhodesia.[31] But while Mhudi's rhetoric appears to endorse notions of deeply ingrained tribal differences, the victimization of the Matabele suggests to me that what Plaatje wants to show is the validity of Mhudi's radical resistance to any interloper and intruder. Might is *not* right, and Ra-Thaga's acceptance of overlordship—whether Matabele or Boer—does involve the ceding of a vital principle of autonomy with regard to the land. Ultimately, it is not the narrative fulfillment of Mhudi's curse on the Matabele that has most resonance in Plaatje's novel but the contemporary, post-1913 fulfillment of Mzilikazi's curse on the Bechuana (including Barolong) collaborators with the Boers. In words whose biblical cadences seem more appropriate than at any other point in the novel, and whose political passion seems more deeply felt than elsewhere, Mzilikazi prophesies that "when the Kiwas [white men] rob them of their cattle, their children, and their lands, they will weep their eyes out of their sockets and get left with only their empty throats to squeal in vain for mercy. They will despoil them of the very lands they have rendered unsafe for us; they will entice the Bechuana youths to war and the chase, only to use them as pack-oxen; yea, they will refuse to share with them the spoils of victory" (175). Had the novel been entitled *Ra-Thaga*, the euphoric romance ending might have drowned out Mzilikazi's curse, suggesting that the future of South Africa lay in good whites and good blacks coming together to build a materially prosperous future. But in choosing Mhudi as his title character and aligning her with the queen of the Matabele, Plaatje subverts that optimistic liberal scenario, providing a parallel, dysphoric ending that is at once more pessimistic yet more assertive of black nationalist rights to the land.

As with Schreiner's depictions of the landscape, therefore, so with Plaatje's. It is impossible to declare that his work is either exclusively conservative or exclusively subversive. Likewise, their respective uses of the novel form also resist such categorization. Even if we decide that Schreiner's work is pioneering, for instance, that there is indeed, as Dan Jacobson writes, "something heroic" in her (re)visionary descriptions of the Karoo, the very nature of literature, the form of the novel, and the English language itself means that no follower in her pioneering footsteps can avoid charges of being at worst complicit with, at best compromised by European culture. Brian Willan writes that Plaatje's novel (and conversely his translations of Shakespeare into Setswana)[32] "was the outcome of a quite conscious and deliberate attempt . . . to marry together two different cultural traditions: African oral forms, particularly those of the Barolong, on the one hand; and the written traditions and forms of the English language and literature on the other" (352).

Such attempts at syncretism did not necessarily earn him the praise of whites or of blacks. Stephen Black, editor of the literary magazine *Sjambok*, which was promoting "realistic short stories of contemporary African life" (Willan 363), impatiently dismissed Plaatje's translations of Shakespeare—"What in God's name the Bechuanas want to read Shakespeare for I don't know, unless it is that they want to feel more like worms than ever" (quoted in Willan 332)—and criticized him in *Mhudi* for having "forgotten Bechuanaland sometimes and remembered only the kingdom of Shakespeare" (quoted in Willan 363). Clement Doke, on the other hand, generally sympathetic to Plaatje and fully aware of Plaatje's commitment to the promotion of Setswana, criticized him for writing in English at all, as "*Mhudi* written in Chwana would have been a still greater contribution, and Chwana sadly needs such additions to its present meagre literature" (Willan 363).

Plaatje's attempt at a "marriage" of African and European traditions, thus, like Schreiner's hybrid text, lays itself open to criticism from all sides. As such, it provides us with an early example of the double-bind faced all over the continent by the later generation of African writers (for example, Achebe and Ngugi) whose opposition to European colonialism initially found literary expression in European languages, but for whom reversion to the vernacular (a) limited audience and (b) carried with it potentially divisive subnationalisms. Even with the contemporary increase of interest in and ascription of value to oral culture, the debate over literary language still rages. Ngugi has given cogent reasons for ditching English and writing in his native Gikuyu (although he is, of course, now exiled from his own tongue by Kenya's postcolonial government), while Achebe continues to defend his use of English. In the new South Africa, committed to nonracialism, language issues are particularly vexed. Any concerted effort to "preserve" a particular language or culture smacks of the kinds of internal divisions of the apartheid era, while privileging any one language threatens the new state's fragile unity by playing into the hands of any group willing to play the nationalist card.[33]

All of the foregoing suggests that, more than a century after *The Story of an African Farm* appeared in print, any representation of African landscape, especially one that, like Schreiner's, claims the weight of moral truth, can cause contention. Even Ngugi, for instance, who rejects the English language in its role as "carrier of culture" (*Decolonising* 13), or Njabulo S. Ndebele, who critiques English for its complicity with imperialism and global capitalism,[34] can be criticized for their totalizing tendency. The English language has also, of course, conveyed counterhegemonic ideas that have had profound influence on culture worldwide. The awarding of Nobel Prizes to "English" writers as diverse as Wole Soyinka, Derek Walcott, Nadine Gordimer, and Seamus Heaney surely provides adequate evidence for Heaney's claim that "English is by now not so much an imperial humiliation as a native weapon" (quoted in Arkins 208–9).[35] One of the features that makes Schreiner's novel virtually the ur-text of colonial hybridity is precisely its attempt to find a language true to the immediate locality that manages to avoid the violence of that imperialist/nationalist confrontation.

This is certainly not a new idea; in fact, it is something of a commonplace and a central idea in Schreiner criticism. Joyce Avrech Berkman sees Schreiner's "revulsion from the binary discourse of her times" leading her to "replace a military articulation of reality" with a "medical counterpart," the "healing imagination" (5) that gives Berkman's study its title. Similarly, Gerald Monsman posits as a main thesis of his book, *Olive Schreiner's Fiction: Landscape and Power*, that Schreiner's "solution to a transformation of the master-servant, male-female, empire-colony hierarchy was not a role reversal in which the disempowered seize control, but a radical role dissolution" (xiii). And it is in these sorts of terms that Christopher Heywood declares that, despite the book's inevitable European ancestry and its focus on European characters, *The Story of an African Farm* does not represent "a false start for the African literary tradition" (30).

Extending Jacobson's analysis of Schreiner's "heroic" opening description which counters European expectations of a night sky to the radical way in which Schreiner debunks "imposed stereotypes" and refuses to accept European anthropological views, Heywood shows how Schreiner instead risks writing from her own experience of the six cultural strands that he identifies as coming together in Cradock (32). In *"The Story of an African Farm*: Society, Positivism, and Myth," Heywood argues that the novel resists the English taxonomic conventions of another Victorian paradigm: the Comtean Positivist paradigm. Heywood suggests three possible divisions of South African cultures into Comte's categories of the primitive (superstitious), barbarian (metaphysical), and Positive (scientific). In each of these divisions, English culture represents the Positive phase of human society while the Khoi (Hottentot), San (Bushman), Nguni (Bantu), Boers, and Germans occupy, in various arrangements, the positions of the primitive and barbarian.[36]

However, even though Lyndall occasionally utters what looks like a Positivist credo, the full effect of *The Story of an African Farm* is to show the inadequacies of Comtean classification. As Heywood points out, the English in the novel are not uniformly civilized: The intellectual, unsettled Lyndall is sharply differentiated from the placid Em; Bonaparte Blenkins is, in Heywood's view, a barbarian (33);[37] and Gregory Rose is scarcely a Positivist model, settling as he does for "the lame ending of a piece of land acquired through marriage" (34). Furthermore, it is the Hottentot (Khoi) maid who translates Blenkins's "incomprehensible English" for Tant' Sannie. Waldo, meanwhile, who plays the role of German artist alter ego to the English intellectual Lyndall, might be seen as primitive either through classification among the impoverished German settlers of the region or through association with the Bushman (San) artist, whose rock paintings Waldo alone seems to appreciate (*African Farm* 49–50). In short, Schreiner's representation of all her characters shows an awareness of (post)colonial hybridity, a radical resistance to what Heywood calls "the straitjacket of ideas offered by the metropolitan cultural world" (38).[38]

But it is chiefly the characterization of Waldo that makes Heywood defend the novel against charges of being a "false start" in South African literature, and he suggests that we might look to Waldo's tentative artistic identification with the Bushman (San) artists (*African Farm* 49) and his ultimate return to and death on the farm as an affirmation of Africanness (Vivan 35). In language reminiscent of Ruskin's descriptions of medieval art, Schreiner introduces "some old Bushman-paintings . . . grotesque oxen, elephants, rhinoceroses, and a one-horned beast, such as no man ever has seen or ever shall" (44). While Em and Lyndall sit "with their backs to the paintings," indifferent, Waldo reveals an intense imaginative sympathy for the "old wild Bushm[a]n that painted those pictures there" (49). The Bushman shares Waldo's (and the medieval gargoyle carver's) unconscious, almost elemental urge to paint: "He did not know why he painted but he wanted to make something, so he made these. He worked hard, very hard, to find the juice to make the paint; and then he found this place where the rocks hang over, and he painted them. To us they are only strange things, that make us laugh; but to him they were very beautiful" (50). In fact, Waldo is moved not to laughter but to an odd state encompassing both "deep excitement" and "a dreamy look." He concludes his excited reverie with the revelation that the very stones seem to be talking to and through him. He is snapped out of his "trance" and returned to the mundane reality of his shepherd's duty by Lyndall curtly assuring him, "It never seems so to me" (50). Any identification thus remains "tentative," but there is at least some acknowledgment of a native tradition of representation not bound by European models, a tradition that might offer a model to build on rather than react against.

It has taken a very long time for white South African culture to advance down the path of identification. In literature, specifically African forms of poetry have only recently emerged in white poets writing in English or Afrikaans. Antjie Krog, for instance, whose explicitly erotic verse and candid confrontations of issues of race and gender first aroused controversy in the Afrikaans literary community in the 1980s,[39] has used

Sotho models in some of her work, using the rhyming of images rather than of sounds, as in Sotho oral praise songs. The praise song has been modified to suit the purposes of the trade union movement, with the poets of Black Mamba Rising using that native form to express their dissent within an essentially European social formation.[40] The general level of visibility of indigenous vocabulary in apparently "English" texts appears to have risen considerably in recent years, and it will no doubt continue to rise under the linguistic dispensations of the "new" South Africa, especially as reflected by policy on education and broadcasting.[41]

As to the language of artistic representation, it is perhaps harder to disentangle "African" from "European" vocabulary. The need for graphic representation in the highly politicized art in the final years of the apartheid regime, for instance, allowed little space for the "native," a category that would have been extremely suspicious, anyway, as possibly playing into the regime's notions of essential differences between "tribes" and races. The Bushmen, of course, played so little part in the political rearrangements that they were left exclusively to anthropologists and Laurens van der Post. Meanwhile, all African art becomes grist for the European mill, one of the most striking examples being the $96 million change British Airways made in 1997 from nationalistically "flying the flag" to flying the world on its tail; one of the designs now adorning BA's airliners uses the traditional patterns and colors of Ndebele murals.

However, even given the idea that language or any set of signs can be reappropriated in any way, it seems to me still valid to locate the source of landscape representation in a specifically European history, and it is interesting to compare the pictures of Dutch/Afrikaner painter Jan Hendrik Pierneef, "long . . . acknowledged as the foremost interpreter of the SA [sic] landscape" (Berman 223), with Schreiner's literary depictions.

The son of Dutch parents, Pierneef (1886–1957) trained at the Rotterdam Art Academy. Back in South Africa he came under the influence of other European-trained artists, such as Frans Oerder. Revisiting Holland in 1925–26, he was further influenced by the Dutch painter and formalist theorist van Konijnenburg. The outcome was a style that expressed the landscape by schematizing forms and separating colors (Fransen 295). Like Schreiner's putative painter, Pierneef squeezed the color from his brush and, according to Hans Fransen, "his palette was so closely attuned to the Transvaal color spectrum that he found it difficult to change over to the more saturated colors of the Cape[42] during his periodic visits to that region" (295). In his linocuts, "simplified to large black and white planes" (296), he squeezed color out completely.

As such, Pierneef looks like the right-seeing artist Schreiner imagined herself to be, whose accurate representation of the South African landscape would counter colonialist conventions. However, Pierneef's "virtually unchallenged position as [South Africa's] most successful artist" (296) shifts attention away from the colonialist/anticolonial question to the issue of settler nationalism. Pierneef's early concerns with form were superseded by his "directing himself to the cause of a hypothetical ideal of 'national art'" (Berman 223). During the 1930s, Pierneef established himself as South Africa's national painter, earning a number of highly significant public commissions, including a series of landscapes for South Africa House in London. Most prominent of his public works within South Africa is the series of murals he designed for the Johannesburg railway station. Marvelous though these may be, the association with the South African Railways system, notoriously segregated both as to passengers and as to job reservation, suggests that these accurate, "native" landscapes, "embrac[ing] views of several quarters of the country, giving expression to the separate character of each" (Berman 225), remain racially exclusive. No less than the words of Langenhoven's national anthem, "Die Stem van Suid-Afrika," they reproduce the Afrikaner mythology of "ver verlate vlakte" (roughly "endless empty plains") waiting for domestication and control, first by wagon, subsequently by railway trains.

I shall return in the final chapter to the effect on public memory and "history" of public memorials, where I will suggest that no mode of memorialization can remain exclusive for long. Schreiner's writing of the South African landscape—like Africa itself "tied by blood and anguish to Europe," as Heywood has it (38)—creates new possibilities for seeing South Africa. Ultimately, however, there is no way of limiting who will turn away from her art, as Lyndall turns her back on the Bushman paintings, and who, like Waldo, will attempt to use it. Neither is there any way of predicting the political applications of any such use, whether nationalist and racially exclusive or in the interests of a healing, holistic vision.

Culture, Cultivation, and Colonialism in *Out of Africa* and Beyond

In an essay written in 1991 entitled "Consuming Isak Dinesen," Susan Hardy Aiken points out that since the filming of *Out of Africa* and *Babette's Feast*, Isak Dinesen has "once again become a pop icon, the subject of fascinated speculation, fashionable imitation, and culinary fabrication" (3). Indeed, since Meryl Streep and Robert Redford first introduced Karen Blixen and Denys Finch Hatton to a mass audience, *Out of Africa* has been put to any number of commercial uses as part of a wave of reactionary nostalgia in western popular culture.[1] The ease with which Blixen's work has been thus co-opted seems to confirm what I argued in the previous chapter, that it is easy to show the complicity of Blixen's and Schreiner's inventions of African farms with hegemonic discourse. One of the consequences of the commercial success of *Out of Africa* has been to facilitate dismissal of Blixen by reading her work backwards, as it were, through the filmmakers' glossing and turning her books into "mere supplements to capitalist technology" (Aiken 4).

Ngugi wa Thiong'o, whose depictions of Kenyan landscape and the struggles over it contrast sharply with Blixen's, reads any connection between the exploitation in and of Blixen's work not backwards but forwards, seeing a "continuity" between Blixen's Africa and postcolonial Kenya (*Moving the Centre* xiii) and seeing Blixen herself as "embod-[ying] the great racist myth at the heart of the Western bourgeois civilization" (135).[2] Such dismissive readings, in Aiken's view, overlook a number of complicating factors, including Blixen's role as a woman in colonial society.[3] In this chapter I propose to explore Ngugi's allegation of racist continuity between the colonial and postcolonial. As in chapter 4, I proceed initially through a literary-cultural analysis of *Out of Africa* in relation to European traditions of the pastoral, and then assess the book's continuing significance by examining wider, more material questions concerning the occupation and commodification of tracts of African land, both in Kenya and in southern Africa from the end of the nineteenth century to the present. Answers to these questions provide ways to demonstrate the persistence long into the postcolonial era of certain colonial attitudes toward culture, cultivation, and conservation, a persistence that in part explains the connection between Blixen's writerly exploitation of Africa and Africans and her exploitability as a medium for those interested in selling exotic colonial chic to a Western audience still hungry for the safari image of Africa.[4]

Let us start where Blixen starts, with the farm which she had. The opening sentence of *Out of Africa* establishes her having (or having had) the farm as the point of departure for the whole book, without any history of prior possession, without any reference to negotiation or purchase, and without the slightest hint that settlers' rights to their farms might have been "secured by murder and sustained by extortion" (Ward 51).[5] Having the farm according to Blixen's formulation, a formulation faithfully repeated in the movie with Meryl Streep's beautifully cadenced voice-over, at once proud and regretful, naturalizes Blixen's presence in Africa. She had a farm the same way one might have brown hair or a bad temper, a particular experience or a disease. Her having the farm is no more a political act than Old MacDonald's having a farm in the nursery song.

The comparison with Old MacDonald may appear trivial, but the apparent innocence of both texts depends on and promotes the assumption that it is part of the natural order of things for individuals to have farms. Moreover, in the same way that the nursery song identifies for children a certain knowledge of various farm animals and what they say, Blixen's work provides a certain knowledge of Africa and what it says, while the limited articulacy of farm animals matches the limited articulation ascribed to Africans. However, while the song implies the more or less autonomous type of farm that we might call a smallholding with its mix of stereotypical farm animals all oinking, quacking, mooing, and producing directly for Old MacDonald, Blixen's 6,000-acre plantation, requiring intensive labor to produce coffee for export, and encompassing the space of some 2,000 squatters, is a horse of a different color, saturated in ideology.

To examine the ideology of having a farm in colonial Africa, we need to question further the very notion of "culture," particularly in that term's relation to "nature," "cultivation," "civilization," "agriculture," and "colony," and especially as they impinge on each other in the late nineteenth and early twentieth centuries. In chapter 2, I referred to Robert Young's argument that Victorian ideas of culture frequently and crucially coincided with race, which in turn led to a link between Arnold's anxiety about anarchy and late Victorian fears about degeneration. By the century's end, Arnold's notion of a singular, though flexible, culture capable of providing a defense against anarchy was becoming less and less tenable in the face of more relativist thinking. For instance, in *The Predicament of Culture*, James Clifford claims that as "evolutionist confidence began to falter" by the turn of the century, "The word began to be used in the plural, suggesting a world of separate, distinctive, and equally meaningful ways of life. The ideal of an autonomous, cultivated subject could appear as a local project, not a *telos* for all humankind" (93).

Furthermore, the shared etymological root of *colony* and *culture* (from Latin *colere,* with a range of meanings including "to cultivate" and "to inhabit") suggests for Young that "colonization rests at the heart of culture, or culture always involves a form of colonization, even in relation to its conventional meaning as the tilling of the soil" (30). Young also notes how the metaphor of cultivation came to be appropriated by city folk, so that from the mid-eighteenth century *cultivated* and *cultured* "took on a class-fix" (31). Both cultivated and a colonist, Karen Blixen is thus able to present her lifestyle on her farm in Africa as the acme of a kind of natural, or at least extrasocial, civilization. "I will be a civilized being," she declares in the section titled "Of Pride." "I will love the pride of my adversaries, of my servants, and my lover; and my house shall be, in all humility, in the wilderness a civilized place." At least at one level, then, she seems to believe that the "civilization" of her house depends solely on her and her will. However, her final sentence in this manifesto-style section seems to make an implied acknowledgment, at least in part, that this civilization is dependent on colonization: "Love the pride of the conquered nations, and leave them to honour their father and their mother" (223–24).

The period of history of a colonized, conquered Africa that this study primarily deals with is thus a period when the notion of culture as a quality you either have or don't have (frequently dependent on race) was under pressure from a newer notion that culture has no opposite, that we inhabit a world replete with different cultures. Valentin Mudimbe, commenting on the dramatic "irruption of the Other in the European consciousness" at this time, quotes Paul Ricoeur's "anguished propositions" that "at the time when we acknowledge the end of a sort of cultural monopoly, be it illusory or real, we are threatened with destruction by our own discovery. Suddenly it becomes possible that there are just *others,* that we ourselves are an 'other' among others. All meaning and every goal having disappeared, it becomes possible to wander through civilizations as if through vestiges and ruins" (Mudimbe, *Invention* 20, 21).

Blixen demonstrates this cultural anguish as much by avoidance as by anything explicit. Her nostalgic invention of the farm she had between 1914 and 1931 takes us back well beyond the contemporary crisis of the late 1930s and produces racialized models of culture and civilization that simultaneously valorize both the apparently timeless authenticity of the Maasai, for example, and Denys Finch Hatton's ancient English lineage.[6] Her life in Kenya is presented not so much as life in another place as life in another time, and this temporal displacement allows her to appear to endorse the modern anthropologist's belief in the plurality of civilizations without denting her faith in the transcendence of aristocratic European culture. In fact, *Out of Africa* and the later *Shadows on the Grass* present Blixen's ability to appreciate other cultures as a mark of her own cultivation and culture. Her readers responded enthusiastically to Blixen's inventions. Because their own worlds were "increasingly defined by the urban, the industrial, the plutocratic, the tame, and the tacky," Blixen's "pristine Africa marked by adventure, freedom, and power" had enormous appeal (Knipp 3). And the African farm, where the wild and the tame, freedom and control, nature and culture, civilizations and civilization meet, is a key site in Karen Blixen's literary invention.

Above all, Blixen's representation of her farm ignores the political. Although she represents it as the place where "Nature" and "culture" meet, the "culture" she describes in and through her self-representation and representation of Denys Finch Hatton, Lord Delamere, and those fellow aristocrats she treats as her peers, is a static, even anachronistic thing. It is not white-settler "culture" (which she largely scorns) but the culture of an earlier age and distant place. Finch Hatton and Berkeley Cole, writes Blixen, were "outcasts," "examples of atavism" whose England was "an earlier England, a world which no longer existed" (184). However, as

Dane Kennedy observes, while Blixen's use of the word *atavism* calls to mind Joseph Schumpeter's theories of imperialism as social atavism driven by irrational, anticapitalist impulses, in fact, "No one had shrewder capitalist instincts than that atavistic circle which included Cranworth, Delamere, the Cole brothers, Finch Hatton, and Grogan."[7] Thus, while Finch Hatton and Cole may indeed be "outcasts," it needs to be stressed that they were "refugees not from capitalism, but from industrialism and its corollaries." In setting the farm up with a fallacious Old MacDonald-esque autonomy as a place where outcasts can feel at home because it, like them, is not really *of* the landscape, Blixen significantly underplays the fact that "property and profit were among the central preoccupations of the society they made in Kenya" (Kennedy 47).

Blixen's displacement of an already achieved "culture" to the new cultural formation of a colony in which "nature" has yet to be tamed carries further complications. Matthew Arnold's notion of culture, or Kenneth Clark's notion of civilization, is something that manifests itself primarily in a domestic environment and hence tends to be associated with cities. Any secondary manifestation in the country is, as Raymond Williams shows, a highly complex one, involving nostalgia for a culture ironically closer to nature and requiring the overlooking of economic conditions that bind the country and the city together. The farmhouse or country manor thus plays a pivotal role in ruling-class attitudes to culture and nature.

It is abundantly clear that Blixen's *Out of Africa*, with its playing up of the natural grandeur of the farm and its playing down of Karen Coffee's position in the local and international economy, clearly conforms to Williams's model of later European pastoral, in which "intensity of attention to natural beauty . . . is now the nature of observation, of the scientist or the tourist, rather than of the working countryman." Likewise, the portrayal of the farmhouse and its aristocratic denizens is in line with Tasso's *Aminta*, in which, according to Williams, "the shepherd is an idealized mask, a courtly disguise" (20). *Out of Africa*'s representation of an Arcadian existence, largely overlooking the displacement of the actual Arcadians, harks back to that original Elizabethan courtier, Sir Philip Sidney, in whose company Blixen claims Denys Finch Hatton would have been at home (*Out of Africa* 186). Even Blixen's care for "her" laborers and squatters, elevating her role within the agricultural community against less scrupulous neighbors, puts *Out of Africa* in the same category as Ben Jonson's *To Penshurst* in which the "moral economy" prevails. Blixen's memoirs present the farm, exactly as *To Penshurst* does, as the site of a "natural order of responsibility and neighbourliness and charity" (Williams 30). Williams's conclusion on Jonson's poem and Carew's *To Saxham* applies, with some provisos, to *Out of Africa:* "What is really happening, in Jonson's and Carew's celebrations of a rural order, is an extraction of just this curse [of labor], by the power of art: a magical re-creation of what can be seen as a natural bounty and then a willing charity: both serving to ratify and bless the country landowner, or, by a characteristic reification, his house. Yet this magical extraction of the curse of labor is in fact achieved by a simple extraction of the existence of labourers" (32).

While it is obviously not entirely the case that Blixen's book overlooks the laborers (the movie, interestingly enough, does a more thorough job of that), it is equally obvious that in her portraiture of Kamante and Farah Aden, Blixen favors the representation of domestic over agricultural labor, particularly when that domestic labor tends to reconfirm her own significance or, as Susan Horton puts it, serves "as a kind of audience in attendance at [her] identity formation" (72). In fact, what is interesting is precisely the inclusion of reified groups of peasantry, laborers, and "natives" at the expense of the boring bourgeoisie: farm managers, accountants, agents, and the like.[8] *Out of Africa* gives the impression that Karen Blixen had unmediated connection with her workforce, that the day-to-day running of the farm depended on her personality as a kind of primum mobile. She may have been unable to predict or control the weather, but the workings of her workers' minds, the nature of their desires, and so on are transparent in the godlike omniscience of her narrative. The gods of Europe—of family and money—feature in Blixen's letters, not her memoirs.

The case of Kamante, the "Savage in the Immigrant's House" whom Blixen presents as some kind of idiot savant as a foil to European sophistication, is particularly revealing in terms of Blixen's extraction of the curse of African labor. Kamante came to her as an orphan from the plains, Blixen writes, just as the baby gazelle Lulu had come to her from the forest (63). He turns out to have had "all the attributes of genius" for cooking, with a particular "gift for making things light" (41). In his culinary art Kamante matches the Ngong Hills' and Denys Finch Hatton's aeroplane's miraculous effects of literal and spiritual elevation, producing egg whites which "towered up like light clouds" (41). However, this skill of Kamante's Blixen presents as some kind of enormous eccentricity, almost a divine practical joke. "Nothing," she writes, "could be more mysterious than this natural instinct in a savage for our culinary art" (41). Furthermore, Kamante has no real appreciation of his own skill, which leads Blixen to comment on the perversity of his preferring his traditional food and his lack of intelligence in occasionally offering her "a Kikuyu delicacy . . . even as a civilized dog who has lived for a long time with people will place a bone on the floor before you as a present" (43).[9] In presenting Kamante's genius in this way, Blixen diminishes the human effort Kamante put into his task, and she hides the fact that his cooking was a job, rather than the art Blixen transmutes it into. Her own role as employer vanishes in such phrases as "he understood to perfection what I wished of him, and sometimes he carried out my wishes even before I had told him of them" (42). Although Blixen declares that Kamante "felt nothing but contempt" for his art, he himself does not comment on what he thought or felt about his skill, and when Blixen does afford him utterance through snippets of dialogue and of letters written to her once she had left the farm, the emphasis on his unfamiliarity with European assumptions and the stiltedness of his English casts him more or less in the role of Fool to Blixen's King Lear, rather than as a fully autonomous being.

In his own language, meanwhile, Kamante was really Kamande Gatura. He was not a stray wild animal like Lulu but a Gikuyu whose connection with the land of Blixen's farm was not to a mythic, asocial Africa but, as with Plaatje's "natives" in South Africa, to a political history of ancestral inheritance and a political present of dispossession. In the 1950s, Kamande Gatura was one of the thousands of Gikuyu imprisoned for taking the Mau Mau oath, a fact that Blixen feels "uneasy" about recording in *Shadows on the Grass* and that prompts her to ask whether this "eternal hermit, the 'rogue' head of game, by his own choice totally isolated from the herd, here at last through a dark inhuman formula experienced some kind of human fellowship?" (*Shadows* 146). The reference to Mau Mau comes as an unsettling shock to readers that Kamante had his existence in a wider society than Karen Blixen's house, a wider society that Blixen still tries to keep at bay by insisting on Kamante's voluntary opting out. Here we see as clearly as anywhere how Blixen's pastoral cuts out the curse not only of labor itself but of the history whereby the conditions of that labor were legitimated. Representing Kamante as cook and loyal domestic servant—one of the civilizing features of her house in the wilderness—in this way allows her to remove any competition for the reader's sympathy. Blixen gives herself license to mourn the loss of her land, while the Gikuyu mourn the loss of Karen Blixen the benevolent landowner.

In thus ratifying and blessing the landowner and her house, then, Blixen's memoirs can be seen to fit Williams's extension of the country/city pattern to metropole/colony. Indeed, they provide a fascinating test case of his claim that "one of the last models of 'city and country' is the system we now know as imperialism" (279). The role of labor on her farm may not be totally overlooked, but the relation of that labor to the system of colonialism—acknowledgment of which would have diminished Karen Blixen's own personal significance—is ignored. Although *Out of Africa* might indeed respect "the pride of the conquered nations," nowhere does Blixen address the process by which they were conquered, the process by which her house could be civilized.

Nor does she address the issue of her own relation to those who did the conquering. Instead, her memoir creates an extratemporal as well as extrasocial African feudal order, remaining silent about the actual place of the Karen Coffee Company historically and in terms of the world economic order. The Ngong Hills weren't a utopia, a "no-place" inhabited only by orphaned totos and gazelles like Kamante and Lulu grateful for a secure home; they already were the home of, among others, Maasai and Gikuyu people for whom, according to Jomo Kenyatta, "land tenure was the most important factor in the social, political, religious, and economic life of the tribe" (22). Blixen's presence on land they had always considered their own was thus part of a violent social displacement, however benevolent she may have deemed herself, and regardless of whether or not individuals like Kamante may have respected her. Susan Horton acutely sums up the ambiguity of her position: "The largest part of *Shadows on the Grass* constructs for her the classic identity of the pioneer going it alone, solving individual health, economic, and educational problems for the natives as if neither she nor they were playing roles specifically designed for them by those policies that were systematically and indeed purposively generating exactly those problems she was setting herself to solve" (218).

The process of displacement and the policies that brought it about included the imposition of all sorts of legal codes and regulations, including taxes. And in the same way that colonization might be fundamental to culture, so taxation is essential to colonization. Here again, etymology supports the claim. In addition to meaning farmer, the Latin word *agricola* could also mean tax collector.[10] Karen Blixen demonstrates that the same dual meaning extends into the French *fermier:* "For some of the years on the farm I had been holding the office of *fermier général* there—that is, in order to save the Government trouble I collected the taxes from my squatters locally and sent in the sum total to Nairobi" (*Shadows* 85). The occupation of farming by whites in Africa—even if those whites saw themselves as independent and idealist aristocrats— was thus a large part of the general colonial occupation of the land. While individual farmers, like Karen Blixen, might present their struggles with drought, disease, etc., as elemental, those struggles are also economic. The farm produces revenue (or fails to produce, as the case may be), just as much as it produces (or fails to produce) any natural agricultural product. What is more, while individual white farmers might see themselves as victims both of natural and political forces, especially of political forces unsympathetic to a farmer's struggles with nature, such farmers—simply by virtue of being white—were necessarily beneficiaries of colonial policies. In short, while Karen Blixen the farmer worried about the rain on her land, Karen Blixen the *fermier* was consolidating Britain's reign over Kenya. Her "ownership" of the 6,000 acres of her farm might be put in quotation marks not just to indicate her questionable right to that land but also to highlight the fact that, in the end, she was always tied to the European system of capital, a fact that became all too obvious when she, too, was forced from the land, and the farm was developed into the suburb which still bears her name.

One of the significant features of early British policy on colonization in Kenya of equating development with agricultural development inadvertently (but perfectly predictably, given the rules of the capitalist game) led to the agricultural underdevelopment of the country. Making land available at rock-bottom prices and favorable lease rates in order to encourage settler-farmers to immigrate actually fueled high levels of land speculation. One of the consequences was that it became far more profitable to own land than to farm it. According to Richard D. Wolff, "By 1930, 64.8 percent of the land available to Europeans was not in any form of agriculturally productive activity" (60). Similarly, in Southern Rhodesia, land and cattle taken from the Matabele in the 1893 war were cashed in "for immediate profit, not long-term development," with most of the cattle going to slaughter houses in South Africa, and land ending up in the hands of a coterie of very rich men (Kennedy 16–17). The consequences—agricultural as well as political—for independent Kenya and Zimbabwe were dire.

Although the South African situation is markedly different, notably as a result of the greater length of white settlement in the respective areas and as a result of the Boers' complex relationship to colonialism, certain key similarities nonetheless exist between the displacement and proletarianization of the indigenous population in all three cases. Key colonial legislation, such as pass laws in Kenya and South Africa, the notorious 1913 Natives' Land Act in South Africa or the so-called *kifagio* or clearing out of the Gikuyu in Kenya, inexorably reduced the viability of African farming. From a position of relative autonomy, as farmers in their own right, Africans were reduced to the status of laborers on white farms; their limited options for other employment, among other factors, made them prey to unscrupulous bosses and kept the cost of their labor artificially low. In addition, white farming in both regions was frequently, though not reliably, supported by various active and direct government subsidies. Particularly in South Africa, where "poor whites" were both a problem and a possible constituency, government policy deliberately aimed to preempt situations in which it became evident that white farming was less efficient, less productive, less profitable than black farming. The racial ideology of British colonialism and of proto-apartheid South Africa could not allow such situations.

In fact, Karen Blixen's openness in *Out of Africa* about the failure of Karen Coffee ought to have given the lie to the myth of white farming's greater efficiency, productivity, and profitability, just as her description of her squatters' plight when she was forced to sell the farm ought to have given the lie to the notion of a natural evolution of a capitalist agriculture in the first place. As Susan Horton comments, in the earliest years of British settlement in Kenya, "The Kikuyu were by and large more prosperous and successful farmers than were European settlers."[11] But by the end of her stay in Kenya, successive colonial administrations had placed legal restrictions on their "'get-ahead' spirit," which in turn "was beginning to transform the Kikuyu into 'Mau Mau'" (209).[12]

Similarly, Tim Keegan and Charles van Onselen, through the Wits

Oral History Project, have shown how the capitalization of South African farming did not come about through some sort of natural selection process whereby the fittest white farming techniques survived, driving peasant and pastoralist to extinction. Rather, the creation of a capitalist South African agriculture depended on massive government intervention through legislation, advantageous economic incentives, and the development of infrastructure in the service of big capital, all underpinned by military and police power. Those farms that were most highly capitalized and seemed to be models of "progressive" farming were not necessarily the most efficient or even profitable[13] and were either playthings of the very rich—"objects of conspicuous consumption" (Keegan 115)—or else, like the fictional farm in Nadine Gordimer's *Conservationist*, a tax write-off.

The stories of African farms that we have in writers such as Blixen, Schreiner, Lessing, and Gordimer present fair reflections of the frequent failure of white farming in Africa, both of its inadequacy to adapt to local conditions and of its vulnerability to fluctuations in international commodity markets. In denying the "natural bounty" of the farm's production, such stories, as I suggested earlier, do not make a perfect match with Raymond Williams's description of *To Penshurst* as a model of the pastoral in English. However, they occasionally make a virtue of their failure in a way similar to the "self-consciously rural mode of display" that Williams identifies in later pastoral in the social imagery of the late nineteenth-century country house novel. As with later works by George Eliot and Henry James, so to some extent and to different ends with Karen Blixen and Nadine Gordimer, the country houses are "the country-houses of capital rather than of land. More significantly and more ritually than ever before, a rural mode was developed, as a cultural superstructure, on the profits of industrial and imperial development. It was a mode of play: an easy realisation of the old imagery of Penshurst: field sports, fishing, and above all horses; often a marginal interest in conservation and 'old country ways'" (282).

The latter catalog of field sports and so on applies perfectly to *Out of Africa* and *Shadows on the Grass* where we recognize that interest in the farm is secondary to interest in the park. While Blixen does very little as a farmer in the memoirs, her hunting experiences provide occasion for some of the most detailed and intense descriptions in the books. She uses them to show herself in an almost elemental relationship with an Africa which in turn makes her and her hunting partner (Finch Hatton) into almost mythic figures outside whose "torchlight there was nothing but darkness" (*Out of Africa* 202).

It also provides occasion for some of the books' most blatant snobbery and fabrication with Blixen relating how she gave lion skins to "the Indian High Priest" (*Out of Africa* 203) and to King Christian X of Denmark, in the latter case claiming to have shot the lion herself (*Out of Africa* 198; *Shadows* 59–67).[14] The letter of thanks from the king is transformed into Blixen's famous "barua a soldani," which, she claims, her squatters viewed as a kind of talisman capable of performing miracles. Their use of it as a source of healing left the letter, according to *Shadows on the Grass*, "undecipherable, brown and stiff with blood and matter of long ago," and Blixen claims, "Within [the letter], in paper and blood, a covenant has been signed between the Europeans and the Africans—no similar document of this same relationship is likely to be drawn up again" (74). That powerful nexus of images and presentation—hunting in an elemental Africa, the consciously heraldic use of the lion, the miraculous power of the letter, Blixen's religious diction ("covenant")—creates an impression of a lost Arcadian romance, an impression whose artificiality was exposed by the discovery in 1969 of "the well-preserved, completely unspotted letter from King Christian X" (Lasson, *Letters* xiv).

That discovery might stand as an example of the disingenuousness of Blixen's pastoral, but my main point at this juncture is that the interest in hunting is one that is bound up with class snobbery and self-aggrandizement. Even Blixen's alleged change of attitude toward hunting over her time in Kenya fits Williams's definition of the new country house dweller who takes "a marginal interest in conservation." In her last ten years in Kenya, despite finding lion hunting "irresistible," Blixen writes, "It became to me an unreasonable thing, indeed in itself ugly or vulgar, for the sake of a few hours' excitement to put out a life that belonged in the great landscape" (58). But who or what is she interested in conserving, and *for* whom or what? Her own linking of reason with notions of ugliness and vulgarity—aesthetic and class judgments—suggests that what she most bemoans the passing of is the aesthetic-aristocratic principle of which she and Finch Hatton were exemplars.[15] Unlike the common mob, they intuitively knew the proper way to hunt, and Blixen's continued attraction to hunting lions in particular—top of the hierarchy in Blixen's mythological bestiary—attests to the way in which the ability to participate in field sports generally is governed by class considerations. For the country house "conservationist," when everybody hunts, the problem is not so much that animal populations are depleted but that the social cachet of hunting itself is diminished.[16]

Specific arguments regarding hunting all reveal the "gentlemanly" aura surrounding it. Schreiner's contemporary, F. C. Selous, whose elephant killing exploits in southern Africa had established him as the "mighty Nimrod" of the Victorian era, became an advocate of conservation by the end of the century, campaigning for "the preservation of African game" by "the prevention of the acquisition of fire-arms by the native tribes, and . . . the total prohibition of all commerce or trade in the skins and horns of wild animals by them or white men" (cited in Taylor 272). Selous proposed, reasonably enough in his own terms, that hunting should only be carried out by the licensed few. But the implication that the "few" should be responsible individuals like himself—that is, non-Africans not involved in trade—neatly reveals a pair of Victorian race and class prejudices.

In 1929 Finch Hatton embroiled himself in a row concerning the ineffectiveness of the Tanganyika authorities to prevent the unsportsmanlike "wholesale slaughter of game from motor cars" (Trzebinski 397–403). Fully endorsing the language of a letter from one Andries Pienaar, Finch Hatton—like Blixen—attacks such slaughter on aesthetic and class grounds, rather than environmental grounds, picking on wealthy Americans who are out to kill as much as possible in order to "figure in magazines as 'Famous Big Game Hunters.'" Finch Hatton is revolted by these activities and shares Pienaar's outrage that their perpetrators "had never been in Africa before, but a single safari sufficed to raise them to the first ranks as the greatest hunters." Finch Hatton's letter to the *Times* (where else?) goaded Douglas Jardine, then chief secretary to the governor of Tanganyika, into a response which, while denying the authorities' ineffectiveness, reproduced exactly Finch Hatton's gentlemanly attitudes. "As a sportsman," he writes, "I bow to no one—not even to Mr. Finch Hatton in my detestation of such butchery," and he categorizes those outragers of "the sportsman's code" as "certain tourists with more money than taste," that is, with new money rather than old.[17] The exchange is a fascinating example of how shared hegemonic class attitudes can shape or misshape the terms of a particular debate, and it reveals all sorts of colonialist prejudice; again, however, what is significant is the way in which the elitism of the "country way of life" manifests itself in attitudes toward field sports and conservation.[18] These attitudes were by no means limited to Kenya, nor have they outlived their usefulness to the West. British settlers farther south (in present-day South Africa and Zimbabwe) were mainly from the lower middle class, without Kenya's relatively high proportion of aristocratic leaders, and thus had to invent the culture which the Delameres, Coles, and Blixens could import.[19] Nonetheless, even a writer usually as critical of the colonial enterprise as Olive Schreiner could redeploy the notion. Although, as Susan Horton points out, Schreiner feels great, though contradictory, admiration for the cultural qualities of African community and Afrikaner individualism (Horton 219–21), the site of "culture" is still England, an England characterized in the male-identified *English South African's View* by "the old oar with which we won our first boating victory on Cam or Thames" (*English South African* 5). Schreiner's identification here of "culture" with the model gentleman/intellectual/sportsman—the ideal Rhodes scholar!—may, given its context, be a strategic one, playing on her audience's presumed prejudices. But other private references suggest that even Schreiner largely subscribed to hegemonic Victorian beliefs regarding "culture."[20]

The persistence of those beliefs into the contemporary era and the buying of "culture" through landownership are nowhere better illustrated than in the works of Nadine Gordimer. *The Conservationist*, in particular, in which the "white" farm is actually farmed exclusively by blacks on behalf of the owner, Mehring, probes the psychology of a rich white South African who uses landownership as a source of cultural capital. Mehring himself has made his money from pig iron, but is uneasy with his wealth and uses the farm as a natural (African) place to escape to when he has had too much (European) capitalist culture. The farm is also (or was supposed to be) the place for recreation for his rich white friends (specifically as a love nest for his mistress). Hence any interest Mehring appears to have for conservation is tainted by his self-interest in preserving a "wild" space for his "cultivated" friends' enjoyment. Even though "he himself was not a sucker for city romanticism," and attempts to make sure that "reasonable productivity prevailed" (22, 23), the actual purpose of the farm as a producer of food is more or less irrelevant to him, as any losses can be offset against tax.[21]

The use of land in this way, as a tax-deductible source of recreation for the wealthy, necessarily prompts consideration of some African countries' greatest tourist asset: wildlife. Here, more than anywhere, Williams's model of metropole and colony comes into its own as "Africa" is sold to the West (although Japanese tourism is increasing, too) as *the* place to see nature red in tooth and claw.[22] Carruthers has shown how in South Africa "the close relationship between the state and wildlife protection has positioned game reserves and national parks closely to the government in power and thus great resistance at grassroots level has taken place. This has often not been to the principles of protected areas, but to the practice of alienating benefits from local people for recreation for the wealthy" (14). With detailed reference to the Kruger National Park, Dongola Wild Life Sanctuary, Pilanesberg National Park, and KwaZulu Natal Game Reserves, Carruthers shows how "wildlife management" could serve as a cover for "forced removal, land reclamation, and game-stocking" (9).

For those outside the continent who cannot afford the actual trip to Africa, there is always the possibility of experiencing it vicariously through film, museum diorama, or theme park.[23] In all three cases, Africa generally connotes wildlife. Documentaries on Africa are more likely to detail the sex lives of Serengeti lions than they are to examine African art, history, or politics. In mass culture, in addition to wildlife documentaries, a string of Hollywood feature films, including *Out of Africa*, continues to trot out the most depressingly stereotypical notions of Africa, the most egregious recent example perhaps being the 1995 Ace Ventura movie entitled *When Nature Calls*.[24] Disney's box-office smash *The Lion King* was not only that corporation's first animated feature film to have been set in Africa; it is also the only one to be completely devoid of human presence. The subsequent Disney version of *Tarzan* dodged the issue of how to represent Africans by leaving them out altogether. Similarly, upscale advertising campaigns for four-wheel drive vehicles and credit cards depict white tourist-adventurers or hardy settlers as pitted against a rugged and demanding "nature."[25] Thus, while the West (or the North, or the First World, or however we formulate it) promotes the "ultimate safari" with lines of pseudo-colonial fashions and high-powered cameras that can capture the most intimate aspects of African (wild)life, it ignores the daily safaris of ordinary African people displaced by the continuing disruption of ordinary African life by European power.

Nadine Gordimer's short story "The Ultimate Safari" takes as its epigraph a small ad from a London Sunday newspaper (the like of which still runs every week) seeking to persuade readers that the romance and adventure of authentic nature are still available to alienated city dwellers in the raw "country" of Africa. The fact that most ordinary Africans are hardly more likely to have come across a lion or elephant than the average New Yorker is to have come across a grizzly bear on Broadway doesn't bother the advertisers, but provides the core of Gordimer's story, in which refugees from the war in Mozambique cross the border from that country into South Africa where they find themselves in the Kruger National Park. There, in South Africa's most vaunted game reserve, they "must move like animals among the animals" (*Crimes* 113) in order to avoid wardens and police. For them the "safari" (Kiswahili simply for "journey," after all; you don't necessarily have to have a Nissan Pathfinder and American Express card) is "ultimate" in the sense of being a matter of life and death; it is emphatically not about buying the biggest thrill. As in a number of Gordimer's short stories, the effect of "The Ultimate Safari" depends on a particular type of narrative irony in which the naïve young refugee tells her story to a savvy metropolitan audience, more aware than she can possibly be of the situation she is caught up in and yet apparently unaware of the human effects of that situation. Gordimer's technique thus hammers home the point that the West is interested in the conservation of Africa, not just in ignorance of Africans but frequently at the expense of Africans.[26]

Defenders of Blixen's writing might argue that her emotional investment in Africa and Africans differentiates her from the resort developers, safari promoters, and others whose investment is overtly financial; that there can be no continuity between her poetic inventions (strictly literary) and the selling of Africa by Abercrombie and Kent, Nissan, and Universal Studios. Such objections miss the point Williams makes that the emphasis on the landlord's "willing charity" is part and parcel of the pastoral mode. Erasing the historically specific conditions of labor on which the cultural capital of book, film, and safari depend is both exploitative and exploitable. For example, the portrayal of Blixen in the film as a sort of proto–civil rights activist whose relative political correctness on issues of race and gender stands out in contrast to the chauvinism of white male settler Kenyan society has next to nothing to do with the specific historical circumstances of Blixen's quasi-feudal "pro-native" attitudes. Rather than explore those circumstances, the movie makes a characteristically self-congratulatory Hollywood move, suggesting that "we" viewers (whites? Americans?) know better now and can afford to mock the ridiculous blimpishness of the Muthaiga Club members.[27] While the actual Karen Blixen cannot be held accountable for such an ahistorical representation of herself, the nature of that ahistorical approach is of the same type as Blixen's practice in *Out of Africa*, itself in line with the wider tradition of European pastoral.

One cannot, of course, dismiss Blixen's genuine effort and affection for the farm and many of its workers. Indeed, the evidence seems to suggest that in many cases she not only loved but inspired love in return. As I suggested in chapter 2, for instance, their loyalty set them apart from her unreliable husband and mercurial lover. However, as in the case of Kamante, they are rarely accorded unambiguous subject status. Frequent references in her letters to "my black brothers" are balanced by unconsciously denigratory lists of the things she loves—"this lovely country, my dear natives, my horses and dogs" (314)—and what she has at her disposal—"my black folk, guns, and dogs" (327).[28] It is, furthermore, a charge repeatedly and justifiably leveled at her that her representation of Kamante as a loyal pet is just one example of her habitual use of animal metaphors to describe Africans. In his article "Kenya's Literary Ladies and the Mythologizing of the White Highlands," Thomas Knipp argues that presenting Africans "as fauna" is one key part of "a two-fold tropology of otherness" (6) that Blixen, Elspeth Huxley, and Beryl Markham all develop.[29] The other mode Knipp identifies in his article, to present Africans in feudal terms, brings us right back to the question of pastoral and the erasure of economic considerations in presenting a benevolent lord of the manor—or in Blixen's case, the benevolent "literary lady" who had a farm.

In the great tradition of English pastoral, the writer shows a marginal interest in conserving the farm, the farm animals, and the old country ways, but ignores the existence of farm laborers. Playing a variation on that theme in *Out of Africa*, Karen Blixen shows a marginal interest in conserving Kenya, its animals, and native ways; however, any pleas she makes on behalf of her farm laborers are muted by her habit of equating them with wildlife, possessions, or the land itself. Thus while it may be anachronistic and unjust to hold Karen Blixen, or Karen Blixen as played by Meryl Streep, accountable for the slew of safaris and safari fashions sold by reference to *Out of Africa,* her original work does indeed lend itself to further commercialization by a culture that has long been involved in the selling of the continent—its people, its land, its natural resources. It is not surprising, then, that the viewing audience of *Out of Africa,* even less than Blixen's original audience in the 1930s, was not invited to consider the political and historical circumstances in which she had her farm, because it seems to come as a tasteless, uncultivated interruption to voice *not* the transcendent spirit of "Ah-frica" but the local, historically specific voices of Africans whose dispossession led inevitably to the bitter anticolonial struggles of Mau Mau and whose continued stifling leaves contemporary Kenya wide open to neocolonial abuse.

Violence and Voluntarism

The Will to Power and the Will to Die

As writers of nostalgic pastoral, both Karen Blixen and Elspeth Huxley extract the curse of labor on their farms in literary ways. A more extreme way to do so physically would be to murder the laborer. In practice, through various legal and extralegal means, this is frequently what happened under colonialism. (I shall be returning to the use of terror and murder as a means of social control in chapter 7.) However, colonial fiction rarely presents violence as white on black, and it is that absence which prompts the analysis that follows—of the connection between violence and voluntarism, or the contention in much white discourse about Africa (as in white Southern writing about slavery) that the element of symbiosis in African European relationships—for example, Blixen's representing Kamante as anticipating her wishes—at least mitigated some of the exploitation. As Valentin Mudimbe observes, the postcolonial condition of many African states has led to a romanticization of the colonial era not just among white memoirists and novelists but also among some historians suggesting that the accident of colonialism "was not the worst thing that could have happened to the black continent" (*Invention* 2).

Still using the insights of Raymond Williams from *The Country and the City*, I will continue to base my argument on specifically "literary" texts, namely Elspeth Huxley's detective fiction (especially *The African Poison Murders*, a.k.a. *Death of an Aryan*, and *Murder at Government House*), where white murderers kill white victims, and Doris Lessing's brilliant first novel, *The Grass Is Singing*, in which a white woman seems in part to will her murder by her black "houseboy" who, in turn, willingly surrenders himself to the colonial justice system and an inevitable death sentence. In addition, I will be examining Karen Blixen's account in

Out of Africa of the death of a worker called Kitosch, victim first of his employer, then of British colonial justice. In this last instance, we have an account of an actual, rather than fictional, example of the way in which what we might call ethnographical knowledge acts in support of forensic detection, a connection vital to understanding the three novels under discussion.

Elspeth Huxley (1907–1997) makes for fairly obvious comparisons with Blixen. Born into an aristocratic family in England, she moved to Kenya at the age of five and lived there until returning to England for her university education. Although she never lived in Kenya again, she repeatedly returned there to her parents' home and repeatedly returned to African topics in her writing. Her first published book was an admiring biography of Lord Delamere (1935), whom she cast as the founder of modern Kenya as a "white man's country." She took up detective fiction in the late 1930s when she was traveling extensively by sea with her husband, Gervase Huxley, who was involved in the tea trade. In addition to her fiction and biographies, she also tried her hand at social documentary in the early 1960s (when so-called "New Commonwealth," that is, black, immigration to England was increasing and when Kenya and other formerly British colonies in African were gaining their independence), publishing *Back Street New Worlds*. Here, according to Wendy Webster, instead of producing "the story of colonisation as one of white people's belonging in a land of adventure, she wrote a quite different story . . . of black people's unbelonging in the metropolis" (529).

Doris Lessing makes for similarly obvious comparisons with Schreiner. Born in 1919 in Persia, she moved with her family to Southern Rhodesia when she was five. As a young woman she was actively involved with a Marxist group opposed to British imperialism, and on leaving Rhodesia in 1949 with *The Grass Is Singing* in her bags, she was unable to revisit the country until it achieved independence as Zimbabwe in 1980. Although much of Lessing's work has been set in and concerned with Africa, she is probably best known as a figure involved with British New Left cultural criticism of the 1950s and with feminist critiques of gender. An extremely prolific writer, in her later years she has excoriated the -isms with which she was involved as a young woman without losing the sharpness and originality of her cultural critique.

If this biographical contrast between the two women resembles the contrast between Blixen and Schreiner, a comparison of their early novels produces an even more telling parallel. If, as Williams contends, the late Victorian country house novel mutates in the twentieth century into a watered-down subgenre of detective fiction, then we can read Huxley's relocation of that country house detective fiction to colonial Kenya as an unusual amalgam of the national model of country and city with the international model of metropole and colony. Lessing's novel can then be read as a masterful subversion of both, with her exposure of the conventionality of the whodunit revealing the actual workings of rural life in colonial Africa. The contrast between the two women's writing plainly resembles the contrast between *Out of Africa* and *The Story of an African Farm*. Huxley reproduces with great dexterity the structure and conventions of the mystery novel, and in so doing remystifies "Africa." Lessing, by contrast, in taking the mystery out of the facts of the murder of Mary Turner, takes the mystique out of the colonial order.

Much later in their careers, both writers produced social commentary on contemporary English society from the perspective of racially indigenous colonial exiles, as well as volumes of memoirs. Again, the contrasts between the two writers repeat the Blixen/Schreiner pattern: Huxley's overt nostalgia (readily packageable in the early 1980s as a TV miniseries) and the racially exclusive version of Englishness produced in her documentary study *Back Street New Worlds*, contrast with Lessing's more future-oriented work (especially evident in *African Laughter*) and with her delight in the multiculturalism of London.[1] While both writers' later work has received fairly extensive criticism, however, their earliest fiction has tended to be overlooked. This chapter aims to fill that critical lacuna and to show how Huxley's and Lessing's inventions of African farms respectively fit into and contest the history of European pastoral and its discursive power.

The farms in Huxley's *African Poison Murders* are not, to be fair, country houses in the Jamesian tradition nor yet in the middle-class tradition of Agatha Christie. They are still to some extent places of work, whose owners think of themselves as sorts of pioneer. Commander Dennis West, for instance, formerly of the China Squadron, had "retired from the Navy and fulfilled his life's ambition to invest his small capital in a farm. . . . The climate was fine. Living was cheap and easy; the country still free from the more rigid fetters of convention, still with a tinge of the frontier about it" (27). Frequently throughout the text there are references to the boundary between farmland and virgin territory; like the "jungle" in *Heart of Darkness,* the forest seems like some sort of malevolent creature always ready to smother human endeavor. Particularly at night, there is the sense that the light of civilization only extends so far: "Beyond lay the bush, a dense black cloak that hid a predatory world of bloodshed and cruelty" (98). Leading up to the climax of the novel, for instance, Inspector Vachell comes to a fork in a path: "One fork went left towards a dam and some cultivation, the other crossed the broad ride that marked the boundary between farm and forest, and plunged into the green depths" (185). Cultivation and civilization, inseparably linked as the markers of an exclusive and unitary "culture" though they may be, are not, in Huxley's imaginary Chania, the completed, buyable commodities of English country house fiction nor even of Blixen's aristocratic pastoral; rather, they are works in progress, and fragile ones at that.

In addition, Huxley might claim that the intrusion of contemporary macro-politics of race through the Nazi Bund affiliations of the farmer Munson makes the story less "detached" and one-dimensional than the model detective story that Williams disparages. However, even the farms' precariousness and the fact that they are working ones cannot hide the way in which Dennis West's or former Harley Street surgeon Sir Jolyot Anstey's "retirement" to them fits the nostalgic models Williams describes. Furthermore, the neat structure and eventual closure of the case puts the novel squarely in the noncritical genre of country house fiction as defined by Williams, in which the country house (however loosely construed) is "the place of isolated assembly of a group of people whose immediate and transient relations [are] decipherable by an abstract mode of detection rather than by the full and connected analysis of any more general understanding" (Williams 249). For instance, although characters make scattered comments regarding fluctuations in commodity prices, there is never any consideration of the reasons for growing pyrethrum or why it is that the Wests' cream should travel "six thousand miles to its market on British breakfast-tables" (1), nor is there any questioning of the assumption that imported cattle and know-how are superior to the native variety. The British presence is generally presented as benign, evoking, for instance, the loyalty of the unnamed askari who saves his superior officer Vachell's life in *Murder at Government House.* While the open racism of Nazism is consistently decried and even ridiculed,[2] British racism tends to be naturalized as neutral observation.

For a book published in 1939, the oddly racist attitude toward racism (that it is an attribute of "the Boche") is perhaps understandable, but the ironies are revealing. Huxley tends to present racial characteristics as given, knowable, and finely discriminated. Markers of these characteristics seem to hark back to nineteenth-century racial attitudes in a manner reminiscent of Robert Knox's *Races of Men* or John Beddoes's *Races of Britain,*[3] and the wider nineteenth-century European project that attempted to define the types of humanity by using the infant "sciences" of statistics, phrenology, craniology, and photography. Thus, even *facial* features are readable as markers of individual character, just as Lambroso or Havelock Ellis believed. Inspector Vachell, Huxley's tall, fair, and handsome detective, for instance, is not quite British, still less English; he is a Canadian who, in Commander West's observation, "looked like a Scot as so many Canadians did. He had the sandy hair and long jaw of the true Scot" (8). In *Murder at Government House,* the narrative observes that it was Vachell's "bony face which betrayed a Scots ancestry" (20). The boniness and length of the jaw are surefire indications not just of ancestry but of the "Scottish" attributes of grit and determination, too.

As a Scot, whatever his own Scottish racial and facial characteristics might be, Vachell himself, the prime observer, is presented as an outsider whose detachment from those around him makes his observation of them appear to be as objective as possible; his role as detective intensifies his own anxiety that emotional involvement with any of his (white) (female) suspects might impair his judgment. The particular emotional involvement he is conscious of in *The African Poison Murders,* which prompts worries about the troubling convergence of the "roads of duty and inclination" (15), is desire for Janice West, the beautiful (naturally) American wife of Commander West. Such anxiety is the very stuff of the detective genre, of course.[4] But in this setting in particular the maze of differences—of duty/inclination, male/female, American/Canadian, English/Scottish—conceals one fundamental similarity: that of whiteness, and the class privileges attendant on whiteness in colonial Chania. The investment that Vachell and all the other white characters of Huxley's novels ignore but which fundamentally precludes objectivity and any "general understanding" of their situation is their investment in an expansionist English culture in which culture is more or less synonymous with race.

That doesn't matter for the novels, though. The various false trails that Huxley so dexterously lays expose all sorts of other oversights and assumptions, but they don't expose the failure to see or read Africa, Africans, or Africanness. The total opacity of Africa is not just assumed but explicitly commented on. As we have already seen, beyond the light of the farms lay the bush, the "green depths," the unsolvable mystery of Africa, that which, unlike Scots' jawbones or European typewriters, gives the European detective no clues. The "African poison" used to kill both Karl Munson and Dennis West is identifiable but virtually untraceable, its symptoms "nothing more nor less than a cessation of the action of the heart" (85). Faced with such a poison, Vachell feels himself in a fog: "How could you get anywhere when you couldn't even depend on doctors to tell you the cause of death?" (83). European science—whether used for pure medical inquiry or for forensic reasons—is thwarted by an Africa that leaves no observable traces behind. Just so does Conrad's "unspeakable" and "dumb" jungle likewise threaten to overcome Marlow's European notions of reason and identity.[5]

In many ways the white detective, assiduously observing others, drawing conclusions from the slightest clues, but troubled by fears about his subjectivity, behaves like an ethnographer, torn by an ambivalent colonial desire.[6] James Clifford, for instance, in an essay on Conrad and Malinowski, talks about the "ethnographic subjectivity" of the early twentieth century as a new development presupposing "the ironic stance of participant observation" (*Predicament of Culture* 93). Vachell's detection is carried out with just such an ironic stance, not just because of the obvious subjective pulls toward attractive women but also because he is aware of the expectations of his superiors. There is a discourse within which he has to keep, and just as Malinowski could write one "official" ethnology of the Trobriand Islanders in his *Argonauts of the South Pacific,* and an "unofficial" one in his *Diary in the Strict Sense of the Term* (Clifford 97), so Vachell frequently has to keep his own observations to himself.

Vachell is most obviously aware of this "official" discourse in *Murder at Government House,* when he is a "newboy" in the Chania CID. On the murder of the Governor of Chania, Vachell's superior, Major Armitage, moves to round up the usual suspects, overriding Vachell's "hunch that this crime isn't the work of a native" (30). Predictably, Armitage finds more or less what he wants—"a Swahili who was suspected of at least two murders, who'd once been employed (he'd been dismissed) at Government House, and who was believed to belong to a Chinyani underworld gang who specialized in housebreaking" (49). Equally predictably, he is way off the mark: The lucky Swahili is now gainfully employed as a night-soil porter—he literally takes shit! It is the more patient ethnographer/detective Vachell who eventually gets his man. This would almost be a joke—and Armitage is certainly presented in caricature fashion with his clipped sentences—if it weren't so serious, and it isn't until *The Grass Is Singing* that we find a white author showing how white detection/ethnography, hardened into outright racist prejudice, produces black criminals. I shall return later to Lessing's novel. For the time being, the point is that even in a genre which apparently seeks to reinforce rationality (Williams's "abstract mode of detection"), there is some awareness that all detection, all ethnography, is inevitably tainted by the subjectivity of participant observation.

It may be, though, that the full force of the detective/ethnographer comparison is stronger when it is framed the other way around—an ethnographer behaves like a detective. Such a formulation more immediately suggests the disciplinary, policing effect of ethnography. Foucault's theoretical work has shown the extent to which institutional discourses "discipline" societies, while Terence Ranger's work on European ideas of the conservatism of African "tradition" and its resultant "immobilization of populations, re-inforcement of ethnicity and greater rigidity of social definition" (Hobsbawm 249) shows the accuracy of Foucault's theories in practice and their applicability to African colonial situations. The development of the apartheid state, with its separation of "tribal" groupings into "homelands," provides the obvious and extreme example of how ethnography can become a practice of policing. In imaginative literature, we might point to the famous ending of *Things Fall Apart*, where Chinua Achebe indicates exactly the same process of discursive policing.[7] The complexity and fluidity of precolonial Igbo society is reduced to a paragraph or two in the District Commissioner's book to be entitled *The Pacification of the Primitive Tribes of the Lower Niger* (Achebe 209).

Given this connection, it therefore comes as no surprise in the first Inspector Vachell novel, *Murder at Government House*, to find Vachell using the American anthropologist Olivia Brandeis as a spy to investigate a secret society thought to be implicated in the Governor's murder. Olivia accepts the task without a qualm and acknowledges, "I should certainly have more chance of finding out *what the Wabenda think* than one of your police detectives" (65; emphasis added). As it happens, her discoveries of "what the Wabenda think" are not crucial to the investigation. In fact, Huxley contrasts the witch doctor Silu's knowledge of Europeans with Olivia's anthropological "knowledge." When she asks to see some of the magic Silu uses to ward off evil spirits, he mocks her expectations by showing her "junk, not magic" (143). And it is Silu, long before anyone else, who realizes who the murderer is—not as a result of any mystical powers but as a result, as Vachell acknowledges, of his application of "psychology" (229). Through the figure of Silu, Huxley gives us a further comparison for the role of the detective, with Olivia telling Vachell that "the functions of a detective in our society resemble those of a witchdoctor among native tribes. The witchdoctor's job, like the detective's, is to hunt down the enemies of society and prevent them from doing further harm" (68).

Like the retired surgeon Sir Jolyot Anstey in *The African Poison Murders* who is "tremendously keen on the natives" (8), Olivia Brandeis appears to give generous, relativistic credit to the African genius, in a way clearly surpassing stereotypical colonialist dismissals of African knowledge. But just as Karen Blixen feels free to speak the minds of her African characters/workers, so Elspeth Huxley leaves unchallenged the right and the ability of the European witch doctor, the ethnographer/detective, to pluck out the heart of Africa's mystery, to close the case on its story. Huxley's detective fiction therefore seems to be of a piece with James Clifford's notion of "ethnographic self-fashioning" in Conrad and Malinowski. Although it "portrays other selves as culturally constituted, it also fashions an identity authorized to represent, even to believe—but always with some irony—the truths of discrepant worlds" (Clifford 94).

A fine example of this muddle occurs in Vachell's mental account of the physiognomy of one Machoka, an askari whom Armitage has arrested on suspicion of his being an accomplice to the Governor's murderer. Huxley presents Vachell as registering both a degree of diffidence as to his own deductive powers and some culturally relativistic musings at the same time as he displays "knowledge" about racial types: "Vachell knew that he had not been in Africa long enough to tell anything about a native's character from his facial expression. It needed years of association with them to do that. But Africans weren't like Chinese, expressionless and wooden-faced to a European stranger's eyes; their features showed great variation. That, he supposed, was due to their lack of homogeneity; like the English and Americans, they were a mixture of any number of races. Machoka, for instance, seemed to be a throwback to the almost pure Hamitic type. He was light in colour, almost as light as a Malay, and although his lips were thick they didn't jut out like rolls of rubber. His front teeth, following the tribal custom, were filed into sharp points, and there were raised tattoo marks on his cheek-bones. Among the Wabenda, Vachell knew, tattoo marks on the cheeks were a sign of high rank" (73).

This paradoxical mix—of awareness of a common heterogeneity, balanced against a series of "us" and "them" discriminations of natives, Africans, Chinese, Europeans, English, Americans, Hamitic types, Malays, and Wabenda; of admitted ignorance and claimed knowledge; of neutrality of tone and racist similes—is not presented critically. There is nothing to deny the suggestion that after sufficient years in Chania, presumably Vachell *would* be able to tell things about "a native's character." This is one of the inconsistencies of Huxley's fiction, as the more liberal attitudes of positively presented characters such as Olivia Brandeis or Sir Jolyot Anstey suggest that European "science" is only one type of knowledge, partial at best, and not inherently superior to African "magic." Indeed, the implications of Vachell's newboy ignorance notwithstanding, the novels tend to present the view, flattering to a liberal noncolonial audience, that the European settler "knowledge" bred by length of stay in Africa tends to be mere prejudice.

Particularly in *Murder at Government House,* tensions appear between a bureaucratic but humanitarian Colonial Office and the reactionary settlers.[8] The District Officer in Taritibu, for instance, who "approved very highly of anthropologists" (145), tartly dismisses the scaremongering suggestion that "a native school-boy secret society is responsible for Sir Malcolm McLeod's murder" as "almost worthy of a settler" (147),[9] while the settlers' spokesman, the fiery Donovan Popple, "believed that he knew more about [Chania's] needs and troubles than most of the outsiders who came in at the Colonial Office's orders for a few years, to sit in Marula behind a barricade of officials and tell everyone who had to make a living in the colony where to get off" (11).

In *The African Poison Murders,* such tensions are not so apparent, but it is still the relative newcomers to Chania who seem to be the more enlightened; the recently settled Wests, for instance, treat their laborers more decently than the longer-established Munsons. Mrs. Munson, in particular, appears as an embittered racist, both jealous and paranoid, critical of the colonial government for twisting justice "to suit the convenience of black pagan apes" (163). Huxley makes her the only character to use such openly insulting, racist language, and matches the ugliness of her character and racism with physical ugliness. When she is first introduced to Vachell, "[h]er squat, lumpy figure was dressed in a khaki twill skirt and a bushman's shirt with bulging pockets. Long strands of hair escaped from the bun into which it was screwed at the back. The idea passed through Vachell's mind that she was wrapped in fat as a dancer might be swathed in shawls. It did not seem to be an integral part of her; there was something essentially jovial about fat, but nothing so easy-going as joviality about the woman who stood in front of him, her feet squarely apart, darting her small eyes from one visitor to the other like a chameleon flicking its long tongue at a couple of flies" (17). Although her obesity is not associated with sexual appetite in quite the same way as Tant' Sannie's in *The Story of an African Farm,* Mrs. Munson seems remarkably close kin to Schreiner's portrait of the Boer woman. And, as Tant' Sannie's sanctimonious claims to Christian decency and morality are satirized by Schreiner, so it is "Mother" Munson's "strange mixture of blunt colloquialism and Calvinistic mock-biblical" that Vachell finds "disconcerting" (130). The significance of the comparison becomes more compelling when we learn that Mrs. Munson has family in South Africa and wishes to go there, "where there are decent people, respectable people fit for my children to grow up among" (163), following the murder of her husband. As I suggested earlier, the publication of *The African Poison Murders* in 1939 might explain this shifting of the stain of racism onto a convenient European other, but the connection with Schreiner suggests that it is part of a more persistent antagonism (partly class, partly intellectual) between the metropolitan English and white settlers on the land.

As Terence Ranger has shown, in the late nineteenth century and early twentieth, white settlers transferred the invented tradition of the gentleman from Europe to Africa. Although they may have "found themselves engaged in tasks which by definition would have been menial in Britain," their "neo-traditional title to gentility" played an important role in maintaining a sense of the "glamour of empire-building" (Ranger 215). Likewise, "with the coming of formal colonial rule it was urgently necessary to turn the whites into a convincing ruling class, entitled to hold sway over their subjects not only through force of arms or finance but also through the prescriptive status bestowed by neo-tradition" (215). We have already glimpsed some of the intensity and complexity of this process in *The Story of an African Farm*, both in Schreiner's representation of Tant' Sannie as less than genteel and in Gregory Rose's boarding-school snobbery toward the uneducated Waldo. More particularly, the Roses are examples of colonists whose local class-inflation was supported by neo-tradition; since their arrival in the colony they have "discovered" that "they were of distinguished lineage," invented a family crest and motto, and named their colonial farm "Rose Manor"—all in an attempt to establish their claim to noble blood (175). Literary awareness of the phenomenon Ranger describes thus dates back to the 1870s or even 1860s (the period which *African Farm* describes), and it clearly persists through the 1930s in the colonial Kenya portrayed by Karen Blixen and Elspeth Huxley, though with varying degrees of critique.

In none of those writers' works, however, does the invention of white class status so prominently and explicitly provide the *content* of the book (rather than "background") as in *The Grass Is Singing*. In this novel, first published in 1950, Doris Lessing meticulously and painfully probes the full intensity and complexity of white settlers' struggle to turn themselves into, and entrench themselves as, a "convincing ruling class." In so doing she completely subverts the ideology of the pastoral that Blixen and Huxley adhere to in their writing of farms and detective fiction, respectively,

The Grass Is Singing is not interested in the "abstract mode of detection" of the "murder mystery" announced by its opening words. Instead, it probes the extraordinarily complex web of power relationships of colonial Southern Rhodesia, relationships determined not just by race, class, and gender but also by location in country and city, colony and metropole, agriculture and industry. An indication of the complexity of these relationships is that each of the story's three main characters can be seen as a victim not just of each other and individual events but also of systems. To state it very baldly: Mary Turner is the victim of colonialist patriarchy; Moses, her murderer, is the victim of colonialist racism; Dick Turner, her husband, is the victim of colonialist capitalism.

Those "systems" are not, of course, so simply separated, but Lessing does show that having a farm in Africa is not the same as having a farm in Europe, nor can it rightly be conceived of in terms of personal mythology. Dick Turner, for instance, whose relationship with the land is presented as being as intense as Karen Blixen's, if not more so, is thwarted at every stage from being able to say, "I had a farm in Africa": "On an impulse, [he] had come to Southern Rhodesia to be a farmer, and to 'live his own life'" (158), but "he was indebted to the Land Bank, and heavily mortgaged, for he had had no capital at all when he started" (47) so that "his 'own' soil . . . belonged to the last grain of sand to the Government" (158).

In addition, the text frequently reminds us—as Huxley's and Blixen's do not—that any notion of white ownership of the land is dependent on the violent displacement of "the natives," along with their coercion into a discriminatory labor system: Lessing describes "contract labor" as "the South African equivalent of the old press gang" and little short of slavery: "White men . . . lie in wait for the migrating bands of natives on their way along the roads to look for work; gather them into large lorries, often against their will (sometimes chasing them through the bush for miles if they escape), lure them by fine promises of good employment and finally sell them to the white farmers at five pounds or more per head for a year's contract" (128). Both Dick's romanticization of "his" land and his "labor troubles" are thus heavily ironized, as he fulminates against the government (to which he is indebted not just monetarily but for his very occupation)[10] for failing to "force the natives to work on the land" or "simply send out lorries and soldiers and bring them to the farmers by force" (159).

His antagonism to the government takes the form we have already seen in Huxley's fiction of long-term settlers on the land railing at urban bureaucrats unduly influenced by English liberalism. But Lessing's settlers are not retirees from Harley Street or the navy. In part reflective of actual demographic differences between white settlement in Kenya and Rhodesia, her settlers arrived with an already existing class antagonism as part of their baggage—antagonism between their "real" world, working or lower middle-class professions, and the "intellectual" world of the privileged British establishment. Charlie Slatter, for instance, who, "from the beginning of the tragedy to its end, personified Society for the Turners" (6), was originally "a grocer's assistant in London" (7), come to lord it over his wife, his children, and especially his laborers, farming "as if he were turning the handle of a machine which would produce pound notes at the other end" (7). He has very effectively bought a local class superiority that is dependent on notions of racial superiority, but within that locally "superior" race/class, there are two special points of vulnerability: gender and "echt" English Englishness, two points that get interestingly confused.

We can see this in the tension between Slatter and Tony Marston, the twenty-year-old just out from England who, as Dick Turner's "assistant" for three weeks, witnesses some of the events leading to Mary's murder. Marston himself has come to Southern Rhodesia expressly to make money and because it offered him a better prospect than "becoming some kind of a clerk in his uncle's factory" (214). In true pastoral mode, however, he initially romanticizes his poverty on the farm as "exciting." By virtue of his being a witness to the events leading to the murder, and a witness with some vestige of faith in "abstract ideas about decency and goodwill" (12), Tony serves Lessing's purpose of being the closest the reader comes to unmasking the ideology of "white civilization" (22).

Elements in his characterization make him familiar to us as the relative outsider, the English newcomer to Africa whose whiteness counts him in, but whose attitudes don't quite mesh. As with Vachell's Canadianness, Marston's Englishness establishes a sort of distance that allows for greater objectivity.[11] However, unlike Vachell, Tony has no authority in the case, and, more like the effete Gregory Rose than the heartily masculine Vachell, he is easily overridden by Charlie Slatter and Sergeant Denham, who deals with (one can hardly say "investigates") the case.

Thus, although Marston has much the same aim as Slatter, Slatter sees him as backed by the cultural capital of an innate *class* superiority. It is perhaps partly anxiety about his own class inferiority that makes Slatter dismissive of Marston's relative lack of "manliness." He sees Marston as "the usual type; the self-contained, educated Englishman who spoke in a la-di-da way as if he had a mouthful of pearls" (212). This tension—between what Slatter perceives as Marston's class superiority and gender inferiority—makes Slatter nervous: "Anything was possible, thought Charlie, from this particular type of young Englishman. He had a rooted contempt for soft-faced, soft-voiced Englishmen, combined with a fascination for their manner and breeding. His own sons, now grown up, were gentlemen. He had spent plenty of money to make them so; but he despised them for it. At the same time he was proud of them. This conflict showed itself in his attitude towards Marston: half hard and indifferent, half subtly deferential" (8). Marston's "soft" face and voice, his education, perhaps even that "mouthful of pearls" feminize him in Slatter's eyes; being a gentleman makes him something both more and less than just plain male.[12]

However, Slatter and Sergeant Denham easily bully Marston, in part by appealing to racial solidarity, but mainly by exploiting his outsider status. Although racially not one of "them" (that is, black), he is yet not quite one of "us" (white male settler). Tacitly persuading him to keep quiet about "anything out of the ordinary" (16) he might have witnessed, Denham tells Marston, "'When *you* have been in the country long enough *you* will understand that *we* don't like *niggers* murdering white *women.*' The phrase 'When you have been in the country' stuck in Tony's gullet. He had heard it too often, and it had come to jar on him. At the same time it made him feel angry. Also callow" (17; emphasis added).

Despite his knowledge and his metropolitan "principles," Marston duly says what is "expected of him" at the trial; a repression of his own interpretation of events which represents his collusion with the white settlers' ideological reticence. Thoroughly disillusioned by what he has seen and by his own behavior, Tony leaves the district shortly after the trial.[13] He is remembered as "the young man from England who hadn't the guts to stand more than a few weeks of farming" (27).

What Tony had seen was, of course, precisely what white settler ideology denied the presence of: interracial desire, specifically the desire of a white woman for a black man. By the time Tony appears on the Turners' farm, Mary and Dick Turner's marriage has already disintegrated; they no longer even share the "double solitude" of marriage and scarcely register each other's existence despite sleeping in the same bed together. Thus Dick notices nothing in the relationship between Mary and the "houseboy" Moses beyond a familiar inability in his wife to understand "the native mind." Tony, however, *has* seen the extraordinary mixture of attraction and repulsion between the two that inevitably culminates in the murder, a kind of sadomasochistic consummation at once feared and desired. Three days before Dick and Mary are supposed to leave the farm, Tony comes across Moses helping Mary to dress and watching her brush her hair with an attitude of "indulgent uxoriousness" (219). Tony is shocked by this evidence of intimacy between the two, and he struggles to comprehend its nature, finally "shrugg[ing] in despair" (223) and dismissing Mary in his own mind as at least half-mad. Significantly, how-ever, he has seen—although he will not say—that "It takes two to make a murder—a murder of this kind" (23), and it is a similar recognition and repression that accounts for the "hate and contempt" that "twisted [Charlie Slatter's] features" (10) as he stared at Mary's dead body. Tony does not initially understand that look, but later "there would be a few brief moments when he would see the thing clearly, and understand that it was 'white civilization' fighting to defend itself that had been implicit in the attitude of Charlie Slatter and the Sergeant, 'white civilization' which will never, never admit that a white person, and most particularly, a white woman, can have a human relationship, whether for good or for evil, with a black person. For once it admits that, it crashes, and nothing can save it. So, above all, it cannot afford failures, such as the Turners' failure" (22).

Thus the dead white woman's body is far more than the catalyst for an "abstract mode of detection." It is the very core of the novel, the object of desire and hatred which "white civilization" attempts to protect and re-press at all costs in order to maintain its own putative integrity or purity and its actual power. In the same way that Marston's "femininity" is po-tentially troubling to Slatter, and requires breaking in, so white settler society, highly patriarchally organized, seeks to exert especially tight control over its women, who are at once, familiarly enough, both the paragons of white civilization and yet acutely vulnerable to degenera-tion.

Given this understanding, what does the violent death of one white woman at the hands of one black man mean? The combination of female victim and black assailant places the novel's critique of colonialism within a framework of potentially uncomfortable stereotypes of white women, black men, and their possible relationships. One recent critic, Katherine Fishburn, goes so far as to suggest that the relative lack of attention paid to *The Grass Is Singing* may be because "Lessing has written what Abdul R. JanMohamed would call a manichean allegory—an allegory that func-tions (however unintentionally in this case) to reinscribe the power and dominance of the white colonial ruling class" (Fishburn 2). There is clearly some force to Fishburn's suggestion, especially if, as Ezekiel Mphahlele does, one reads Moses' motivation for murder in purely per-sonal terms as stemming from his belief that "Mary was leaving the farm because she has found new love" (*African Image* 138). I would suggest, however, that Lessing's rendering of the dual, systemic victimization of Mary and Moses (for his murder of her ensures his own death) deliberately and successfully turns the stereotypical notions on their heads.

Mary's destroyer should be construed not just as Moses—whatever his personal motivation—but as colonialist patriarchy. First abused and abandoned by a drunkard father, then pushed into a stifling marriage by social pressure, Mary's gender has victimized her from the start. In her dreams she confuses Moses with "her father menacing and horrible" (192), and in one particularly graphic instance she imagines Moses first murdering her husband and then approaching her: "slowly, obscene and powerful, and it was not only he, but her father who was threatening her. They advanced together, one person" (192).

At the same time, her murderer is equally victimized by colonialist patriarchy in the form of Mary's extreme racism. As a result of her totally segregated town upbringing, Mary "could not understand any white person feeling anything personal about a native" (69). She shares the prevailing white farmers' objectifying attitude in the novel toward African laborers as "the geese that laid the golden eggs" (7). Consequently, with the progressive deterioration of her marriage, with her husband's deepening economic failure as a farmer, and her almost total isolation from any company—white or black—she has no way of comprehending or coping with her desire, both socially and individually unspeakable, for Moses, nor with his pity for her.

Unable to forget that she had once whipped Moses across the face, she is torn by guilt and fear of revenge, attraction and repulsion, so that the memory of his semi-naked body as he washed, "that thick black neck with the lather frothing whitely on it, the powerful back stooping over the bucket, was like a goad to her" (166). These violently ambivalent responses produce the final climactic scene of the novel in which Mary seems to will (or is unable not to will, perhaps) Moses into murdering her[14] as the only possible consummation of their sadomasochistic master-servant relationship. She "knows" that Moses is waiting for her, and feels "in a trap, cornered and helpless. But she would have to go out and meet him" (241). Complete with the melodramatic bursting of a storm, and forked lightning glinting off Moses's plunging knife, the murder is thus a violent parody of a midnight assignation that both parties must keep, according to a script already written.

After the murder, Moses initially makes as if to flee from the scene of the crime, but "when he had gone perhaps a couple of hundred yards through the soaking bush he stopped, turned aside, and leaned against a tree on an ant heap. And there he would remain, until his pursuers, in their turn, came to find him" (245). His subsequent arrest, trial, and execution are foregone conclusions; everyone, including Moses, knows that Moses is "as good as hanged already" (9) by allowing himself to be apprehended. But it is precisely here, in Moses's indifferent submission to the inevitable processes of the institutionalized racial violence of colonial law, that we see the brilliance of *The Grass Is Singing*, because here Lessing's subversion of the pastoral mode—her exposure of the systems that run farms, countries, and empires—coincides with her subversion of the genre of detective fiction.

Crudely put, *The Grass Is Singing* is a murder story. Unlike in Huxley's fiction, however, only one murder is committed, and the suspense is provided by withholding not the identity of the murderer but the reason for the murder. The action of the story is provided not by the detective's exhaustive tracing of a skillfully hidden murderer and his retrospective re-creation of the murder but by the explicit exposition of the events leading to the murder. Nothing factual is hidden. The climax is therefore not the detection of the murderer, but the act of murder itself. Using a form that perfectly fits her content—the novel opens with a news report of Mary Turner's houseboy's arrest and confession—Lessing shows that, when it comes to apparently black-on-white crime in colonial Africa, no detective is necessary because the criminal has already been produced by official, institutional discourse. The narrative presents "people all over the country" reading the news report with "a little spurt of anger mingled with what was almost satisfaction, as if some belief had been confirmed, as if something had happened which could only have been expected" (1).

The novel then shows the enormous discrepancy between what "people all over the country" understand of the case and what actually happened. In other words, although the apparently salient facts of the case—that Moses, a black farm laborer, had murdered Mary Turner, his white employer—are explicit from the start, nevertheless, because so much depends on repression—particularly repression of desire—and because the narrative is partial in presenting the point of view of Mary, rather than her murderer, at the level of motivation much still remains implicit, in fact, very vague indeed.

As such, the novel reverses the procedure of conventional detective fiction. Catherine Belsey defines the "project of the Sherlock Holmes stories," for instance, as being "to dispel magic and mystery, to make everything explicit, accountable, subject to scientific analysis" (111).[15] "The stories begin in enigma, mystery, the impossible, and conclude with an explanation which makes it clear that all logical deduction and scientific method render all mysteries accountable to reason" (112); however, Belsey goes on to point out that a deconstructive reading of those stories reveals to what extent they depend on an ideological reticence, particularly with regard to women and women's sexuality.

According to Robert Young, just such a reticence characterized culture and race theory in the nineteenth century, which were linked by a suppressed "third term"—sexuality (*Colonial Desire* 97). Although Young's demonstration of the prevalence of a "sado-masochistic structure of inter-racial sexual relations in the colonial period" (108) refers primarily to white male/black female sexual relations, his description of the imbrication of race, class, and gender coincides with Lessing's fictional representation. In Blixen, Schreiner, and Huxley the separateness of African and European races and cultures is preserved by, among other things, silence about interracial sexual desire. In articulating that silence, Lessing reproduces in fictional form the set of racial, cultural, and sexual relationships that Young describes.

Hazel Carby's article "'On the Threshold of Woman's Era': Lynching, Empire, and Sexuality in Black Feminist Theory" is relevant to my earlier speculations as to the kind of feminist affiliation that might have been achieved through a meeting of Ida B. Wells and Olive Schreiner (see chapter 1). The same set of relationships therefore link the full legal sanctioning of Moses's death to the extra-legal but "institutionalized practice" of lynching in the 1890s in the United States. According to Hazel Carby, under that institution, just like Charlie Slatter and Sergeant Denham in *The Grass Is Singing,* "white men used their ownership of the body of the white female as a terrain on which to lynch the black male" (Carby 309). Carby's analysis of the logic whereby violence against black men was justified through their demonization as rapists of white women stresses the intimacy of the link between "internal and external colonization, between domestic racial oppression and imperialism" (304) in much the same way as Young does in *Colonial Desire.* Lessing pushes further to reveal the link within white colonial society between domestic gender oppression and racial oppression.

The Grass Is Singing, in sum, attempts to demonstrate how ideological reticence—both in the literary genre of detective fiction and in the actual contact zone of colonial desire—works to produce a misleading set of apparent "facts" that are already explicit, already accounted for, and scientifically (in this case, forensically) analyzed. Going well beyond Huxley's intermittent relativism, in which European science and African magic occasionally appear as parallel sets of knowledge, equally partial, equally (in)valid, Lessing's novel, then, is a much more radical and coherent attempt to expose the ideological basis of European knowledge, forensic or otherwise. European science whether of the racial or forensic varieties is a particular kind of "*méconnaissance*" and, far from producing the objective knowledge it aspires to, actually produces a highly self-interested discourse of knowledge as power.

So far I have confined my comments to fictional representations, limiting my historical comments to one or two observations by Terence Ranger. However, in looking at Karen Blixen's account of the death of the worker Kitosch in *Out of Africa*, we can see one example of the way in which actual European forensic practice inflicts violence on black Africans. Countless equally egregious, or more egregious, examples could be found in the annals of all colonial states, but what I am attempting to show is the way that, even though ostensibly "pro-native," the ideology of the pastoral in Blixen's work extracts labor, replacing analysis of systems of power with myths.[16]

Briefly, what Blixen describes is the case of a worker named Kitosch who was so badly beaten for riding his employer's horse back home (rather than leading it) that he died from his injuries. In court, although the district surgeon declares that death was "due to the injuries and wounds that he had found on the body" (*Out of Africa* 241), the evidence of two defense doctors who claimed that it was Kitosch's own "wish to die" that had caused his death is sufficiently persuasive to the jury for them to find the settler employer guilty not of murder but of "grievous hurt" (242). Blixen relates the entire event in exemplary style, formally reporting the statements of those involved in a series of witheringly detached and sardonic sentences. The contrast between the medical experts' conditional conclusions and the patent facts of the matter are evident, for instance, from Blixen's use of "might" in the following sentences: "If Kitosch had not taken this attitude, he would not have died. If, for instance, he had eaten something, he might not have lost courage, for starvation is known to reduce courage. [The doctor] added that the wound on the lip might not be due to a kick, but might be just a bite by the boy himself, in severe pain" (242). Such medical evidence—all too depressingly familiar from other cases of prison "suicides" and "accidents"—is clearly specious, and Blixen's sarcasm draws attention to its speciousness.[17] However, the conclusion she draws from the case comes as a surprise.

Rather than taking the case as an example of the rottenness of the state of British justice in Kenya, she takes Kitosch's "wish-to-die" literally[18] and transforms him into a figure of "beauty," who "embodied the fugitiveness of the wild things who are, in the hour of need, conscious of a refuge somewhere in existence; who go when they like; of whom we can never get hold" (243). Thus, rather than look at the event as evidence of the asymmetry of power relations between two interacting groups, Blixen reestablishes the separateness of African from European: The slave again is ascribed a power that puts him beyond the reach of the slave owner.

As my comments on Blixen's representations of the slave/slave owner relationship would indicate, this latter move might in fact be seen as in keeping with all of Blixen's thought; its emergence at this point, however, jars. By what sleight-of-hand has she transformed Kitosch, a man who was beaten to death, from murder-victim into a figure of beauty and freedom, "the fugitiveness of the wild things"? I would argue that it is her own ethnographic urge—which drives her to differentiate among and within races, nations, cultures, tribes—that allows her to ignore the grossness of the Kitosch case and turn it into something ethereal. In so doing she reproduces the same kind of reasoning as that displayed by the defense doctors, and although her motives might be more honorable than theirs, she reaches equally ludicrous conclusions.

For instance, using language that reminds us of that used against Tony Marston, the first defense doctor cited claimed to speak "with authority" on the "will to die," "for he had been in the country twenty-five years, and knew the Native mind" (241). Blixen's sarcasm here undercuts the doctor's "authority" and "knowledge." As with Huxley's and Lessing's settlers, length of stay in the colony seems merely to have hardened prejudice rather than facilitated learning. However, Blixen herself is no less categorical in her declarations about "the Native mind," prefacing the account of the court proceedings with comments on the difference between "Native ideas" of justice (whereby "a compensation for his death should now be made to his people") and European ones in which "the problem of guilt and innocence at once presented itself" (239). This distinction echoes earlier comments in the section entitled "A Shooting Accident on the Farm" where Blixen speaks with "authority" similar to the doctor's about "the Native mind" and its attitude to justice: "To the African there is but one way of counter-balancing the catastrophes of existence, it shall be done by replacement; he does not look for the motive of an action. . . . The Native will not give time or thought to the weighing up of guilt or desert: either he fears that this may lead him too far, or he reasons that such things are of no concern of his. But he will devote himself, in endless speculations, to the method by which crime or disaster shall be weighed up in sheep and goats" (93–94). If there is any sarcasm here, it is directed against "the African" and his "endless speculations" of value measured in the currency of sheep and goats. It seems that in cases such as the shooting accident on the farm, where she herself is part of the judicial process, Blixen presents "knowledge" of the "Native mind" in a less critical manner than when anyone else is in judgment. It is not so much that there is no reifiable "Native mind" to know. It is that Blixen, by virtue of her superior intellect and intuition, can know it more accurately than other white settlers. In other words, it does not matter whether Blixen is disdainful of European or of African justice. Her disdain is not directed to systematic criticism of either and analysis of their interactions; it merely forms part of her self-invention as a mythic figure in a mythic landscape. Thus, Kitosch's brutalized and devalued body is etherealized and ascribed a mythic value in a way that allows Blixen herself apparently to transcend the materiality of her circumstances.

As with much of Blixen's work, the move is reminiscent of the self-aggrandizing transvaluation of Yeats's use of symbol. But if we compare the "beauty" ascribed to Kitosch with the "terrible beauty" born out of the Easter Rising, we can see quite how willful Blixen's reading of Kitosch's death is. Whereas the leaders of the 1916 rebellion actually did lead a rebellion and actively resisted British colonial power, Kitosch's only act of resistance was to ride rather than lead a horse; for that "offense" he was beaten to death. Blixen's account almost suggests that there is no need for active resistance, systematic resistance to colonial rule, since no matter how oppressive the rule, Africans will always have the freedom of "wild things" to "go when they like." Thus, again, in reimagining Kitosch as having no less autonomy ultimately than Karen Blixen, the apparently autonomous and transcendent farmer, Blixen forgets her complicitous role as *fermier*, part of a system whose personal, ethnographic, and forensic knowledge of Africans was always put to nonreciprocal uses of control.

3

"In Africa"

Qui donc saura nous faire oublier telle ou telle partie du monde
Où est le Christophe Colomb à qui l'on devra l'oubli d'un con-
    tinent
[Who then can make us forget such or such a part of the world
Where is the Christopher Columbus to whom one might en-
    trust the forgetting of a continent]
Guillaume Apollinaire

X stands for the unknown.
Malcolm X

X-ing Out Africa to Produce
Something New

Ever since Pliny recorded the statement "ex Africa semper aliquid novi," it seems that Europe has expected the novel, the exotic, the previously unknown out of Africa. Blixen alludes to the reference in the English title of her first memoir, but although her exoticizing purports to be of a relatively benign variety, by the time *Out of Africa* was published, Africa's exoticism had become so closely associated in Western discourse with wildness, barbarism, and darkness that any expectations of novelty had ironically transmuted.[1] For most European colonial writers, to travel to or settle in Africa was to travel *back* in time,[2] to experience the freakish novelty of primitive or traditional societies untouched by European modernity. In this allochronic discourse,[3] Africa figures, as Christopher Miller has it, as a "trope . . . recounting a colonial history, designating a difference" (10) representing either a lost Eden (as in much of Blixen's work) or a living Inferno (as in *Heart of Darkness*).

The discourse of darkness reflects European ethnocentrism and ignorance that misconstrued the white space of gaps on maps and that can still shrink the continent's vastness to the scope of a suburb in the manner of the *New Yorker*'s famous map of the World. Despite its inaccuracy the label has stuck,[4] hiding the fact that the naming and mapping of Africa by Europe has never been a neutral, objective Enlightenment. Rather, it has always been hand in glove with enslavement, conquest, and colonization, part of that European activity which has shaped and distorted the continent physically and imaginatively, determining even the political map of contemporary Africa through the arbitrary boundary drawing by European powers at the Congress of Berlin in 1884.[5] Two years before the Berlin Conference, Ernest Renan, one of the chief European theorizers of the nation-state, declared that it was not language, race, religion, or geography which determined the idea of a nation. Rather, it was the common will of the people of that nation. There is no place in his thinking, however, for the externally imposed will of imperialist power, and he takes no account of the difficulties of the coming to nationhood of states defined by geographical lines that confound and compound diverse cultural, religious, ethnic, and linguistic groups.[6]

One of Renan's memorable dicta regarding nation-formation claims that forgetting plays a key role (Renan 66); what he had in mind was presumably some sort of communal hatchet burying.[7] However, when the "forgetting" has been done for (and of) you—as Africa has been forgotten by Europe and America, physically and imaginatively x-ing out whole societies, not just surnames—then nation-building depends on rather different memorial re- or deconstruction. This chapter, playing on the homophone of Malcolm X's adopted surname (to indicate the crossing-out of his African lineage) and the Latin *ex* as in Pliny's "ex Africa semper aliquid novi," allows me to comment on the manner in which European discourse has tended to ascribe enriching or enlightening value to European experience in Africa while erasing indigenous African experience.[8] In particular, it situates Blixen's ahistorical and nostalgic memoirs and Schreiner's historically specific novella *Trooper Peter Halket of Mashonaland* in relation to Conrad's *Heart of Darkness;* the contrast between the continued popularity of *Out of Africa* and the canonical centrality of *Heart of Darkness,* on the one hand, and the canonical invisibility of *Trooper Peter Halket* indicates the degree to which the West's discourse on Africa remains allochronic and consequently self-exculpatory. Despite all the canon reform of the last twenty years or so and the burgeoning of the field of postcolonial studies, writing, like Schreiner's, which impolitely insists on exposing the brutal effects of European colonization, or Euro-American neocolonialism, tends to receive less attention from literary scholars than texts that lend themselves to ahistorical thematic approaches.

Africa and the Colonists: Schreiner's and Blixen's Sense of History

We have already seen that Schreiner's and Blixen's African inventions are, to varying degrees, consistent with the dominant trope of difference that Miller describes, Schreiner's case being the more ambivalent. We have had evidence, for instance, that Schreiner might be an exemplary case of the inability of European anti-imperialists to evade the imperialist ideology that "forgot" Africans and African history. It is there not only in her early fiction's racist representation of Africans but also in the much later, "scientifically" argued *Woman and Labour*. Her overlooking of Africans and African history produces mere traces of indigenous culture in *African Farm*'s Bushman paintings discussed in chapter 4, while her attentiveness to European voices results in her jarringly uncritical faith in "civilizers" like Sir George Grey.[9] Further, while her worldview was colored by "progressive" notions of history as exemplified by Mill's faith in the perfectibility of humankind, such belief in the ameliorative effects of her interventions was not racially neutral; it depended on Herbert Spencer's so-called social Darwinism, which placed Aryans at the top of a racial hierarchy and discouraged hybridity except in cases of "mixtures of nearly-allied varieties of man" (Young 19). We saw the results of this belief in Schreiner's discussion of the sexual repulsion between refined Europeans—such as Charles Darwin and George Sand—and the most uncivilized non-Europeans she could think of—Fuegan men and Bushman women (*Woman and Labour* 261–62; see chapter 2). Therefore, while Schreiner's evolutionary faith informed her feminism, socialism, and pacifism by positing the future possibility of a society free from class, race, or gender domination, and a society free from war, it also, especially in her early work, enabled her "forgetting" of Africans and African history. Nonetheless, in Schreiner's rejection of the imperial romance mode we can see how clearly her generally interventionist, future-regarding sense of history diverges from Blixen's fatalistic, nostalgic sense.

Blixen's rejection of a progressive view of history involves a kind of remembering and forgetting quite distinct from Schreiner's evolutionary thought, even though, like Schreiner's, it too simultaneously resists and reproduces, potentially at least, some of the West's more standard ways of forgetting Africa and African history. In the brief section in *Out of Africa* entitled "Of Natives and History," Blixen posits what initially looks like a standard progressive, evolutionary view, racialist in the notion that "the people who expect the Natives to jump joyfully from the stone age to the age of motor cars, forget the toil and labour which our own fathers have had, to bring us all through history up to where we are" (251). Even though by birth Blixen is part of that collective "we" who are more familiar with the age of motor cars than with the stone age, she clearly disdains those "people" for forgetting the toil and labour of their own history.[10] Her disdain becomes more apparent as the section proceeds, and Blixen distances herself further from her fellow white settlers' cynical response to the news that "nine young Kikuyu, from the Church of Scotland mission, had come and asked to be received into the Roman Catholic Church, because they had, upon meditation and discussion, come to hold with the doctrine of Transubstantiation" (251). Laughing at Blixen's news, the settlers "explained" to her "that the young Kikuyus had seen a chance of higher wages, of lighter work, or of getting a bicycle to ride on, at the French Mission, and had therefore invented their conversion in regard to Transubstantiation" (251–52).

Blixen, in her turn, dismisses the settlers' racist cynicism, insisting that Father Bernard, the local Catholic priest, "knew the Kikuyus well" and suggesting that the conversions and the reason for them were perfectly sincere. Her own reasoning, however, depends on a complex application of the evolutionary view of history that sets different peoples at different stages of historical "development": "The minds of the young Kikuyu may now be walking on the shadowy paths of our own ancestors, whom we should not disown in their eyes, who held their ideas about Transubstantiation very dear. Those people of five hundred years ago were in their day offered higher wages, and promotion, and easier terms of life, even sometimes their very lives, and to everything they preferred their conviction about Transubstantiation" (252). So far so clear: The young Kikuyu are just like our own ancestors except that they're five hundred years behind in development. In defending the Kikuyu this way, Blixen paradoxically asserts human sameness through cultural difference, a move whose potential racism is revealed in the very next sentence: "They [our ancestors] were not offered a bicycle, but Father Bernard himself, who had got a motor bicycle, attached less value to it than to the conversion of the nine Kikuyus" (252). This reference, suggesting that Father Bernard, a twentieth-century white man, shares the values both of "our ancestors" and of the Kikuyu converts, completely undermines the racial, cultural, and historical determining of difference that frames Blixen's response.

Her conclusion to the section involves a similarly paradoxical endorsing and undercutting of a linear notion of history. Imagining an ingenious scheme whereby "we" could allow "them" to "catch up with us, three years to our hundred," Blixen imagines the Kikuyu "in twenty years . . . ready for the Encyclopaedists, and then they would come, in another ten years, to Kipling. We should let them have dreamers, philosophers, and poets out," writes Blixen, "to prepare the ground for Mr Ford" (252). Again, this all sounds patronizingly accepting of the Western idea of progress, but Blixen immediately turns that idea on its head by bending the line of history into a circle. "Where shall they find us then? Shall we in the meantime have caught them by the tail and be hanging on to it, in our pursuit of some shade, some darkness, practising upon a tomtom?[11] Will they be able to have our motor cars at cost price then, as they can now have the doctrine of Transubstantiation?" (252).

Like Schreiner, she appears bound by western ideology, intuitively testing the limits of a counterhegemonic version of history, but unable fully to articulate it without some recourse to the hegemonic model. However, while Schreiner's testing of the limits depends on pushing the progressive model to one particular logical extreme—that utopian future time of freedom described earlier—Blixen's testing involves bending the line of the progressive model so that it ends up chasing its own tail. For her, what is significant in history is not one's ameliorative impact on a particular society but one's individual struggle with "destiny."[12] This is a stock feature of her fiction and equally of her representations of Africans as oscillating between "self-defeating arrogance and a stoic surrender to whatever the powers that be handed them" (Horton 223), and Horton is surely right in ascribing this representation to projection.

Her account of her dealings with Kinanjui, the Kikuyu "chief," provides further evidence of the self-serving nature of Blixen's forgetting-and-remembering of Africans and African history. I put "chief" in quotation marks because Kinanjui's very status depended on British colonial expectations of African "tribal" customs and had little to do with actual precolonial Kikuyu practice. As such, Kinanjui reveals to what extent Blixen necessarily inherited a "history" of "Africa" that already depended on a British discourse in which forgetting and remembering appear in invented traditions. As Terence Ranger puts it: "The most far-reaching inventions of tradition in colonial Africa took place when the Europeans believed themselves to be respecting age-old African custom. What were called customary law, customary land-rights, customary political structure and so on, were in fact *all* invented by colonial codification" (Hobsbawm and Ranger 250). In fact, customary political structure among the Kikuyu did not involve the institution of chiefdom as such, so as Wunyabari O. Maloba writes, "When the British sought for local agents of colonialism they chose people who had no traditional power." These "chiefs," such as Kinanjui, "owed their offices to British colonial administration and not to the traditional institutions . . . and served without being unduly worried about their popularity with their subjects" (27).[13]

Thus, when Blixen introduces "the big Chief Kinanjui" in *Out of Africa*, she can only partly explain the forgetting involved in the history of Kinanjui's elevation. She describes him as "a crafty old man, with a fine manner, and much real greatness to him, although he had not been born to be a chief, but had been made so, many years ago, by the English, when they could no longer get on with the legitimate ruler of the Kikuyus of the district" (127). In other words, while she is aware of some of the politics behind his appointment, she doesn't question the fundamental issues of "African" chiefdom and presumed tribal identity. Like most, if not all, Europeans Blixen "failed to comprehend that ethnic populations encompassed substantial diversity and that ethnic affiliations were not infrequently competing or contradictory" (Ambler 32), frequently in her work falling back on monolithic versions of Kikuyu, Masai, Somali, Kavirondo, Arabs, and other ethnic groupings even when the details of her subject matter belie those groupings' monolithic nature.[14]

One such instance becomes evident in Blixen's discussion of Kinanjui and his role in resolving the dispute over the accidental shooting of two boys on the farm (*Out of Africa* 81–137). While playing with a shotgun, Kabero, the seven-year-old kitchen-toto of Blixen's farm manager, had accidentally wounded four other children (one, Wanyangerri, very seriously) and killed one, a boy named Wamai. After the shooting, Kabero vanishes into the Masai reserve, and Blixen presides over the local "kiama" to settle the question of compensation for the dead and wounded boys.

By the time Blixen introduces Kinanjui into the story, she has already, after some considerable effort, worked out what she considers to be a fair and equitable settlement acceptable to all parties. Apart from the obvious complexity of arbitrating justly in any case of accidental death, one of the factors that makes the settlement in this case so knotty is that it involves a complicated web of intermarriage, adoption, and trade between and among Masai and Kikuyu clans—precisely the sort of intercourse that undercuts the totalizing tendencies of tribal terms. Kaninu, for instance, the father of the boy who accidentally did the shooting, "was on good terms with the neighbouring Masai tribe, and had married four or five of his daughters off to them," and even Kinanjui himself had apparently "sent . . . more than twenty of his daughters to the Masai, and had got a hundred head of cattle back from them" (102). Moreover, Wamai, the boy killed in the shooting, was the adopted son of Jogona; on those grounds, Wamai's birth parents—members of "the Nyeri people, who belonged to a low class of Kikuyu, and had all the look of three dirty and shaggy hyenas that had slunk one hundred and fifty miles upon Wamai's blood-track" (107)—disputed Jogona's compensation award of forty sheep. Blixen clearly despises these Nyeri ambulance chasers, using animal metaphors to describe them not only as scavengers but also as parasites, sitting "with no more manifestation of life than three ticks upon a sheep" (108). She is more than satisfied when their claim is turned down by the D.O., and her description of them walking "scowling back to their own village, without having got anything *off the farm*" (113; emphasis added) suggests to what extent Blixen thought of all the people on the farm in proprietorial, or at least paternalistic, terms as "her" people even more than Kikuyu, or Somali.

Most important, however, Blixen's own account of the case fully reveals the arbitrariness and constructed nature of "tribal" identity, at the same time that it uses the terms *Kikuyu, Masai, Somali,* and so on in essentialist ways. Thus, while Kabero (Kaninu's son, and the boy who had done the shooting) becomes Masai in the space of a five-year stay in the Masai Reserve (121),[15] and while "the hearts of Kaninu's daughters were turning like the hearts of the Sabine women of old" (103), the climax of the section, where Blixen describes the full and final public settlement of the case, pits Kinanjui as quintessential Kikuyu and Farah as archetypically Somali. And typically for Blixen, she sees them both in terms of animals and of slaves or slave owners.

Imagining an almost immemorial, virtually unchanging history of an Arab slave trade totally free from European influence, Blixen presents the Kikuyu as long-suffering sheep getting "through their destiny, as they got through it now, on their immense gift for resignation" (134). Unlike the birds of prey, the invading Arabs, or "the Native bird of prey of the highlands," the Masai, they neither died under the yoke nor stormed against fate; instead, "they were friends with God in foreign countries, and in chains" (134). Meanwhile, the Arabs' "young illegitimate half-brothers" (132), the Somali, who "in the old time . . . could marry with the daughters of the Masai only, out of all the tribes of the country" (133) occupied a special position as the Arabs' seconds-in-command, as a result of which "their relation to the Natives was nearly exactly that of the sheepdog to the sheep" (133).[16] Thus, when Farah—himself peripheral to the matter in hand—and Kinanjui meet at the settlement, Blixen makes their meeting represent something essential, elemental, and extratemporal: "Farah and Kinanjui met here, the sheepdog and the old ram. Farah stood up erect in his red and blue turban, black embroidered Arab waistcoat and Arab silk robe, as thoughtful, decorous a figure as you would find anywhere in the world. Kinanjui was spreading himself on the stone seat, naked but for the mantle of monkey furs on his shoulders, an old Native, a clod of the soil of the African highlands. . . . It was easy to imagine the two, a hundred years earlier or more, holding a converse over a consignment of slaves" (135). Although she herself is present, and although she herself has final, formal authority—as her drawing up and signing the document of settlement indicates (137–38)—she remains absent from the representation of the "meeting," thus repeating the forgetting of British presence involved in her figuring the Kikuyu as sheep among Arab and Masai birds of prey and Somali sheepdogs.

One might argue, however, that in thus forgetting the European role, Blixen is not just, deplorably, attempting to find an alibi for European behavior, as Walter Rodney would presumably aver, but that she is also, or instead, laudably attempting to create her own sort of afrocentric history in which Europeans do not play the role of pervasive influence they think they do.[17] This contention would fit the oscillation of aloofness and identification we saw in her setting herself apart from the "we" who are from the motor-car age, it fits with her outsider status as non-British, and it fits with the complex mix of identification and alterity we find in her representations of Kinanjui himself.

Kinanjui is more than an old ram, vulnerable and long-suffering. He is also grandly impressive and elephantine. Blixen's comparison of Kinanjui with an elephant verges precariously on the edge of the patronizing, even mocking: "He was always an impressive figure tall and broad, with no fat on him anywhere; his face, too, was proud, long and bony, with a slanting forehead like that of a Red Indian. He had a broad nose, so expressive that it looked like the central point of the man, as if the whole stately figure was there only to carry the broad nose about. Like the trunk of an elephant, it was both boldly inquisitive and extremely sensitive and prudent, intensely on the offensive, and on the defensive as well. And an elephant, finally, like Kinanjui, would have a head of the very greatest nobility if he did not look so clever" (130). However, even though her portrait may exemplify Fanon's settler's bestiary, the elephant does not merit ridicule in Blixen's eyes. Her respect for it is up there with her respect for that other grand animal, the lion, and in thus representing Kinanjui as elephant to her lioness, Blixen's use of the bestiary here produces not so much demeaning difference as ennobling sameness.

Two further details of the description just quoted lend credence to my contention: Kinanjui's having "no fat on him anywhere," and his resembling a "Red Indian." In the former case, Blixen's aversion to fat manifested itself in her own anorexia, a condition exacerbated physiologically by her syphilis, but also a willed "badge of defiance to the *hyggelig,* a lightness not only of the flesh: it contradicted Westenholtz solidity" (Thurman 66).[18] That lightness and leanness, that spareness is one of the features she projects onto the African landscape; indeed, in the opening description discussed in chapter 4, Blixen declares that "the geographical position and the height of the land combined to create a landscape that had not its like in all the world. There was no fat on it and no luxuriance anywhere" (13). A little later she declares that "the chief feature of the landscape, and of your life in it, was the air" (13). All this leanness then gets picked up by Blixen's "tribe of deerhounds," which "went well with African scenery and the African Native. It may be due to the altitude— the highland melody in all three. . . . It was as if the great, spare landscape . . . was not complete until the deerhounds were also in it" (67). What I am arguing is that Blixen's reference to Kinanjui's leanness is, as frequently, a projection. Only the lean are here where they ought to be in the landscape of Blixen's farm, that "refined essence of a continent" (13).[19] Thus, no matter how patronizingly, Kinanjui is accorded Blixen's highest accolade of belonging in the aristocratic-cum-feudal "Africa" she invented.

The second feature that suggests Blixen's tone should not be read as mocking is the reference to Kinanjui's resemblance to a "Red Indian." Blixen knew about "Red Indians" through her father's stories and writing. Wilhelm Dinesen had spent more than a year in America in the early 1870s and, according to Judith Thurman, his "assumption about Nature as the great moral force and [his] sense of Western culture as 'the betrayal of the original distinction of mankind' Isak Dinesen would take up in *Out of Africa*" (Thurman 15). Thurman stresses how Blixen, in emulating her father's romanticism and disparaging her mother's domestic values, was deeply affected by Wilhelm's stories: "When she went to Africa she was extremely proud to enjoy that relationship of mutual respect with the Africans she imagined Wilhelm had had among the Chippewa and Pawnee" (Thurman 27).

Her sense of affinity with the lean and aristocratic Kinanjui reaches its height in a later section of *Out of Africa* when both he and she at their moments of crisis and loss—Kinanjui's death, the loss of her farm—fall victim to the shrinking effect of bureaucratic colonialism. Indeed, the section entitled "Death of Kinanjui" is embedded in the final, most elegiac section of *Out of Africa*, "Farewell to the Farm." Kinanjui's death, the death of Finch Hatton, and Blixen's departure, which all occurred in the first six months of 1931, represent the passing of the last vestiges of authentic "Africa" before the farm gets swallowed up by the "development" of the suburb of Karen, when the refined essence of the continent is destroyed by rude concrete, bricks, and tarmac roads. In these last pages, Blixen, like her father in America some sixty years previously, aligns herself not with the European "we" whose technology had allowed her to see Africa from, in, and as air, but with the native other, finally unable to escape the smothering embrace of European economic expansion.

Such an alignment might have appeared merely self-serving. What makes Blixen's account of Kinanjui's death so moving, though, is that it also appears to be a genuine account of her own tiredness and cowardice. For when she writes that Kinanjui, about to die, "sent for me" (286), she is no longer lord of all she surveys but effectively a squatter, too, unable to perform—Prospero-style—any more of her colonial magic. Thus when she learns of the reason for Kinanjui's summoning her, she "sat and listened with a heavy heart" (289). She was needed not as a fellow African aristocrat to share a last moment of mutual respect but as an intermediary to pull one last string to allow the old collaborator at least to die more or less among his own people. Specifically, Kinanjui wanted to avoid being taken by the local mission doctor to die in hospital; instead, he asked Blixen to let him go to her house. She, mindful that this house was no longer her own, tired out by dealings with businessmen and lawyers, and anticipating blame for Kinanjui's death should he die on the journey or on arrival, refuses his request: "I had not got it in me any longer to stand up against the authorities of the world. I did not have it in me now to brave them all, not all of them" (290). In addition to her own self-reproach, she feels the reproach of Farah, whose "eyes and whole face darkened with surprise" (290), as well as the silent reproach of Kinanjui himself and his entourage. To be eliciting the very stoicism she normally preferred to observe or practice hurts her. Kinanjui "looked," she writes, "as if something like this had happened to him before, which very likely it had" (291). Then she goes on: "'Kwaheri, Kinanjui,' I said— Good-bye. His burning fingers moved a little against my palm. Already before I had got to the door of the hut, when I turned and looked back, the dimness and smoke of the room had swallowed up the big outstretched figure of my Kikuyu Chief. As I came out again from the hut it was very cold. The moon was now low down at the horizon, it must have been past midnight. Just then in the manyatta one of Kinanjui's cocks crew twice. Kinanjui died that same night, in the mission hospital" (291).

This is the tone of which Blixen is a real master: while "my Kikuyu Chief" smacks of patronization, it still avows an intimacy; while the sense of guilt evoked by the sound of the cocks crowing presents a chastened, poignantly subdued self, that self is once more implicitly valorized by the suggestion that her silence almost matches Peter's denials of Christ. The remainder of this section continues in much the same vein, simultaneously building up and cutting down the significance of Karen Blixen, the lone African European stoically withstanding (or failing to withstand) the forces of a barbarous civilization that ultimately made of Kinanjui's funeral an "altogether . . . European and clerical affair" (292). Blixen writes herself as African more clearly here than anywhere else in the book, affirming her attraction to the Kikuyu practice of leaving the dead "above ground for the hyenas and vultures to deal with," a practice that allowed the body "to be made one with Nature and become a common component of a landscape" (291).

Her anger against the Christian takeover of the funeral service produces a "they" which declares her distance from the European authorities of church (especially) and state and from all those processes that were transforming lean "Natives" into Christian converts, "fat young Kikuyus with spectacles and folded hands, who looked like ungenial eunuchs" (292). "If they wished to impress the Kikuyu with the feeling that here they had laid their hand on the dead chief, and that he now belonged to them, they succeeded. They were so obviously in power that one felt it to be out of the question for Kinanjui to get away from them" (292). In fact, even the tall, lean Kinanjui himself appears to have been shrunk and distorted, squashed fat as it were, to fit into "a nearly square box, surely no more than five feet long." Like Blixen, he has finally been brought home to a family of no real kin where fat and rectitude rule.

In this section, therefore, we see Blixen inventing a self very strongly identified with the "African." Like Kinanjui the archetypal African, this African Blixen cannot escape the clutches of European colonialism. However, in her memorialization of "my Kikuyu Chief" Blixen has forgotten her earlier recognition of Kinanjui's *lack* of authenticity, the fact that he owed his chiefdom to British colonial intervention. To use a proverb she might have appreciated, those who run with the hare cannot hunt with the hounds, and in the same way that it was inevitable that Kinanjui was finally claimed by the European authorities he had served, so it was inevitable that Blixen too should feel the insistence of Europe's claims. By specifically bemoaning the missions' role—something from which she assumed she could legitimately claim distance[20]—in taking over Kinanjui's funeral, Blixen diminishes the role of colonial and imperialist economics, a system to which she was inextricably bound and literally indebted.[21]

Commenting on their constant oscillation between identity and alterity in their self-inventions vis-à-vis Africans, Susan Horton observes that "Dinesen and Schreiner came to think of themselves as in-betweens who could turn that status into something positive by becoming go-betweens, intercessors, and mediators" (Horton 222). Ultimately, though, such attempts to act as go-betweens, dependent on temporary suspension of their European identity, depended on a conscious and unconscious forgetting of both Europe and Africa. Indeed, it is possible that Blixen is right to see the death of Kinanjui and her loss of the farm as equivalent, marking the end of one phase of colonial European African collaboration. And her sadness at the beginning of the anticolonial interregnum might further be justified not just by the fact that bureaucrats and politicians took over from farmers and chiefs but also by the fact that what emerged from anticolonialism in Kenya turned out to be a new kind of collaboration at the state level, producing a neocolonial African elite that still collaborates with Europe in that ultimate system of spatial control, nationalism, and that still remains in hock to European economic imperialism.

It has produced an Africa, furthermore, that gives the West a new binarism: the faces of famine and of fat-cat "wabenzi," that comprador class which has used its own forgetful memories of Africanness to keep the people down.

The Violence of the Canons

> When genocide becomes part of the cultural heritage in the themes of committed literature, it becomes easier to continue to play along with the culture which gave birth to murder.
> **Theodor Adorno**

> I write about violence as naturally as Jane Austen wrote about manners. Violence shapes and obsesses our society, and if we do not stop being violent we have no future. People who do not want writers to write about violence want to stop us writing about us and our time. It would be immoral not to write about violence.
> **Edward Bond**

The contradictions of Blixen's attitudes to colonial and precolonial Africa and Africans and the complexities of her own (and Kinanjui's) resistant yet collaborative self-positioning in respect to British authority were by no means unique. Simon Gikandi, "born in the shadow of colonialism, under a state of emergency in Central Kenya" (xix), prefaces *Maps of Englishness* with an observation that despite his people's detestation of colonial rule they passionately "believed in the efficacy and authority of colonial culture" (xix). Such observations underpin Gikandi's specific reading of Englishness as "a cultural and literary phenomenon produced in the ambivalent space that separated, but also conjoined, metropole and colony" (xii). While Blixen's memoirs acknowledge some of the spatial conjoining of metropole and colony, as we have seen she still manages to reproduce the trope of "Africa" as a site of otherness by resorting to the kind of allochronic discourse Johannes Fabian describes in which the other's difference is established by his/her occupation of a different historical time. Such an allochronic approach leads her to produce an ahistorical "Africa" which invites a symbolic reading requiring an aesthetic response rather than a critical reading prompting an active response. In this regard *Out of Africa* is a kind of obverse of *Heart of Darkness,* and the continuing circulation of both texts in the West bears witness to the West's Manichaean memorial construction of Africa as Eden or Inferno. The absence from the canon, by contrast, of Schreiner's *Trooper Peter Halket of Mashonaland,* which emphatically conjoins metropole and colony both in space and in time, and no less emphatically undermines the efficacy and authority of colonial control, indicates to what extent this culturally powerful construction of Africa depends on a particular forgetting—of the history of European violence. The huge discrepancy in canonical status of *Heart of Darkness* and *Trooper Peter Halket* prompts broader questions about the definition, value, and function of literature in the West, particularly in relation to violence and the use of terror, and the artist's consequent aesthetic and social responsibility.

These are questions with relevance not only to recent African cultural history; they are fundamental, it seems to me, to all literary production. The starkness of their appearance in the literary production of colonial and postcolonial encounters ought simply to alert us to the violence of apparently "politer" texts[22] and the collective violence of texts-as-canon. That recognition implicitly supports Pierre Bourdieu's notion of symbolic power and feminist, postcolonial, and deconstructionist canon reformers' notions of the potential epistemic violence of cultural canons. I contend that the discrepancy between the canonical positions of *Heart of Darkness* and *Trooper Peter* to a large extent depends on something like Bourdieu's notion of politeness, the authors' capacity "to assess market conditions accurately and to produce linguistic expressions which are suitably euphemized" (Thompson 20). Although Bourdieu does not apply his ideas specifically to literary canon formation, his description in *Language and Symbolic Power* of the academic rehabilitation of Heidegger as dependent on a particular kind of "structural censorship" strikes me as analogous to the enshrining of *Heart of Darkness* in the English literary canon. As Bourdieu has it, this structural censorship "is imposed on all producers of symbolic goods, including the authorized spokesperson, whose authoritative discourse is more subject to the norms of official propriety than any other, and it condemns the occupants of dominated positions either to silence or to shocking outspokenness" (138). Conrad's focusing on an abstract "horror" at the heart of darkness, rather than shockingly horrific events, represents just such a censorship.

Unlike the shockingly outspoken Olive Schreiner, Conrad appears to have had a shrewd intuition that the canon tolerates only certain types of violence and its representations. The rest it silences.

To avoid the risk of setting up my own binarism between the reception of two works representing violence, however, I first need to back up and reiterate that even the apparently apolitical, and "civilized" nature of a text like *Out of Africa*, through its *non*representation of violence, tends to occlude the violence of colonial politics. As my comment above on "texts-as-canon" hinted, this is not just a question of textual content; it is, more significantly, a question of reception, and as such it highlights the potential epistemic violence of cultural canons.

In a typically memorable, typically suggestive, typically category-collapsing dictum, Walter Benjamin declared: "There is no document of civilization which is not at the same time a document of barbarism" (*Illuminations* 256). Benjamin's claim is never more persuasive than when the document in question stems from an encounter between those assumed to be civilized and those assumed to be barbaric (however ironically those terms are deployed). It should be clear that although *Out of Africa* explicitly documents one European woman's notion of civilization, the book itself does not quite have the same canonical status as a *public* "document of civilization" as Conrad's *Heart of Darkness* does. Neither, in its politeness and decency and its explicit respect for separate Masai, Kikuyu, Somali, and European attitudes, does it risk the self-questioning circularity of Conrad's novella, which claims Kurtz's looking at his own barbaric heart of civilized darkness as a "moral victory." Nor in its "ordinariness" does it portray anything as "spectacular" as Marlow's descent into the Inferno. However, Blixen's nostalgic representation[23] of an Edenic Africa, with its silence on the violence of imperialism, fascinatingly complements the image of a Hellish Africa depicted by Conrad.

In fact, Blixen herself might have relished this connection. I have already drawn attention to the fact that, through the influence of Georg Brandes, she was powerfully drawn to Nietzsche, whose attempt to push beyond metaphysics she admired. As Thomas R. Whissen points out, she frequently includes traces of the diabolical in her artist-figures (71), and she liked to think of herself as similarly going beyond good and evil. She certainly prefers the Satanic-creative to uncreative good, and in 1926 in a very long "confessional" letter to her brother she compares herself to Lucifer, explaining:

"I conceive of it as meaning: truth, or the search for truth, striving towards the light, a critical attitude,—indeed, what one means by *spirit*. The opposite of settling down believing that what one cares for is and must be best, indeed, settling into the studied calm, satisfaction and uncritical atmosphere of the Paradise. And in addition to this: work . . . a *sense of humor* which is afraid of *nothing*, but has the *courage of its convictions* to make fun of everything, and life, new light, variety." (*Letters* 249)

Hence, although it may seem like a wrench to compare Blixen's and Conrad's Africa, through the Nietzschean and/or Manichaean sense of the equivalence and mutual dependency of good and evil, in providing the sites for invention of figures who attempted to embrace their fate regardless of conventional morality—namely, Blixen's writer-persona Isak Dinesen[24] and Conrad's Kurtz—both Africa as Eden and Africa as Inferno equally represent the European will to power over Africa and Africans.

Such a contention is nothing new, at least, not in its separate parts. Susan Horton stresses throughout *Difficult Women, Artful Lives* the vital role Blixen's Africans played in her self-construction: "The European subject becomes real to itself by seeing its reflection in the eyes of another," says Horton. "Becoming real to herself by seeing her reflection in their eyes, Dinesen becomes real and important to European and American audiences by reporting those reflections" (195). It is precisely that *use* of Africans to validate European identity that Achebe objected to in 1974 in his germinal essay "An Image of Africa: Racism in Conrad's *Heart of Darkness*." Having demonstrated how Conrad uses Africa and Africans as mere "setting and backdrop" or as a "metaphysical battlefield devoid of all recognizable humanity," Achebe, full of righteous exasperation, expresses amazement that nobody has seen "the preposterous and perverse arrogance in thus reducing Africa to the role of props for the break-up of one petty European mind" (*Hopes and Impediments* 12).

Achebe calls Conrad "a thoroughgoing racist" (*Hopes* 11). Rather than pursuing that line of personal attack or Frances B. Singh's line of inquiry into the "colonialistic bias" of the text itself, I want to pursue Achebe's claim that *Heart of Darkness*'s reception (and *Out of Africa*'s) in the West over time has precipitated a racist image of Africa, part of the "white racism against Africa" which Achebe writes has become "such a normal way of thinking that its manifestations go completely unre-marked" (11–12). While the specific texts sporadically provide evidence of at least some antiracist, anti-imperialist attitudes,[25] and while Conrad's in particular displays moments of extreme cultural relativism, reversing the gaze, and imagining how the English might respond to an invading force, still the overall effect of their canonical status precipitates this Eurocentric sediment that Africa is a place for white folks to go to lose their minds, their lives, or their paradise.[26] As cultural artifacts *now* (that is, independent of Conrad/Blixen or the texts' biases), as "documents of civilization" *Heart of Darkness* and *Out of Africa* are largely emptied of their potentially disruptive content and can be made to fit into that liberal canonical position that is neither wholly imperialist nor radically and impolitely anti-imperialist. To borrow from Bourdieu again, such an approach opens up the way to look at the "authority" of *Heart of Darkness*, that status which makes it *the* point of reference for Euro-American writing about the Congo and in part accounts for the frequency of its appearance in anthologies. Bourdieu insists that if we look "in language for the principle underlying the logic and effectiveness of the language of institution" we are forgetting that "authority comes to language from outside" (109)

When *Heart of Darkness* is taught in English courses in high school and university, however, teachers still tend to look "inside," offering the text up as a "great work of literature," exemplifying Conrad's narrative technique of impressionism, his handling of allegory, imagery, or what have you, or providing a case study of different literary critical responses.[27] Its appreciation by these aesthetic criteria tends to anaesthetize the western reader's political awareness.[28] Even in Robert Kimbrough's compendious, superauthoritative Norton critical edition, the fact of the death of some 5 million people in the Congo easily slides from view,[29] while, in his third edition, Kimbrough responds to canon-broadening moves by adding the voices of George Washington Williams, "a black American who was in the Congo at the same time as Conrad" (Kimbrough xiv), and some "newly chosen essays by Third World writers" (blurb description). Meanwhile, *Trooper Peter Halket* doesn't get the academic treatment at all outside South Africa.[30]

It is tempting to claim that Schreiner's marginalization as female and colonial immediately denies her the cultural capital and symbolic power of the male metropolitan Conrad. Indeed, following Bourdieu, those two circumstances do deny her the recognized authority that in someone more "sure of his cultural identity" (Bourdieu 125) might have allowed her transgressive speech to be effective. However, given Conrad's hyphenated and highly accented Englishness at the time of writing of *Heart of Darkness* and in his own lifetime, Conrad's own "cultural identity" was also not that secure.[31] What we need to explore, therefore, is not biography but Schreiner's and Conrad's respective modes of euphemization, the rhetorical strategies they use in order to reach their audience, and persuade their readers that an operation they are deeply implicated in is rotten to its core.

Conrad's novella is a frame-story. An unnamed narrator recounts the story he heard from Marlow about Kurtz. Thus Kurtz's experience, which is presented as encapsulating the story's "true" significance, is deflected through at least two layers of narrative and interpretation.[32] Additionally we are told that Marlow's stories are different from the usual seamen's yarns because the meaning of an episode for him was "outside, enveloping the tale which brought it out only as a glow brings out a haze, in the likeness of one of these misty halos that sometimes are made visible by the special illumination of moonshine" (Conrad 9). Throughout the tale this haziness is compounded by hiatuses, lacunae, ambivalence, instances of misunderstanding and outright lying, and a generally skeptical attitude toward the power of words to represent anything accurately. Kurtz's "unspeakable" acts remain unspoken, and the heart of darkness itself resists verbal illumination. First-time readers[33] of *Heart of Darkness* could not be said to "know" what Kurtz has done. What the text reveals is auto-referential—its own epistemological crisis.

Fredric Jameson describes Conrad's impressionistic style as schizophrenically defying classification, "floating uncertainly somewhere in between Proust and Robert Louis Stevenson." It has elements of late Victorian realism, and of the romance of Victorian adventure stories, at the same time as it displays in emergent form both the alienated and fragmented subjectivity of modernism, and features of popular or mass culture (*Political Unconscious* 206). Schreiner's style in *Trooper Peter Halket* is less ambivalent. Although, like *Heart of Darkness*, her opening sets her focal character apart in the darkness, and although his encounter with the mysterious "Jew of Palestine" stretches the credibility of the text's apparent realism, the result of Peter Halket's solitary musing and ghostly meeting is to lay bare exactly what he had expected to do in Af-

rica, what he had done, and the utter hypocrisy of the conventional justi-
fications for such expectations and deeds. First-time readers of *Trooper
Peter Halket* could not *fail* to know that Peter has killed, raped, and plun-
dered. Through spectacular representation the text reveals the vicious-
ness and hypocrisy of British-sponsored activity in Mashonaland and
Matabeleland.

Although Schreiner's text has no equivalent of Conrad's epistemological comfort zone around the facts of Peter's longer-term presence in
Africa, like Conrad's it does initially—politely—draw a reader in by establishing the potential goodness, or essential decency, of the main character. Schreiner draws attention to Peter's youth and malleability by referring to the scattering of "a few soft white hairs, the growth of early
manhood" on his face (4). Son of a washerwoman from a fairy-tale "little
English village" (7), Peter retains the carelessness and thoughtlessness of
the schoolboy who preferred fishing or bird-nesting to school. He is just
an ordinary boy, in short, of the "boys will be boys" variety.[34] Schreiner,
however, will not let her readers enjoy the false comfort of an unthinking
attitude to thoughtlessness; although memory of his mother acts as a
kind of vestigial conscience, as a trooper, Peter has behaved as thought-
lessly and carelessly as if shooting Africans and raiding their kraals were
no different from killing fish or stealing birds' eggs. "As a rule," writes
Schreiner, "he lived in the world immediately about him, and let the
things of the moment impinge on him and fall off again as they would,
without much reflection." On this particular night, however, he "fell to
thinking" (6).

In his thoughts, balanced against the dream of achieving fame and fortune, and establishing his mother in "a large house in the West End of
London, the biggest that had ever been seen, and another in the country"
(9), lurk more painful recollections of the kinds of "unspeakable" act that
Heart of Darkness cloaks in general mystery: "niggers they had shot";
"the kraals they had destroyed" (5); "the skull of an old Mashona blown
off at the top, the hands still moving" (15); the rape of a black woman "he
and another man caught alone in the bush" (15). In one particularly
graphic image which hideously revises the pastoral idyll of his childhood,
Schreiner has Peter recalling himself "working a maxim gun, but it
seemed to him it was more like the reaping machine he used to work in
England, and that what was going down before it was not yellow corn,
but black men's heads; and he thought when he looked back they lay

behind him in rows, like the corn in sheaves" (15). Peter's dawning sense of his own responsibility has no unequivocal equivalent in *Heart of Darkness*, as we are never privy to the details of Kurtz's thinking, and Marlow himself only observes brutality rather than perpetrating it.

In terms of rhetorical strategy, then, for engaging their audience, we might conclude that the two texts work in a pair of opposite ways: first, while Conrad's provides a genuine comfort zone of epistemological dubiousness, Schreiner's provides the doubled certainty of realistic vision enhanced by spiritual vision; second, while Schreiner sets up the assumed innocence of the Englishman only to question that assumption, Conrad uses it in order to maintain a stance of apparently impartial aloofness. Indeed, Marlow is as seasoned as an observer as he is experienced as a seaman; apparently well acquainted with his own and others' vices and virtues, he can be tempted, but will not fall. Presented almost exclusively with his point of view, Conrad's contemporary British readers, like the reviewer in the *Manchester Guardian*, could presume that Conrad was making no "attack upon colonisation, expansion, even upon Imperialism" (White 179).[35] Sharing *Peter's* point of view, Schreiner's contemporary readers were starkly confronted with the conscience-troubling likelihood that their notions of innocence were deeply flawed.[36]

In dominant Victorian discourse, "work" held high rank among the cardinal virtues. Set against both "thought" and "idleness," "work" represented a virtually unquestioned good.[37] The attitude appears to have been widespread across Europe. King Leopold himself argued that in accustoming the population of the Congo to "general laws . . . the most needful and the most salutary is assuredly that of work" (quoted in Kimbrough 79). Thus, in exposing the "work" of imperialism as less than innocent, involving the "working" of maxim guns to reap black men's skulls, Schreiner's text is openly, impolitely subversive. Unlike Marlow, who uses routine work as a kind of prophylactic against thought,[38] jungle fever, and the brutal cynicism of the "pilgrims," manager, and so on, Peter's lack of a trade means that his work *is* imperialism red in coat and blood. *Africa* doesn't get to him. What gets to him is Cecil Rhodes, the Chartered Company, and the desire for money—in short, the *European* working, or working over, of the world.

Indeed, even though it is in a faltering, untheoretical, and entirely self-interested way, Peter recognizes that "work" is a cover. He anticipates making his fortune at a time when "the Mashonas and Matabeles would have all their land taken away from them, and the Chartered Company would pass a law that they had to work for the white men; and he, Peter Halket, would make them work for him. He would make money" (9–10). That final pair of sentences turns "them work[ing] for him" and "money" into more or less interchangeable grammatical objects of the verb "make." Peter, Schreiner suggests, seems to have grasped that labor can be commodified, and elsewhere he explicitly contrasts those who work with those who make money: "It's not the men who work up here who make the money; it's the big-wigs who get the concessions!"[39]

The comparison with King Leopold and the charade of turning the local populace into workers is obvious. Indeed, Conrad, too, points to the commodification of labor, notably in his description of the "gloomy circle of some Inferno" near the Company Station where exhausted workers have come to die (20). And Conrad is no less explicitly moralistic than Schreiner about the economic exploitation of Africa; he describes the aim of the Eldorado Exploring Expedition as being "to tear treasure out of the bowels of the land . . . with no more moral purpose at the back of it than there is in burglars breaking into a safe" (33). However, even these explicit statements don't do away with Conrad's comfort zone for specifically British readers. Marlow himself, for instance, is not involved in the commodification of the labor; he is not a part of the fictional, ludicrously named Eldorado Exploring Expedition. These imperialists, after all, are not British, and the Congo is not part of that "vast amount of red" on the map of Africa which Marlow declares "good to see at any time, because one knows that some real work is done there" (13). Schreiner, by contrast, has Peter *wanting* to commodify African labor and working for a real-life British company headed by a real-life British businessman/politician, Cecil Rhodes.

By refusing to let her British audience distance themselves from someone else's imperialism, Schreiner thus risked antagonizing the very readership she aimed to transform. As Gerald Monsman astutely comments, "The fictional problem is somehow to find a device that will allow the English to identify themselves with their victims; that is, equally with the natives to feel powerlessness and to sense that their culture could be subject to arbitrary destruction" (Monsman 114). According to Monsman, Schreiner overcomes this problem by making "the aggressor the victim of his own system" (115) and setting up "a parallel between Peter's conversion and that of her readers" (115). Here, through an apparent similarity, a crucial difference between *Trooper Peter Halket* and *Heart of Darkness* becomes apparent: While the final representation of both Peter Halket and Kurtz shows each to be the victim of his own aggressive system, Kurtz is the more successfully euphemized.

At the soft heart of *Heart of Darkness*, Conrad makes Kurtz "the victim of his own system" so spectacularly that he appears to be virtually the victim of his own bodily system, his very nervous system. For facing up to the fact of that self-destruction Marlow elevates Kurtz's whispered cry "The horror! The horror!" into "the expression of some sort of belief" and "an affirmation, a moral victory paid for by innumerable defeats" (69, 70). Whereas Peter's conversion leads to transforming action—the freeing of a Shona captive that leads to Peter's own sacrificial death—Kurtz experiences a classical moment of anagnorisis, a self-knowledge mediated by Marlow that makes of Kurtz a kind of tragic hero whose "moral victory [was] paid for by innumerable defeats, by abominable terrors, by abominable satisfactions" (70). This anagnorisis is experienced more or less vicariously with the reader having to depend on Marlow's interpretation of Kurtz's famous last words. As Marlow says, "It is not my own extremity I remember best. . . . No. It is his extremity that I have seemed to live through" (69). The shared nature of this interpretive experience is prefigured by the earlier scene in which Conrad connects the two men at the physical level, by having Marlow tracking down the escaped Kurtz and bringing him back to the steamboat. So loyal is Marlow to his "Shadow" at this point that no one else knows of the little sortie, and Conrad adds still further symbolic weight to the two men's shared specialness by alluding, however faintly, to Christian legend. By the time Marlow manages to get Kurtz back to the boat and stretched out on his couch, he recalls, "My legs shook under me as though I had carried half a ton on my back down that hill. And yet I had only supported him, his bony arm clasped round my neck—and he was not much heavier than a child" (66). Although it may be merely a suggestion, Conrad appears here to be playing with the legend of St. Christopher carrying the Christ-child across a river. It is surely a perversely Manichean process that allows Kurtz's revelation of horror to occur almost simultaneously with his symbolic apotheosis.

Be that as it may, however, Conrad has proved so successful in euphemizing Kurtz and Marlow that critic after critic has been drawn into reading with the grain, focusing on Marlow's abstract ahistorical interpretation and inevitably distancing generations of literature students from the African victims of imperialism. Patrick Brantlinger, for instance, asks with some incredulity how it was "possible for [Lionel] Trilling to look past Kurtz's criminal record and identify the horror with the fear of death or with African savagery" (270), but then goes on to assert the reasonableness of Trilling's conclusion given the direction of Conrad's writing. "Conrad himself," says Brantlinger, "identifies with and ironically admires Kurtz" as a spiritual hero for "staring into an abyss of nihilism so total that the issues of imperialism and racism pale into insignificance" (270).

Schreiner's purpose, by contrast, was to go beyond providing her audience with the private, readerly luxury of catharsis and to keep the focus squarely on the material consequences of imperialism and racism. To do so she uses a different but perhaps even more familiar allusion to Christian tradition. Like the New Testament Peter, her Peter Simon goes well beyond merely passive self-knowledge. In coming to a revelation about the system that has spawned him, he undergoes a personal transformation which in turn causes him to try to transform the system. His self-separation from what his fellow white men have been doing leads him to direct physical involvement with the Captain of his troop, but in place of Marlow's support of and loyalty toward Kurtz, Schreiner offers us an image of Peter's confrontation and defiance of the Captain. After first attempting to persuade the Captain to let the Shona prisoner go and to allow Peter to "go and make peace" (112), Peter finally creeps out of the camp under cover of darkness and sets the prisoner free. The inevitable noise caused by the prisoner's flight rouses the camp and in the ensuing mayhem Peter is shot dead. Schreiner foregrounds the Christlike, sacrificial nature of all this when she writes, "One hour after Peter Halket had stood outside the tent looking up, he was lying under the little tree, with the red sand trodden down over him, in which a black man and a white man's blood were mingled" (131). Dying in an act of blatant defiance of the Captain aligns Peter with African victims of colonialism, and in doing so makes him a victim of a system he has rejected, and which, Schreiner hoped, her readers would actively reject.

It didn't happen that way. In fact, as we have already seen, it was one of Schreiner's gravest disappointments: "In spite of [*Trooper Peter's*] immense circulation I do not believe it has saved the life of one nigger, it had not the slightest effect in forcing on the parliamentary examination into the conduct of affairs in Rhodesia and it cost me everything" (Rive 333).[40] Hers had been a deliberate appeal to the British public, in the lifting or turning down of whose thumb Schreiner saw the decision between war and peace (Rive 299). What does the British public's deafness to that appeal betoken?

Gerald Monsman suggests that Schreiner's problem lay in her ignoring the limits of fiction. Comparing her fictional technique unfavorably to that of H. G. Wells in *The War of the Worlds,* Monsman argues that Wells's fictional device of having the English experience Martian colonization generalizes his attack on imperialism. Wells, writes Monsman, "has little of Schreiner's desire to censure a specific abuse, little sense that his fiction could participate in history" (120). As such, his "presentation avoids Schreiner's explicit didacticism," can be "technically" more successful, more "fictionally adept," and work "more effectively" (120, 121), exactly the sorts of judgment that have been used to enshrine *Heart of Darkness* in the canon. But what can it mean to say that a fictional text is "effective," when accepting the limits of fiction in the first place has assumed virtual nonparticipation in history? And what sort of intervention on Schreiner's behalf might have been "effective" in saving African lives or indicting Cecil Rhodes?

As was seen in chapter 1, two years after the publication of *Trooper Peter Halket,* Schreiner again addressed a polemical work to the British public when she produced her *English South African's View of the Situation.* Her aim, clearly stated throughout the work, was to avert the looming Anglo-Boer War. She hoped to persuade the British public that they were being hoodwinked by Rhodes and his fellow capitalists into waging war on the Transvaal for the ostensible purpose of freeing British inhabitants there (the so-called "Uitlanders") from Boer oppression, when their real aim was control of the recently discovered Witwatersrand gold. Again, despite considerable support for her position, the work failed to have the desired effect. War duly followed, among other things introducing the world to the horrors of modern trench warfare and concentration camps. Although Rhodes died before the peace was signed, the Randlordship he stood for survived and prospered, and in due time the racial policies he had pioneered in the Cape came into effect in the new Union of South Africa.

Schreiner appears, then, to have been doomed to failure in her efforts at immediate political intervention whether she employed a fictional (read "aesthetic") or nonfictional (read "political") medium. What this suggests is that we should not ascribe the disappearance from the canon of *Trooper Peter Halket* to its failure to observe the limits of fiction, limits which are themselves political fictions. Schreiner is out largely because her political content was, and remains, impolite—shockingly outspoken and insufficiently euphemized.

Readers have two ways of coping with such impoliteness: attacking it and ignoring it. In contemporary reviews, according to First and Scott, "Most of the provincial dailies and the London papers revered [*Trooper Peter's*] style and ignored its politics." The only review to label it "political" did so pejoratively: the reviewer in *Blackwood's* (interestingly enough—since that is where *Heart of Darkness* first appeared) describing it as a "political pamphlet of great bitterness, linked on to the very smallest thread of a story that ever carried red-hot opinions and personal abuse of the fiercest kind into the world" (First and Scott 230). Trying to *not* see the politics of *Trooper Peter Halket of Mashonaland* represents a will to blindness about politics in general and the violence of political systems in particular.

Such blindness has many and varied manifestations, all showing how spectacular representation of violence can get discredited as overstatement. In *Shamanism, Colonialism, and the Wild Man,* Michael Taussig describes the way in which newspaper accounts of the atrocities in the Putumayo rubber boom of the early years of this century "involved the barely conscious tension of fascination and disgust, binding the fantastic to the credible" (33). Taussig goes on to quote the evidence of the British vice consul in Iquitos to a British House of Commons Select Committee, who thought on reading the newspaper accounts that "they were rather fantastic in the horrors they depicted. Such a horrible state of affairs seemed to me incredible. . . . I really thought . . . that they were in a way fabricated" (35). This "real-life" difficulty of recognizing as credible what seems fantastic is part of the problem of representing colonial violence to the metropolitan center. Taussig introduces it via complex connections between the violent, even genocidal pursuit of the rubber trade in Columbia and in the Belgian Congo, and two outsider-insider representers of the trade's atrocities—the Anglo-Irish Roger Casement, and the Anglo-Polish Joseph Conrad. While Casement's reports for the Congo Reform Society displayed a "studied realism," Conrad's "way of dealing with the terror of the rubber boom in the Congo was *Heart of Darkness*" in which, argues Taussig, his aim was *"to penetrate the veil while retaining its hallucinatory quality"* (10; original emphasis).[41] Taussig is more generous to the mistiness of Conrad's style than I am, positing that "the mythic subversion of myth, in this case, of the modern imperialist myth, requires leaving the ambiguities intact—the greatness of the horror that is Kurtz, the mistiness of terror, the aesthetics of violence, and the complex of desire and repression that primitivism constantly arouses" (10). In my view, it is precisely that "mistiness of terror" which sufficiently euphemizes Conrad's work to allow it to become canonical[42] and which anaesthetizes political response to *Heart of Darkness*.

Taussig sums up Conrad's own position on the possibility of an active, specifically political response to circumstances by contrasting Casement's activism (and ultimate execution) with Conrad's "resolutely [sticking] to his lonely task of writing, bathed in nostalgia for Poland, lending his name but otherwise unable to assist Casement and Morel in the Congo Reform Society, pleading with hyperbolic humility that he was but a 'wretched novelist inventing wretched stories and not even up to that miserable game'" (11). Clinging to his role as a producer of fiction, Conrad remains free to produce euphemistic representations of violence that more closely resemble the halo of Marlow's style than the bitter kernel of Schreiner's. In *Heart of Darkness*, readers are not really required to ask whether or not they find the representation of violence credible, fantastic, or in a way fabricated, since Marlow's impressions constantly distance readers from the acts themselves.[43]

Presumably in an attempt to avoid the anesthetic effect I have just described, and to add documentary credibility to her literary representations of violence, Schreiner notoriously included as a frontispiece to the first edition of *Trooper Peter Halket* a chilling photograph of three Africans hanging from the branches of a tree as eight white men and one black casually look on. Two of the men appear to be smoking cigars, and one is smoking a pipe. They look for the world like a group of deep-sea "sport" fishermen with their prize marlin. In the body of the text, Schreiner has Peter refer to the "spree they had up Bulawayo way, hanging those three niggers for spies" (34). According to Peter's secondhand account, "They made the niggers jump down from the tree and hang themselves; one fellow wouldn't bally jump, till they gave him a charge of buckshot in the back; and then he caught hold of a branch with his hands, and they had to shoot 'em loose" (35). Any critical mention of

Trooper Peter Halket appears to have to include reference to this combination of photograph and textual account.[44] Arthur Keppel-Jones's history *Rhodes and Rhodesia: The White Conquest of Zimbabwe, 1884–1902* identifies the three hanged men as "rebels" who had been caught looting and burning. Keppel-Jones cites Frederick Selous, who wrote an autobiographical account of the Matabele and Mashona rising of 1896, as being "satisfied that justice was done" in this case, but adds that Selous "does not say by what law the death penalty was imposed for looting and burning" (462).[45]

The point is that, in using a photograph, as Monsman has it, to "prepare for the symbolic enactment at the end by wedding the literary text to the social context" (Monsman 121), Schreiner is using a medium whose spectacular authenticity can still be disclaimed by those who rewrite lynching as execution. The "social context" is not as stable as it might seem. In *its* literary context, the text of the photograph can be read as *in*authentic, still to be discredited. Geoffrey Wheatcroft, in his study *The Randlords: South Africa's Robber Barons and the Mines That Forged a Nation*, writes that two generations after it was written "copies of [*Trooper Peter*] could still be found in homes in Rhodesia; few of them preserved intact the original frontispiece" (208).[46] This latter evidence of white Rhodesians' incredulity and denial, presumably accompanied by the violence of tearing, might stand as an image of the (white? European? male?) incredulity and denial implied by the tearing out of the canon of Schreiner's novella.

What is curious is that Schreiner's readers still appear to be confronted with the possibility that her accounts of more or less casual brutality might appear too excessive to be authentic. Quoting Peter's boastful account of how he had "had two huts to myself, and a couple of nigger girls," Gerald Monsman, for instance, comments, "One cannot help feeling Schreiner may have been overdrawing Peter's insensitivity" (116). She may well have been overdrawing it as far as public taste was concerned, but as far as realistic representation is concerned, she was probably underdrawing it.[47] Monsman's response, however, in line with the *Blackwood's* reviewer's dismissal of the book as a "political pamphlet of great bitterness, linked onto the very smallest thread of a story," or Wheatcroft's dismissal of it as "no great work of literature, but a heartfelt cry of rage at the cruelty of imperialism" (208), suggests that the book's spectacular nature still devalues it as literature with a "deeper meaning."

However, if that "deeper meaning" depends on transferability of a work's "message," Schreiner's text could easily have been seen to transcend the immediate and local had the canon not privileged a very particular set of "universals." In fact, the recognition in *Trooper Peter Halket* of the links between racial and sexual subjugation on the one hand and economic and military power on the other still has great urgency.

Despite repeated reminders, such as Ken Saro-Wiwa's execution in Nigeria, that contemporary African economic-driven military terror may be linked still to metropolitan lives—in the gas that fuels cars, in the coltan that goes into cellphones, in the diamonds that adorn fingers, ears, and necks, even in the chocolate we feed our children—the persistence of an allochronic discourse on Africa in mainstream Western media serves to perpetuate cultural, economic, and actual violence against Africans. The connectedness of the system may appear even more obscure to a contemporary consumer than they were in Conrad's Congo or Schreiner's Mashonaland, and the agents of their violence locally may have become more easily forgettable as they have become "independent" and black, but much the same system Schreiner attacks in *Trooper Peter Halket* still operates. As Chinua Achebe recognizes, the same attitude of othering keeps the neocolonial African poor in their poverty by using about the poor "the very words the white master had said in his time about the black race as a whole": "*You see, they are not in the least like ourselves. They don't need and can't use the luxuries that you and I must have. They have the animal capacity to endure the pain of, shall we say, domestication*" (Achebe, *Anthills of the Savannah* 37; original emphasis).

What is most troubling to me right now as I type this page, courtesy of a state-supported American university, with a bond capacity equivalent to the amount Tanzania recently spent on an air defense system, typing on one of thousands of university computers collectively drawing enough electrical power to light Soweto,[48] is the applicability of Achebe's attitude to the very idea of the postcolonial, whether in regard to postcolonial nation formation or postcolonial canon formation. Everywhere across Africa attempts at replacing the colonized state with something autonomous and new—Nyerere's African socialism or the ANC's original redistributive policies, for example—have been stifled and limited first by the jostling of giants in the cold war, and latterly taken in hand by the World Bank and the IMF. Academic postcolonialism, likewise, finds itself unable to avoid co-option; replacing colonial canons with something autonomous and new results in some new citations, to be sure, but the dependence on iterability has made little impact on the disciplinary nature of the academy or on the mainstream publishing industry's commodification of knowledge.[49] Every decoding is another encoding, after all, and it appears impossible to step outside the cultural memory bank created by canonical discourse. Without the canonical status of *Heart of Darkness*, neither Achebe's essay nor my own work would be readable; the cultural capital of Achebe's reputation and of my literary profession depends on that bank.

On the other hand, if we reread texts like *Trooper Peter Halket* not with the view to creating a new, and newly forgetful, canon of postcolonial literature but with a view to carrying on Schreiner's historically conscious struggles against "the inner darkness of self and outer darknesses of system" (Monsman 185), maybe we are still able—gradually, perhaps imperceptibly—to have some progressive political impact.

Graves with a View

Atavism and the European History of Africa

The discovery of primitiveness was an ambiguous invention of a history incapable of facing its own double.
Valentin Mudimbe

But what is the object of the colonist's "first step"? It is
to mark a line in the ground, to open a clearing, to remove obstacles.
Paul Carter

Even death is a purchase.
Nadine Gordimer

In one of the key meditative moments in *July's People*, Maureen Smales,
displaced from her white suburb to a settlement in the bush, is forced to
question what she calls the "humane creed" and its dependence on "va-
lidities staked on a belief in the absolute nature of intimate relationships
between human beings" (64). When it comes to the first universal category she can think of—love—Maureen realizes fairly rapidly that "The
absolute nature she and her kind [that is, white South African liberals]
were scrupulously just in granting to everybody was no more than the
price of the master bedroom and the clandestine hotel tariff" (65; original
emphasis). What appears to surprise Maureen more is the possibility that
even death—supposedly the universal leveler—might be economically
determined, that "even death is a purchase" (65). She goes on to consider
that one of her husband's "senior partners could afford his at the cost of
a private plane—in which he crashed. July's old mother . . . would crawl

. . . bent lower and lower towards the earth until finally she sank to it—the only death she could afford" (65). Like de Kok's "Small Passing" and like the quotation from Achebe's *Anthills of the Savannah,* Maureen's thoughts probe the limits of liberal humanism and raise vexing questions about the economy of death, especially in racialized colonial Africa where the intimate relationship between your being and the land figures differently according to whether you can be thought to belong to the land or whether the land belongs to you. This chapter addresses these questions first by showing how in their memorials and memoirs Schreiner and Blixen as white colonial writers wrote themselves or their fellow colonialists into the very landscape as an ultimate claim on and to Africa, while black Africans with an a priori connection to the land use different figures to reclaim the land with their own memories and memorials. Typically, however, Schreiner also offers us a counternarrative that opens the way out of a simple black-white dichotomy, with *Trooper Peter Halket of Mashonaland* providing a model for nationalist reclamation through the motif of resurrection and insurrection.

When Paul Carter talks about the colonist's first step being to "mark a line in the ground, to open a clearing, to remove obstacles" (24), he did not have in mind the kind of ground clearing involved in digging graves; graves, however, may be markers of the colonist's ultimate declaration of belonging—the posthumous equivalent of boundaries' and boundary fences' declarations of ownership. The graves of Schreiner, her political enemy Cecil Rhodes, and Denys Finch Hatton, for instance, show how white settlers' graves in Africa—and the subsequent narrative treatment of those graves—lay physical and symbolic claim not just to parts of Africa but to the notion of *being* African, literally grounded in African history.

It is something of a truism that, while a sense of teleological history first emerged in the Western imagination about the time of the European Renaissance, it was the nineteenth century which first exhibited widespread anxiety about its own historicity. In his *Lectures on the Philosophy of History,* Hegel draws the distinction between *res gestae* and *historia* (60) and declares that only those cultures which have produced "subjective annals" actually have an "objective history" (61). This claim inevitably leads to his privileging of literate cultures and hence to the dismissal of "Africa" as being without history (91–99). While a Hegelian attitude legitimates European authority, Francis Fukuyama's 1992 declaration that history has ended suggests that just at the time when African authority might finally be seen to be legitimated—with the passing of the last European-ruled African nation—the post-Hegelian view sees nothing to legitimate.[1] In the face of this dual refusal of legitimacy, postcolonial writers of African history might perhaps take consolation from this chapter's attempted deconstruction of European atavism, for the making of the graves of Cecil Rhodes, Olive Schreiner, and Denys Finch Hatton into historical markers involves a process that counters Enlightenment Europe's alleged attitudes toward history.

In his 1970 introduction to the Penguin edition of Schreiner's *Story of an African Farm*, in line with the Hegelian rationale, Dan Jacobson poses as a problem the specific lack of settler history in South Africa: "A colonial culture is one which has no memory," that is, "a vital, effective belief in the past as a present concern, and in the present as a consequence of the past's concerns" (7). He then describes how at the age of eight or nine he climbed to the summit of Buffelskop with his parents to see Olive Schreiner's grave. He describes both the view from the grave and his own reactions:

> The view beneath was of a red and brown expanse stretching flat to the horizon on all sides, interrupted only by stony kopjes like the one on which we were standing, and by the glint of water from a half-empty dam that was shaped like a thumbnail and looked no bigger than a thumbnail, too, from the height we were at. I can remember how impressed I was by the sunscorched aridity and solitude of the scene; and also how obscurely creditable or virtuous I felt our own presence there to be. (9)

Jacobson's description and response, mediated by his own memory and inherited affection for Schreiner, resonate with the notes struck by Schreiner herself in her descriptions of the inhospitable Karoo landscape with its "sunscorched aridity and solitude" and the consequent sense of creditability and virtue. There seems to be a shared way of seeing that endows the Karoo with that historically questionable "emptiness" examined in chapter 4, which in turn leads to a quasi-Romantic subjective response.[2] Furthermore, in both Jacobson and Schreiner, through the latter's choice of burial place, we see how colonial discourse—however anticolonialist it may be—makes claims on the land by creating memory and hence history. The grave allows a sense of continuity to extend from

1894 (when Schreiner picked out the site) to 1921 (the year of her reinterment) through the 1930s (the period of the young Jacobson's visit) to the 1970s and Jacobson's introduction—and now to this work.

In short, while writing the Karoo landscape was problematic for Schreiner, providing an ambivalent critique of colonial culture by reproducing the trope of absence, emptiness, and negativity, her burial on Buffelskop was less ambiguously complicit with white discursive power. Writing an atavistic history through her grave, she marks the very landscape itself in a gesture at least as potent as marking the page.[3] Whatever the aims of her ahistorical landscape representation, Schreiner's actual historicization of that landscape through her grave shares its assertive way of seeing, an "over-looking" that both sees all and neglects to see, with her onetime friend and political enemy Cecil Rhodes. Like Rhodes's grandiose memorial and the statue of him in Cape Town's Company Gardens (both situated on the slopes of Table Mountain with tremendous views out across the hinterland), the grave at the summit of Buffelskop offers a perfect physical prospect, lying in wait it seems for Cronwright-Schreiner[4] or Jacobson to come along and finish the painterly/political task before the land can be thoroughly claimed for and as history. In Schreiner's fiction, by contrast, the prospectless Waldo is quietly absorbed into nature as a humble chicken perch (300).

It may appear unfair thus to link Schreiner and Rhodes, the latter the very epitome of the imperialist and a man who left his physical mark on southern Africa in many more ways than in his grave. The similarity of the two final resting places, however, overrides Rhodes's and Schreiner's political differences and suggests an ultimately shared attitude toward themselves as Europeans in Africa and African history. That the making of the grave sites into historical markers involves a kind of atavism which counters Enlightenment European attitudes toward history adds a further ironic twist to their implanting themselves in Africa.

The "imposing and dominant" (Stead 4) site that Rhodes chose and which he called "The View of the World" was located among the sacred rocks and caves of the Matopo Hills in present-day southwestern Zimbabwe. Among the Matabele, the site was known as "The Home of the Spirit of My Forefathers," as it was already the burial site of the Matabele ruler Mzilikazi, whose presence there already has its own history of conquest and violent displacement.[5] Rhodes's choice of burial site therefore suggests not just a writing over of African history but a similarly atavistic notion of history and how to assert one's place in it, in both Rhodes's and Mzilikazi's minds. Indeed, W. T. Stead (whom we need to treat with some caution on this matter)[6] even records Rhodes's "very quaint" and "childlike" belief that he would return to the earth after his death and "be able to recognize and converse with those who had gone before, and that both he and they would have the keenest interest in the affairs of this planet" (Brantlinger 190). This may not quite be an attempt to set himself up for ancestor worship, but it comes remarkably close.

In *Rule of Darkness,* Patrick Brantlinger's chapter on "Atavism and the Occult in the British Adventure Novel" analyzes a mode of writing in late Victorian England which he calls "Imperial Gothic"[7] and which "combines the seemingly scientific, progressive, often Darwinian ideology of imperialism with an antithetical interest in the occult. Although the connections between imperialism and other aspects of late Victorian and Edwardian culture are innumerable, the link with occultism is especially symptomatic of the anxieties that attended the climax of the British empire" (Brantlinger 227). Further, Brantlinger suggests that the intrusion of the occult is an indication of a sense of the failure of Christianity and of faith in Britain's future. If we accept his thesis, we might see both Rhodes's and Schreiner's graves as compensatory moves for other failures of personal and social natures, symptomatic of the anxieties attending their achievements. The two graves, then, might be seen to represent some final success and fixity, and while we might read Schreiner's more generously as symbolic of her desire to belong *to* the land whereas Rhodes's resists any reading but of ownership *of* the land, both nonetheless assume vast acreage in prospect.

A comparison of the narrative treatment of the graves reveals further similarities. Ruth First and Ann Scott narrate the reinterment of Olive Schreiner both movingly and critically, using Cronwright-Schreiner's biography as their chief source. They pick out a number of moments where Cronwright-Schreiner actively mythologizes in his account of the burial: he saw a large eagle that he "could not remember having seen before" and which seemed to him "like the Bird of Truth from *African Farm* welcoming them to Olive's last resting-place"; and in his speech over the sarcophagus he said that "nature now seemed to him almost visibly permeated by Olive's spirit" (332). First and Scott see in Cronwright-Schreiner's reading/writing of the scene his making of Olive into a "child of nature" through which he could "contain his basic disapproval of her 'strange and incredible' personality" and see her "absorption in nature" (cf. Waldo!) as a symbol of her "inability to produce, or be part of the 'real' world" (332). However, they record without comment Cronwright-Schreiner's thanking the African workmen for having carried her coffin, appropriate, he said, "because she had always been their champion" (332). Although this is a gesture toward recognizing the labor frequently overlooked in the pastoral tradition, the African workmen still remain nameless, while Schreiner is written into history through the literature of England, a verse from *In Memoriam.*

In Stead's account of the burial of Rhodes, the huge labor of carrying Rhodes's body from the house in Muizenberg where he died, thence to Groote Schuur in Cape Town, and thence well over a thousand miles to the Matopos is erased by Stead's repeated use of the passive voice: "With an energy worthy of the founder of their State, a road *was constructed* from Bulawayo to the summit of the Matopos. Along this, followed by the whole population, the body of Mr. Rhodes *was drawn* to his last resting-place. The coffin *was lowered* into the tomb, the mourners, white and black, filed past the grave, and then a huge block of granite, weighing over three tons [but alone at the scene in possessing individual agency!], sealed the sepulchre from all mortal eyes" (Stead 192, emphasis added).

Two photographs, from Cronwright-Schreiner's edition of Schreiner's letters and Stead's *Last Will and Testament of Cecil J. Rhodes* further emphasize the point. Beneath a picture of the anonymous African workmen carrying Olive's coffin up Buffelskop (the gradient is steep) appears the caption: "Olive Schreiner's body nearing the very summit of Buffel's Kop (5,000 ft.), 13th August, 1921" (facing page 370). Stead's photograph of "The Scene at the Burial of Mr. Rhodes" has an equally labor-erasing caption: "The coffin is being lowered into the tomb, and the picture shows the slab, weighing three tons, which covers the coffin" (191).

Cronwright-Schreiner and Stead are clearly responding to a particular contemporary moment (and I don't wish to impugn the sincerity of their mourning), but it is a moment of balanced forces with glances both to past history and history to come, and their writing of the graves writes them into history at the expense of the indigenous population. The private response to the loss of someone loved is not finally separable from the public ceremony. It seems legitimate, therefore, to treat the two men's accounts as equally public documents, even though the two ceremonies do not appear equally public.

In the case of Schreiner's grave, we have already seen in Jacobson's introduction how it lends itself to readings by people other than the circle of her family and intimate friends, and we shall see later that Etienne van Heerden treats this public record as still potentially disruptive. In the meantime, it remains to be pointed out that although First and Scott critique Cronwright-Schreiner's original "text," they do so on private rather than public grounds, that it was his way of "contain[ing] his basic disapproval of her 'strange and incredible' personality'" (332). They don't offer the reading I'm suggesting of settlers' graves representing the final claim on the land and therefore history of that land; that their being committed into the ground represents a commitment to the land that makes them a part of the land, hence both African and natural, innocently there and very difficult to erase or escape from.

That same process of making African, natural, and innocent occurs with Karen Blixen's representation of the life, death, and burial of Denys Finch Hatton. Unlike Rhodes and Schreiner, Finch Hatton lives on in nothing but memory, memoir, and memorial; he has no mines, no scholarships, no farms, no books to his name. To be sure, Errol Trzebinski has devoted a full-scale biography to him, and Robert Redford—an unlikely but telling casting choice for an English aristo—turned him into a Hollywood symbol (of what, though, exactly?), but without Karen Blixen it is difficult to imagine him taking a place in history as an individual. Whereas Rhodes and Schreiner would have left considerable marks on the history of their time and ours even without their grandiose graves with a view and are thus relatively easy to assess in terms of their *actual* cultural legacy, the effect of Finch Hatton's memorialization is of necessity less material, hence harder to assess but more insidious. In Denys Finch Hatton, then, I would contend that we have the most overt case of mythmaking, and it is therefore interesting to consider the cultural effects of this mythmaking.

Part of the problem is posed by his, and Blixen's, aristocracy. Rather than belonging to either of the two rising Victorian groupings represented by Rhodes and Schreiner—the openly capitalist bourgeoisie or the intellectual class—Finch Hatton belongs, at least in Blixen's representation of him, not only to a class—the aristocracy—but to a class order of the past, the rural, quasi-feudal order. *Out of Africa* (which has always been a difficult book to categorize), and to a lesser extent *Shadows on the Grass*, may best be seen as an extended example of pastoral elegy in which Finch Hatton becomes the scholar-pilot whose death is a synecdoche for the death of the ideal farm, rather than, as Gordimer has it, "a purchase."

As I suggested in chapter 5, in heroizing both farm and Finch Hatton, Blixen creates a kind of utopian African feudal order that largely disregards the *actual* place of the Karen Coffee Company, geographically and in terms of the world economic order. Having displaced the "Natives," the farm was willy-nilly a part of colonialist capitalism, not the kind of organic local feudal order Blixen projects. This is not to say that *Out of Africa* ignores economics though the movie again tellingly does. It presents Blixen living *as if* she could ignore economics.[8]

As we also saw in chapter 5, all of this confirms at least two of Raymond Williams's arguments. To reiterate: First, the pastoral is a tradition that tends to erase the violence of economic relations and the harshness of labor conditions; it is precisely that violence and harshness which builds the country house and its lifestyle, represented in *Out of Africa* by Berkeley Cole's insistence on the finest glassware to drink his breakfast champagne from when out shooting animals (184). Second, the pattern of power relations whereby city capital dictates what goes on in the country is repeated in colonial and neocolonial situations where the metropole calls the tune in the colony.[9]

In the tradition of pastoral, *Out of Africa* hides these power relations, but it does so all the more beguilingly because it appears so guileless. The subjectivity of the whole memoir makes it difficult to see the object relations involved as part of a system at all, and the generosity of the subjectivity makes it difficult to see them as exploitative. For instance, if we look at Blixen's very moving account of Finch Hatton's death and burial, we find writing full of mystification and mysticism. Part of the mystification is the result of Blixen's omission of the fact that she and Finch Hatton had quarreled.[10] Part is more standard colonialist stuff: the assumption that there will be "boys" to carry your coffins for you or, aping Stead's style, that your coffins can *be* carried for you. The mysticism occurs throughout: Blixen suggests that Finch Hatton knows he's going to crash his plane, making that event—possibly caused by inexperience or even plain cramp, making it hard for Finch Hatton to cope with vicious air currents—into something fated.[11] After the crash, when Blixen and her friend Gustav Mohr are searching for the grave site Finch Hatton had picked out, not only does the cloud lift but it lifts when they are at the very site they have been looking for. When the "boys" begin digging the grave, Blixen becomes aware of an echo, an echo she promptly endues with life—"It answered to the strokes of the spades, like a little dog barking" (304). Sometime after the burial Blixen witnesses a cockerel biting off the tongue of a chameleon and reads that as a "sign" and a "spiritual answer" from "Great powers" that "This was clearly not the hour for coddling" (315). After Blixen has left Africa, she learns that some lions had been seen on Finch Hatton's grave and concludes, "It was fit and decorous that the lions should come to Denys's grave and make him an African monument" (308).[12] Blixen's phrasing in this last example plays on what one might call the "natural heraldry" of the lions, as if nature recognized Finch Hatton's noble lineage. In contrasting the heraldic lions on Nelson's column ("made only out of stone"), Blixen not only links Finch Hatton to the grand memorials of British history but even elevates her lover above the admiral. The grammatical ambiguity of "and make him an African monument" is also striking: Does Blixen mean that the lions turned Finch Hatton ("him" as direct object) into an African monument, or does she mean that they made one *for* him (indirect object)? Either way, we again see the way in which the European presence is naturalized as African.[13] The former reading effects that naturalization even more thoroughly and explicitly than the latter.

Blixen's writing, as here, is imbued with the melancholy charm of the elegy and is frequently wonderful in more than one sense. While it is perhaps unfair to give it Patrick Brantlinger's label of "Imperial Gothic," Finch Hatton meets (in part at least) two out of the three requirements Brantlinger identifies as the characteristics of imperial Gothic. First, Blixen represents him as outside the pale of "ordinary" colonial life, and suggests that his success as a safari organizer was due to his skill as a tracker and hunter—skill that suggests "individual regression or going native" (Brantlinger 230).[14] Second, as an aristocratic sportsman he exhibits a certain heroic "manliness," while his flying gives him additional opportunities for "adventure and heroism" that imperial Gothic sees as diminished in the modern world (230). Blixen is quite explicit in seeing both Finch Hatton and Berkeley Cole as exiles not just from England but from their rightful heroic time, placing Berkeley Cole as a character out of Dumas's *Vingt ans après* and Finch Hatton as an Elizabethan courtier. Of the pair she writes, "No other nation than the English could have produced them, but they were examples of atavism, and theirs was an earlier England, a world which no longer existed" (184). She goes on to suggest that the "particular, instinctive attachment which all Natives of Africa felt towards Berkeley and Denys . . . made me reflect that perhaps the white men of the past . . . would have been in better understanding with the coloured races than we, of our industrial age, shall ever be" (186).[15] Thus does Blixen use a nostalgic, innocent reconstruction of a class order to reconstruct her nostalgic, innocent, preindustrial racial one.

A harder-nosed interpretation of Finch Hatton would see the other memorial to him that Blixen describes—a bridge at Eton—as placing him in a Tom Brown-ish tradition of the English public schoolboy assured of his own superiority both at home and abroad, one of the Blues who ruled Blacks,[16] or a type of Forster's English character who hasn't really grown up and whose feelings haven't been allowed to develop fully.[17] Even Errol Trzebinski's generally fawning biography suggests that he had something of a "Peter Pan" complex, and one is reminded of another phrase of Patrick Brantlinger that "Africa was a place where English boys could become men and men could behave like boys with impunity" (190).[18]

Blixen's romantic idealization of Finch Hatton makes him into a figure like Rupert Brooke's "The Soldier" whose dust not only enriches some corner of a foreign field but makes it "for ever England" (Silkin 76). In fact, Finch Hatton is not unlike Brooke himself: Both were born in 1887, had similar public school and Oxbridge educations, and earned reputations for style and good looks that made them attractive to men as well as women. Of more direct significance here, it is their "fields" that connect them. The memorial to Finch Hatton at Eton that Blixen describes bears the motto "Famous in these fields and by his many friends much beloved" (*Out of Africa* 307). The connection between Eton's fields of play and England's fields of battle is well established, and in this specific context the links between playing fields, battlefields, and the fields of the ideal rural England become irresistible; the connection hammers home the point that the pastoral mode is anything but transparent in its representation of a "natural" landscape. It is extraordinary that Blixen can deploy this Brookeian trope two decades after Wilfred Owen had exposed "The old lie: Dulce et decorum est / Pro patria mori" (Silkin 178), and even more extraordinary when we consider that Brooke's 1914 poem already feels anachronistic when read against Hardy's skeptical Anglo-Boer War elegy "Drummer Hodge." Here Hodge—a music hall comedian's stock term for the boorish, comic, country bumpkin—is shoveled in "uncoffined" not into any recognizable field (of battle, play, or farm) but into the strangely empty, "corner"-less Karoo "veldt" (Silkin 75–76). Hodge's assimilation into the flatness of this land has more in common with Waldo's becoming his own cairn in *African Farm* than with any of the graves with a view of Rhodes, Finch Hatton, or Schreiner and points not only to the class implications of the claiming of natural grandeur for the graves but to the very notion of "England" itself. The England that fought the Anglo-Boer War was one consisting of ummarked generic "Hodges" used by big-name politicians, mine owners, and power brokers to make their mark on the land. No doubt such exploitation is always a feature of war, but that the same "England" can still be romanticized in Finch Hatton indicates a sad failure to recognize its violence.

Although Patrick Brantlinger links the occultism of "Imperial Gothic," via a citation from Adorno, to fascist politics (245), a link that the underlying violence of Blixen's romanticization of Finch Hatton's supports, the occult is perhaps more commonly associated with resistance than with control. In late Victorian England and America, the occult could be marshaled as a resistance strategy to dominant ideology, notably by feminists, socialists, and abolitionists,[19] but, for the purposes of this essay, the occultism of indigenous African practice has been used fairly consistently in opposition to European colonialism and the fascist-style administrations which that depended on.

Such opposition has not always been successful or even recognized. But if we return to South Africa, we find a momentous event involving ancestral beliefs shaping the history and landscape of the Xhosa people at the very time when Olive Schreiner was a very young child and moving from one mission station to the next in the British-defined Eastern Cape Colony. Under the twin pressures of colonial military conquest and a devastating epidemic of lung-sickness in their cattle, the Xhosa carried out a drastic purging of the "pollution" in their land. A young girl, Nongqawuse, prophesied that if they slaughtered all their cattle and destroyed all their grain, the world would become as new again, the ancestors would return with healthy herds and ample grain, and the white settlers would be driven into the sea. Some ninety percent of the Xhosa followed Nongqawuse's advice, with the result that 40,000 starved and Sir George Grey was able to take such efficient advantage of the desperately weakened survivors that, as Robert Ross says, "Many Xhosa today are convinced that Grey himself was hiding in the reeds by the Gxarha, whispering to Nongqawuse" (53).

Colonialist and subsequently apartheid history of the Cattle-Killing of 1856–57 read it either as a kind of "mass-suicide," almost as if the Xhosa were reacting purely to internal impulses, not to external pressure, or as a plot against the colonial authorities (Ross 52–53; Switzer 71). Current attitudes, particularly following the work of Jeff Peires, see the Cattle-Killing as an act, in part at least, of cultural resistance. Les Switzer points out, "For most believers, the cattle-killing movement was their last hope to preserve the old way of life" (71). What is interesting is that what looks like an unadulteratedly "African" response—based on the prophecy that the Xhosa ancestors would return to allow the creation event (*uHlanga*) to be repeated—is affected by Western traditions; whilst the first prophets of *uHlanga* saw it incorporating all people, Xhosa and non-Xhosa, "settler antagonism . . . soon prompted the believers to declare that whites were not eligible to enter the promised land (they had killed the son of God)" (Switzer 70). In other words, it is not only Xhosa beliefs which drive the movement; Christian beliefs, too, are used as a kind of prototype of "liberation theology" against the colonial powers.[20]

Uses of such resistance feature in fiction, too, from the colonial period through the apartheid era and beyond, with notable appearances in Schreiner's *Trooper Peter Halket of Mashonaland*, and Percy Mtwa and Mbongeni Ngema's *Woza, Albert!* In Schreiner's polemical novella, as we have seen, Trooper Peter is visited by a mysterious stranger—"a Jew of Palestine" (21)—who gradually makes Peter aware of the indefensibility of the British slaughter in Mashonaland. Finally, Peter, whose name alone associates him with Christ's disciple, enacts the ultimate Christian sacrifice by freeing a Shona captive due to be lynched the next day and dying in his place. His body remains, unmarked except by a makeshift cairn (133), "lying under the little tree, with the red sand trodden down over him, in which a black man's and a white man's blood were mingled" (131). As we have seen, Schreiner's impolitely direct attack on Rhodes's policies and strategies excoriates a world where brutal capitalism hides behind the rhetoric of Christianity and improving civilization.

Three-quarters of a century later, Gordimer's *Conservationist* similarly uses the trope of resurrection as insurrection in her exposure of the spuriousness of the mining capitalist's pose of environmental concern. As we touched on in chapter 5, Mehring uses his farm not only as a kind of psychic safety valve in the manner of Huxley's and Blixen's classic modernist retreats to "nature" but also, motivated by financial pragmatism, as a tax write-off. In order to critique both his psychic attraction to and legal ownership of the land, however, Gordimer makes the unusual move for her of deploying local African (specifically Zulu)[21] religious beliefs. Gordimer uses these beliefs—that the original creation of humankind (*uthlanga*) in Zulu took place in a liminal cavelike place, combining earth and water, and might be repeated again—to produce a kind of national allegory that in some ways pushes beyond Schreiner's. *The Conservationist* opens with the discovery of an unnamed dead African among the reeds (also *uthlanga* in Zulu) of a dried up *vlei* [marshland] on Mehring's farm. The local police are too lazy to investigate the man's death and shovel him uncoffined into a makeshift grave in the *vlei*, and everybody gets on with their business. The African farmworkers run the farm more or less independently of Mehring, while Mehring finds himself becoming more and more alienated. As Mehring begins to crack up, however, a huge storm, brewed in the Mozambique Channel, sweeps southwest into South Africa. In flooding the farm, this allegorical deluge simultaneously cuts Mehring off from it and resurrects the unnamed dead African. The narrative shifts to the farmworkers' perspective for the book's final brief chapter, as they prepare to give the unnamed man a formal burial. In a gesture that appears to indicate that Mehring has accepted the extent of his unbelonging to this piece of land he owns, we learn that Mehring cannot attend the funeral because he is "leaving that day for one of those countries white people go to, the whole world is theirs" (266). Left to their own devices, the farmworkers finally bury the dead man, reclaiming both the land and their own right to it. Witbooi, one of the workers, even "provide[s] a pile of medium-sized stones to surround the mound as he would mark out a flower-bed in a white man's garden" (267). Gordimer closes the novel with a more distanced fade-out, but one that pointedly reasserts the dead man's rightful repossession of the land as a part of an unbroken ancestral chain of belonging: "There was no child of his present but their children were there to live after him. They had put him away to rest, at last; he had come back. He took possession of the earth, theirs; one of them" (267).

While Gordimer uses Zulu religion to allegorize the restoration of Africa to the African, nearly a century after *Trooper Peter Halket*, Percy

Mtwa and Mbongeni Ngema's *Woza, Albert!* uses a strategy almost identical in form and motivation to Schreiner's allegory. Instead of an attack on Rhodes and the mowing down of Shona and Ndebele "rebels" or on the atavistic ironies of white capitalism, *Woza, Albert!* attacks the hypocrisy of white South Africa claiming to be a Christian state while mowing down demonstrators at Sharpeville, Soweto, etc. The play imagines what would happen were Christ (Morena) to return to contemporary South Africa, and shows his daily-increasing anger and outrage at the treatment of black South Africans. Morena is killed while walking across the water from prison on Robben Island, but rises again on the third day in the very graveyard where the character Zulu Boy (still nameless after all these years) has now got a job as caretaker. In a final scene blending Christian mythology and traditional African beliefs, Zulu Boy persuades Morena to raise the heroes of South Africa's liberation struggle from the dead. Performances of *Woza, Albert!* would normally be followed by the singing of "Nkosi sikelel' iAfrika" and by the chant and response "Mayibuye!" [Let it return], "iAfrika." In *Woza, Albert!* Christianity, the belief in ancestors' continued presence beyond the grave, memory, and history all come together, prefiguring the return of Africa to itself. The narrative line of colonialist history, a chain of white writing of and on the land, is thus challenged by the resurrection/insurrection of African "ghosts."

The struggle necessarily continues after the formal removal of apartheid. In his autobiography, *Long Walk to Freedom*, Nelson Mandela resurrects an idyllic rural African landscape in recalling his birthplace and early childhood in Qunu in the Transkei. He reclaims this landscape, which had already, some seventy years earlier, been marked by the colonialist exploitation of the effects of the Cattle-Killing, and re-presents his "authentic" place of origin as a kind of framing device in his own history. Mandela recounts, for instance, how, on his release from jail, a visit to his mother's grave brought home to him the contrast between the past and the present: "When I was young, the village was tidy, the water pure, and the grass green and unsullied as far as the eye could see. Kraals were swept, the topsoil was conserved, fields were neatly divided. But now the village was unswept, the water polluted, and the countryside littered with plastic bags and wrappers" (506). And in his moving conclusion Mandela again recalls that time of childhood when he felt that he was "free to run in the fields near my mother's hut, free to swim in the clear stream that ran through my village, free to roast mealies under the stars and ride the broad backs of slow-moving bulls" (543). Clearly, the weapon of memory can be wielded in any number of ways in writing the land.[22]

If we return for one last time to Schreiner's grave on Buffelskop, for instance, we can see that Etienne van Heerden's practice in the story "The Resurrection of Olive Schreiner"[23] is more in line with Mtwa and Ngema's act of cultural disruption than it is with Cronwright-Schreiner's attempt at stabilization; it looks less to past history and making Schreiner an African memorial, than to the future in which she might be a potentially unifying force, breaking the racial impasse of apartheid.

While researching the Schreiner documents in Cradock Public Library—what clearer emblem of the official repository of history-as-writing/writing-as-history?—van Heerden's narrator reflects back to his childhood and the violence surrounding a visit to town by the prime minister. Son of an English-speaking mother and Afrikaner father, the narrator stages a symbolic resurrection of Olive Schreiner. Together with his friend Willempie, son of the laborer Windpomp killed in the story, he steals Schreiner's bones from the sarcophagus on top of Buffelskop, weaves them together with wire, dresses them in an old dress of his mother's, and hangs the effigy on a "cross . . . made from old fencing-droppers and a sawn-down telephone pole" (180). The whole process is conceived of as an act of rebellion—resurrection as insurrection again—driven by a confusing array of motives: the narrator's identification with his "brave ancestors, the Rebels, who would not bow before the British Empire" (179); the town librarian's declaration that "Olive understood this country. She could unite. She could write life back into the country" (166); and the narrator's and Willempie's sense of grief and outrage at the murder of Willempie's father at the hands of the local white civil defense force commando.

The unifying purpose of their rebellion is undercut by reminders of the terrible divisions in South African society, and its efficacy is obviously in question. Van Heerden emphasizes the weakness of their gesture by making Schreiner's skeleton "not complete: one arm was—crazily—only shoulder and hand with fingerbones" (180). Nevertheless, the story ends back in the Cradock Library with a reassertion of "Olive Schreiner" as written, available, and potentially unifying history, still a presence:

What can I say?
> Thy voice is on the rolling air,
> I hear thee where the waters run,
> Thou standest in the rising sun . . . ?
> Yes, that too. (183)

Although it's a "crazy" sort of leap, van Heerden's qualified fictional optimism in the face of the violence of apartheid matches the qualified optimism of Albie Sachs,[24] who was maimed by a car bomb in Maputo in 1988 and is now one of South Africa's leading jurists. Like van Heerden's fictional Schreiner skeleton, Sachs was left without an arm but amazingly without bitterness, imagining only "soft vengeance" in an idealistic culture of gentleness and love where the rule of law is not a weapon exploited by rulers and lawyers. Postcolonial Africa (including the "new" South Africa) clearly has a history—that sense of Jacobson's of the past being an integral part of the present; and its graves—whether unknown or grandiose—are markers both of violence and of sacrifice. But here at the "end of history," what future is there for a "new" African history? In the same way that it is possible to rewrite the statute books and still not remove de facto apartheid,[25] even a rewriting of history texts, with the inclusion of oral history and so on, may not be adequate to reorder the dominant way of seeing embodied there by the memorialization of Rhodes on the backside of Table Mountain and enshrined in his "View of the World" at the top of the Matopos.

However, if, as the epigraph from Paul Carter asserts, the colonist's first step is to mark the land, and even if those markings seem historically indelible, perhaps this book in its tentative postcolonial space-clearing offers some kind of contestation. Like any book of this nature, it is unable to catch up with the history it is trying to sketch, but it may yet mark the history to come.

Notes

Introduction

1. See Gurnah, "Settler Writing in Kenya: 'Nomenclature Is an Uncertain Science in These Parts.'"

2. See Berkman, *The Healing Imagination of Olive Schreiner*.

3. In a crystalline summary of Bhabha's project, Robert J. C. Young stresses that "in making ambivalence the constitutive heart of his analyses, Bhabha has in effect performed a political reversal at a conceptual level in which the periphery—the borderline, the marginal, the unclassifiable, the doubtful—has become the equivocal, indefinite, indeterminate ambivalence that characterizes the centre" (*Colonial Desire* 161).

4. See Wilentz, *Binding Cultures* xxvii–xxxiii. For further discussion of motherhood and writing, and a cautious link between African and African American "rememory" through mothers, see also chapter 3.

5. See, e.g., Simon Gikandi and Ian Baucom, whose work probes the connections between Englishness and empire, whether in Africa, India, or the Caribbean.

6. See Felski, *The Gender of Modernity* 145–73.

7. See, e.g., Nuttall and Michael, *Senses of Culture* 1–23.

8. See, e.g., Leon de Kock's special issue of *Poetics Today*. He uses the image of the "seam" as "the site of a joining together that also bears the mark of the suture. . . . On the one hand the effort of suturing the incommensurate is an attempt to close the gap that defines it as incommensurate, and on the other this process unavoidably bears the mark of its own crisis, the seam" (276). In my own work I have been fascinated by the way contemporary white and black South African poets have attempted to reinscribe themselves in a South Africa more conscious of its Africanness but still prone to racial and class segregation. See Lewis, "This Land South Africa: Rewriting Time and Space in Postapartheid Poetry and Property."

9. In borrowing the terms *spectacular* and *ordinary* I am referring to Njabulo Ndebele's *Rediscovery of the Ordinary*, in which he calls for (black) South African writers to move beyond the idiom of spectacular protest literature to a literature in which interiority is prized and the political is mediated through the psychological.

The term *rememory* comes from Toni Morrison's *Beloved*; see chapter 3 for a fuller discussion. Poets resisting the normalization of South Africa according to the dictates of Euro-American market capitalism would include Jeremy Cronin, Lesego Rampolokeng, and Seitlhamo Motsapi. See also Anthony O'Brien's *Against Normalization: Writing Radical Democracy in South Africa*.

10. For a critique of such binarism, see Chrisman's introduction to *Rereading the Imperial Romance: British Imperialism and South African Resistance in Haggard, Schreiner, and Plaatje*, in which she insists, for instance, that "metropolitan dissent was theoretically possible and actually practised" (7), and adds, "The cognitive and physical boundaries between metropolis and colony were all more mobile than [Fredric] Jameson's scheme can allow for" (10).

11. While most of my commentary in this introduction responds to political change in South Africa, the book's concern with land ownership and occupation is plainly relevant to current concerns in Kenya and Zimbabwe.

12. Although *Not Out of Africa* appears to have been spurred by Lefkowitz's reading of *Black Athena*, the texts and scholars Lefkowitz debunks in the book are earlier, more hyperbolically and polemically Afrocentric books such as George James's *Stolen Legacy*, Cheikh Anta Diop's *Civilization or Barbarism*, and the work of Dr. Yosef A. A. ben-Jochannan. For a comprehensive account of the controversy, see Jacque Berlinerblau's *Heresy in the University*.

13. Kenyan philosopher Henry Odera Oruka bridges the universalist/ ethnophilosophical gap by linking the oral transmission of Kenyan sages' ideas with the mediation of Socrates' ideas by his disciples. See Samuel Oluoch Imbo's excellent *Introduction to African Philosophy*.

14. See, e.g., Senghor, *African Socialism* 72-75.

15. See, e.g., Soyinka's famous rejections of négritude and of the bolekaja critics (Chinweizu et al.) in his article "Neo-Tarzanism: The Poetics of Pseudo-Tradition."

16. See also Peter Merrington's article "A Staggered Orientalism: The Cape-to-Cairo Imaginary," in which he describes the discursive construction of the Cape as Mediterranean.

17. Liberalism, as Rob Nixon notes, becomes an especially problematic term when writing about South Africa from the vantage point of an American institution because the very notion "resonates quite dissimilarly in the two societies" (79); "in the USA liberalism has tended to connote left of center, while in South Africa it has stood as a right of center term" (81).

Chapter 1. The Invention of the "I"

1. Judith Thurman identifies the source of the epigraph as Nietzsche in his "On the Thousand and One Goals" (*Isak Dinesen* 50). Linda Donelson identifies the source as Tacitus, translating from Herodotus's "poetic description of the ideal education of a Persian noble, especially a king." Blixen may also have been aware of the quotation in its English form in Byron's *Don Juan* where the three goals are also cited as Persian in origin. The appeal of both Nietzsche and Byron lies in their "aris-

tocratic radicalism," a quality that gave Georg Brandes the title for a series of lectures on Nietzsche in 1888. Blixen's brother, Thomas Dinesen, who was very close to his sister and spent some years on the farm with her but was left out of the narrative of *Out of Africa* by mutual agreement, was amused by some of the book's inaccuracies. With regard to the epigraph, he told Thurman that "my sister couldn't ride or shoot an arrow, and she never told the truth" (*Isak Dinesen* 200).

2. Although not published until after Schreiner's death, both *Undine* (1929) and *From Man to Man* (1926) were at least partly composed simultaneously with *The Story of an African Farm*, and their historical settings overlap.

3. The choice of science fiction as a mode for feminist writers has a long and distinguished history, beginning with Mary Shelley's *Frankenstein*. Of Schreiner's contemporaries, one might mention the experimental fiction of Lady Florence Dixie's *Gloriana* or Charlotte Perkins Gilman's *Herland*. More recently, writers as diverse as Margaret Atwood, Doris Lessing, Octavia Butler, and Buchi Emecheta have all used science fiction to present feminist critiques of current issues. Here it might be added that Blixen's choice of the Gothic, when considered in the light of her fascination with Einstein's theories of relativity, might be considered to be in the same mode, as a version of time traveling. Else Cederborg, for instance, declares that "she would . . . have been able to appreciate good science fiction writers as kindred spirits" (introduction to *On Modern Marriage*, 29).

4. Her role as governess may have made her vulnerable to less than mutual sexual advances from her employers. In one such case, with the Colesberg agent and auctioneer George Weakly, Schreiner told Havelock Ellis that "he tyrannized her and tried to kiss her, but exerted a fascination over her: finally he 'did something which made her leave'" (First and Scott 72).

5. Henry Havelock Ellis, whom Schreiner found particularly sympathetic (she called him her "other self") was a pioneer sexologist; Bryan Donkin was Freud's physician; and Karl Pearson, a professor of mathematics at London University, was a leading figure in the emergent fields of statistics and eugenics.

6. In a move that seems to be the male intellectual's equivalent of a gentleman's preferring blondes but marrying brunettes, Karl Pearson married Mrs. Cobb's younger sister, Maria Sharpe, five years later. According to First and Scott, Maria "had been brought up to dance, play croquet, and appreciate the great cathedrals of Europe. She was gifted at watercolor and well read in the literature of the day. Pearson asked her to be the club's secretary and from then on they worked closely together. In both class and cultural terms the relationship made sense" (170).

7. Emily Hobhouse was a feminist activist who exposed the terrible conditions that Boer and African prisoners experienced in British concentration camps during the Anglo-Boer War. Constance Lytton was a prominent suffragette in Britain.

8. I have already mentioned Vera Brittain's reference to *Woman and Labour* as "the Bible." The earlier influence of *African Farm* was equally profound. The novel sold more than 100,000 copies by the end of the century, and its radicalism was notorious (First and Scott 19). Edith Lees cited *African Farm* and Ibsen's play *A*

Doll's House as the two most significant literary events of the 1880s that "drove thinking women further towards their emancipation" (Clayton 46). Its appeal to women appears to have cut across class, however, extending well beyond the middle-class intelligentsia. In *The New Girl: Girls' Culture in England, 1880–1915*, Sally Mitchell cites one working-class reader as "feeling that *much* of what I have been thinking so strongly is here expressed," while a pupil at Cheltenham Ladies' College remembered a smuggled copy of the book setting the sky aflame and turning the girls into "violent feminists" (212, n.12). According to Mitchell, nearly every auto-biographical account of pupil-teachers in the last decades of the nineteenth century mentions reading *African Farm* "with bated breath and great excitement as a thrill-ing, liberating, and highly secret experience" (37). Doris Lessing recalled that *Afri-can Farm* "was the first 'real' book she had read with Africa as a setting" (First and Scott 94). While black South Africans could not identify with the "nameless, shad-owy, 'woolly Kaffir maids,'" Lauretta Ngcobo for one regards her communication with Schreiner as no less than "sacred" as a result of Schreiner's socialism, pacifism, and feminism: "You could not find a more potent keg hurled at South Africa" (Ngcobo 189, 190). Because he recognizes the African workers' reticence as "laced with agony," Ezekiel Mphahlele can declare that "Olive Schreiner's warmth and compassion never escapes us" (*African Image* 123). Schreiner's work was tremen-dously influential across a huge social range of readers.

9. The casual use of this epithet, and Schreiner's use of the term *Kaffir*, which is now considered equally offensive, is probably not intended as derogatory, but it does indicate how completely racialized Schreiner's thinking was. In step with much nineteenth-century thought, she appears to have believed, almost without question, that the white races were the most evolutionarily advanced and that there was a "hiatus" between races and classes in "totally distinct stages of civilization" (*Woman and Labour* 260). Unlike most racists, however, this meant that Schreiner felt whites had a moral responsibility to shoulder their "burden" of superiority. In this respect she resembles Blixen, whose attitude toward Africans involved not just racial but class attitudes of noblesse oblige. Paula Krebs argues that Schreiner strategically maintains the sense of racial difference between black and white in order to consider black South Africans as a political constituency without alienat-ing a British readership unable to cope with the idea of racial miscegenation (Krebs 112–15).

10. Krebs's *Gender, Race, and the Writing of Empire: Public Discourse and the Boer War* highlights the alliance of male financiers, newspaper owners, and politi-cians both in South Africa and in England in shaping opinions promoting and sup-porting British military intervention. Citing J. A. Hobson, she presents the case that "Fleet Street was manipulated by the English-language press in South Africa," which itself was manipulated by South African mining interests (25).

11. Repeatedly in her letters in 1899 Schreiner stresses sentiments like "while we don't want to fight, if Chamberlain is determined to drive us to war, it will not be the walk over the field that they dream of" (Rive 351), eerily reminiscent of the original

jingo rhyme "We don't want to fight but by jingo if we do we've got the men, we've got the guns, we've got the money, too!" As with many of her prophetic utterances concerning South Africa, Schreiner was uncannily accurate in predicting the course of the war that followed: "It will take from 100,000 to 150,000 men to do it. We shall fall back on our wide desert plains and hills, and as fast as they beat us in one place we will rise in another" (Rive 363).

12. Milner sent a polite reply, but the futility of Schreiner's intervention became apparent even to her, when Milner's famous dispatch to Colonial Secretary Joseph Chamberlain referring to the British Uitlanders in the Transvaal as "helots" was published on July 6, 1899 (Rive 368).

An equally ineffective attempt at intervention was her urging her brother Will in case of war to "send home a deputation of women to see the Queen" (368).

13. See Gordimer's "The Prison-House of Colonialism." Gordimer could not have known that Schreiner had reproduced her comment almost verbatim in a 1905 letter to Fred Pethick Lawrence, in which she states, "The native question is the *real* question of South Africa" (letter in University of Cape Town archives, reference number UCT MMP D61/217). Between the end of the Anglo-Boer War and the formation of the Union of South Africa (1910), Schreiner's letters repeatedly express horror at the connivance of the former white enemies in jointly oppressing South Africa's black population in order to create a pool of cheap labor.

14. For a concise discussion of the issues of women's representivity in South African autobiography, see Nuttall and Michael's essay "Autobiographical Acts" in *Senses of Culture* 298–317.

15. Or we might consider a further twist by invoking, as Claire Kahane does, the distinction Barthes makes between the closed-circuit of classic nineteenth-century realism and the notion of "figuration," a notion that implicates text, reader, and writer (Kahane 8). In Kahane's reading of *African Farm*, the text's multiple voices and reversals of gender (a feature she refers to nonpejoratively as its "hysterical structure of fragmentation") pushed the novel "beyond the constraints of conventional linear narrative form and opened up new possibilities for representing the subject. In this sense Schreiner's narrative voice is a precursor to present-day representations of a subject-in-process, representations privileging hysteria as a subversive mode of discourse that articulates a dis-ease with the cultural ordering of desire" (84).

16. As with Gordimer, Suzman's political position is generally assumed to be defined by race rather than by gender concerns. She is far more likely to be seen as a lone voice for black rights than as one of very few female voices in the apartheid era parliament.

17. Schreiner's relative lack of political theorization may be indicated by comparing her participation in the Men and Women's Club with her friend Eleanor Marx's refusal to join on the grounds that she wanted to devote her time to fighting for socialism, "the highest and most important work" she could do (cited in First and Scott 147).

18. For further discussion of *None to Accompany Me,* and the general isolation and marginality of the white woman writer, see chapter 3.

19. Curiously enough, *Closer Union* is the title of her 1909 pamphlet dealing with the constitutional talks that led to the eventual formation of the Union of South Africa in 1910. It is perhaps indicative of the way Schreiner came to integrate the personal and the political. About this time, for instance, in a letter to Mrs. Francis Smith, she wrote about the English suffragettes: "It's not what they are trying to *get,* it's what they are becoming—they *are* breaking free" (*Letters* 281).

20. Although I have not found any reference to Brandes's work in Schreiner's correspondence, she owned a 1906 copy of Brandes's *Recollections of My Childhood and Youth.*

Chapter 2. Of Masquerades and Masks: Miming and Alterity

1. Cf. First and Scott 208. On one occasion Schreiner apparently asked Cronwright-Schreiner to be photographed with his shirt sleeves rolled up so as to show off his manly forearms.

2. See esp. chapter 4 ("The So-called Dependency Complex of Colonized Peoples") of *Black Skin, White Masks,* in which Fanon shows that Mannoni's reading of aggressive black men in Malagasy patients' dreams seems driven by Mannoni's own desire to universalize black self-alienation, and overlooks the material circumstances which included the French colonists' actual employment of black (Senegalese) troops (83–108).

3. For further discussion of the sadomasochistic master-slave relationship in a specifically colonial context, see my analysis of *The Grass Is Singing* in chapter 6.

4. See, e.g., *Shadows on the Grass* 101–3, where Blixen relates how her "people of the farm" humored her desire to be taken seriously as their doctor. She feels that they have decided to "indulge" (103) her by coming to her even with relatively insignificant ailments. Even as a judge, she claims to be "used" in some way by being turned into a symbol or, as she puts it, "brazen-serpented" (*Out of Africa* 98). For information on Clara Svendsen's life with Blixen, see Thurman, *Isak Dinesen* 352–56.

5. See chapter 6 of this volume.

6. For further discussion of *Trooper Peter Halket,* see chapters 7 and 8 of this volume.

7. Havelock Ellis himself was well known for his naturism (even in frigid England), and as a young woman Schreiner was also apparently wont to sunbathe in the nude (Chapman, Gardner, and Mphahlele 22).

8. More recent studies of Englishness in the age of imperialism that make similar arguments include Simon Gikandi's *Maps of Englishness* and Ian Baucom's *Out of Place: Englishness, Empire, and the Locations of Identity.*

9. Entropy itself was a discovery of the Victorian age and one that seemed counter to the positivism of attitudes toward science in general and Darwinian evolution in particular. Young links the idea of entropy to the racial concept of degeneration

(100), while Gillian Beer's essay on "The Death of the Sun" also highlights how a physics explaining that all bodies in motion slow down and come to rest was hard to reconcile with notions of progress and perfectionism. Keeping the empire going thus necessitated a struggle against entropy, against the tendency to disorder. In the more familiar terms of Matthew Arnold, culture needed to be consolidated as a bastion against anarchy.

10. See also Krebs's chapter on Schreiner in *Gender, Race, and the Writing of Empire* in which she argues that Schreiner approaches racial questions differently with respect to black South Africans and Boers. Schreiner's deployment of an evolutionist understanding of race suggests that the Boer and English "races" might merge to produce a hybrid (but still white) South African race. Schreiner resists, however, "the prevailing discourse of evolution for discussing Africans; instead, she discusses Africans as a political and economic category, as a class. This reversal enables her to avoid the fraught area of miscegenation while taking Africans seriously as a political group" (114–15).

11. A similar distinction is frequently made in Blixen's fiction, too. For instance, in "The Dreamers," the Englishman Lincoln Forsner, on board a dhow plying between Lamu and Zanzibar, talks of the "blue and voluptuous South" (350), more or less eliding the Mediterranean world with the Orient.

12. Some of her phrasing is downright frightening. In *On Modern Marriage*, for instance, Blixen talks about "undesirable specimens" (91) and the "bettering of the race" (92); introduces ideas of bloodstock breeding (93); and makes the chilling suggestion that in the future the only children considered illegitimate will be those who "do not possess full value as human beings, and whom it will not benefit the race to pay full value for" (89).

13. See also Anna Davin's "Imperialism and Motherhood," where she points to the specifically South African context of the Anglo-Boer War for promoting fears regarding infant mortality and "national standards of physique" (89). Chrisman argues, however, that the case of Olive Schreiner should make us resist assumptions of a completely homogeneous metropolitan discourse on women and empire (7).

14. I use the phrase "mastery" advisedly. Keeping the masculine form shows to what extent acting as a white woman (i.e., as an employer) meant acting as a (white) man.

15. One might also add, of course, that as a Dane, Blixen is not as thoroughly implicated in the administration of colonial Kenya as, say, Elspeth Huxley. The continued presence and relative effectiveness of the various Scandinavian aid programs in East Africa in recent years perhaps attests to the way a certain national and political nonalignment can in part counter a racial and economic identity.

16. See also Michelle Adler's article on Lady Florence Dixie and Sarah Heckford, two Victorian women travelers in South Africa who also struck masculine poses. Adler quotes Kay Schaffer: "To speak with authority she must wear a male disguise" (90).

17. See chapter 7 for further discussion of the mask of "work" in colonialist contexts.

18. Nomenclature is problematic here. Although the derogatory overtones and inaccuracy of the terms *Bushman* and *Hottentot* have resulted in their being replaced by San and Khoi, I have retained them here because neither Schreiner nor Blixen knew of any alternative. In this context, therefore, *Bushman* and *Hottentot* should be understood as a kind of shorthand for "the people Schreiner and Blixen would have called Bushman and Hottentot." For a discussion of the image of the Hottentot in European discourse on sexuality, see Sander Gilman's essay mentioned above. Sara Baartman, the "Hottentot Venus" whose genitals provided enormous fascination in London and Paris in the 1820s, has been the subject of considerable interest in light of post-apartheid KhoiSan and Coloured nationalism. See, e.g., Steven Robins's "Silence in My Father's House: Memory, Nationalism, and Narratives of the Body" 129–37. Baartman's remains were formally returned to South Africa only in 2002 and were buried in a ceremony presided over by South African president Thabo Mbeki, whose speech lambasted European "barbarism."

Chapter 3. The Childless Mother and Motherless Child, or the Orphanhood of the White Woman Writer in Africa

1. See chapter 2 for comments on the perceived role of motherhood in providing good, healthy imperial subjects. In South Africa, the Truth and Reconciliation Commission's final report includes fifteen pages on apartheid disruption of family life. Far from protecting and supporting the family as a "core structure in society," the apartheid state "generated a crisis in South African family life" (5:142). Although not as thorough and organized, colonial rule in Kenya similarly disrupted traditional patterns, forcing women and men off the land and into the cities. As Jean Hay has it, "Women who moved to Nairobi, Kisumu, or other cities looking for work to support themselves—or to escape an unhappy marriage—sometimes had few alternatives to informal prostitution, and women living on their own faced a great deal of criticism and suspicion about their activities" (192).

2. As Anthony O'Brien reminds us in *Against Normalization*, the very word *location* has specific, raced meaning, capable as it is of referring to the township slums "in which women of the South and especially the African South have been constrained or seduced to live" (133).

3. For discussions of the role of memory and forgetting in post-apartheid South Africa, see Sarah Nuttall and Carli Coetzee's book, *Negotiating the Past: The Making of Memory in South Africa*. I owe the link to Morrison's idea of "rememory" to an anonymous reader of this text in manuscript; the reference is to Marianne Hirsch's "Maternity and Rememory: Toni Morrison's *Beloved*." Extending the discussion to the United States and the experience and representation of family life among African Americans brings to mind the work of Hortense Spillers. In her essay "Mama's Baby, Papa's Maybe," Spillers attacks Daniel Patrick Moynihan's 1960s report on the "Negro Family" for freezing "'ethnicity' itself [as] a total objectifica-

tion of human and cultural motives. . . . Apparently spontaneous, these 'actants' are *wholly* generated, with neither past nor future, as tribal currents moving out of time." Spillers insists on an historical understanding of the disruption of African family systems by the "orphaning" of the slave-child who neither belonged to the mother nor was related to the owner. Given that history, any continuing matrifocal "ties of sympathy that bind blood-relations in a network of feeling, of continuity" represent "one of the supreme social achievements of African Americans under conditions of enslavement" (Spillers 74).

4. The priority given to the case of Amy Biehl (the American Fulbright scholar killed by township youths in Cape Town in 1993) both by Sindiwe Magona's *Mother to Mother* and by the filmmakers of *Long Night's Journey into Day* suggests that we might even extend the range of racial reconciliation internationally.

5. The role of orphanhood in southern African black women writers might make for an interesting comparison. Bessie Head actually was an orphan, and she used the trope in her fiction. Zoë Wicomb's *You Can't Get Lost in Cape Town* "kills off" the narrator's mother, only to resurrect her for the final story. In Tsitsi Dangarembga's *Nervous Conditions,* Tambu effectively separates herself from her birth parents when she moves away to school. Dangarembga's 1996 film *Everyone's Child* raises the huge problem of AIDS orphans.

6. Judith Thurman cites the telegram as being in the Karen Blixen Archive in Copenhagen. Linda Donelson denies its existence and includes the text in the category of "Famous Mistakes" published about Blixen. However, the existing telegram Donelson cites from Finch Hatton makes reference to an earlier telegram, and the exchange as she re-creates it from that point matches Thurman's description (*Isak Dinesen* 246).

7. Cf. Horton, *Difficult Women, Artful Lives* 78–82.

8. See Nancy Chodorow, *The Reproduction of Mothering,* and Regenia Gagnier's *Subjectivities.*

9. This term, of course, has none of the high seriousness of professional psychoanalysis, but I'm rather fond of the omphalos as an idea simply because it gets us away from that sex/not-one binarism of Lacan/Irigaray. Everybody has a belly button, after all.

10. I am aware that the gendering of all these terms is rather loose and has come under fire from recent theoreticians wary of essentialism. However, the anxieties felt by Schreiner and Blixen do lend themselves to the Gilbert and Gubar thesis that the woman writer of the nineteenth century felt that there was a kind of "infection in the sentence" resulting in a "radical fear that . . . the act of writing will isolate or destroy her" (*Madwoman* 49).

11. Furthermore, the structure of *Shadows on the Grass,* like *Out of Africa,* resists the linearity of chronology.

12. Schreiner: "On that day when the woman takes her place beside the man in the governance and arrangement of external affairs of her race will also be that day that heralds the death of war as a means of arranging human differences. . . . The

knowledge of woman, simply *as woman*, is superior to that of man; she knows the history of human flesh; she knows its cost; he does not" (*Woman and Labour* 176).

13. See also Thurman's comment that Blixen's position on a given issue changed not just over time but also in reaction to those in authority: "The impulse to defend her independence—to set herself apart from the herd, to be unique—remains constant" (208).

14. See Blixen, "The Roads Round Pisa," *Seven Gothic Tales* 37.

15. For further tangential comment on the role of the uncanny and the politics of home in writers mentioned in this essay, see both Lars Engle, "The Political Uncanny: The Novels of Nadine Gordimer," and Homi Bhabha's introduction to *The Location of Culture* (in which he discusses Gordimer's *My Son's Story* alongside Morrison's *Beloved*).

16. In *Discourses of Difference: An Analysis of Women's Travel Writing and Colonialism*, Sara Mills scrupulously avoids the potential essentialism of gendering style, arguing rather "that women's travel texts are produced and received within a context which shares similarities with the discursive construction and reception of male texts, whilst at the same time, because of the discursive frameworks which exert pressure on female writers, there may be negotiations in women's texts which result in differences which seem to be due to gender" (6). For Mills, therefore, the interest in colonial women travel writers lies in the clash between two discourses—of femininity and of imperialism. The latter calls for "action and intrepid, fearless behaviour from the narrator, and yet the discourses of femininity demand passivity from the narrator and a concern with relationships" (21–22). These conflicting requirements are "discursively productive" as they "enable a form of writing whose contours both disclose the nature of the dominant discourses and constitute a critique from its margins" (23). Although Catherine Barnes Stevenson is much less theoretically punctilious than Mills, her biographical approach remains useful to my argument here. For further discussion of this issue, see also chapter 4.

17. I am thinking not only of Schreiner's view that a community where mothers took their rightful place in the foreign affairs of the state would be a community unable to pitch its children into war, but also of Ingrid de Kok's poem "Small Passing" (in *Familiar Ground*), discussed later, in which the white mother of a stillborn child is comforted by black mothers who "will not tell you your pain is white."

18. JanMohamed's book, *Manichean Aesthetics*, was published in 1983. I am also quoting from his 1986 essay, "The Economy of Manichean Allegory: The Function of Racial Difference in Colonialist Literature," in which his arguments are offered in condensed form.

19. Gordimer has continued her work on behalf of black writers' organizations and arts organizations such as the Windybrow Arts Centre in Johannesburg. In addition, she has insisted that conference organizers who invite her to conferences outside South Africa must also invite younger, aspiring black writers. These efforts have not inoculated her from criticism. In 2001, the Gauteng educational council

temporarily "banned" *July's People* on grounds of its supposedly racist portrayals of black characters.

20. I am aware that this is a slightly tendentious comment, especially in light of later stories and novels such as *My Son's Story*. However, it seems to me that Gordimer will be remembered as a chronicler of the soul of white South Africa under apartheid. As JanMohamed notes, "When she does enter the world of the Other, as in *July's People*, it is primarily to examine the dependence of whites on their African servants" ("Economy of Manichean Allegory" 101).

21. In fact, Vera's position at the end of the novel fits fairly closely with Gordimer's 1959 suggestion that "all that the new Africa will really want from us will be what we can give as 'foreign experts'" (*Essential Gesture* 36). The peroration of Gordimer's "That Other World That Was the World" sounds a much more confident note, with Gordimer claiming she "may now speak of 'my people'" (*Writing and Being* 134).

22. An obvious example is *A Sport of Nature*, in which the female protagonist, Hillela, is married to a prominent leader in the liberation struggle. These two produce a child, one of the only such cross-racial children that survives in Gordimer's fiction. In her short stories, such as "The Moment before the Gun Went Off" or "Town and Country Lovers," the emphasis tends to be on the brutally invasive nature of apartheid law in aborting interracial relationships. In her two most recent novels, *The House Gun* and *The Pick-up*, Gordimer further extends her range of exploration of interracial relationships by describing, respectively, an interracial gay household and the marriage between a white South African and an Arab immigrant to South Africa. For an article comparing the successful asexual accommodation of Vera with Zeph in *None to Accompany Me* with the broken sexual relationships in *Burger's Daughter*, *My Son's Story*, and *A Sport of Nature*, see Alice Knox's "No Place like Utopia: Cross-Racial Couples in Nadine Gordimer's Later Novels."

23. It seems handy to hang on to these terms in a chapter dealing in part with European anxiety about human evolution. It would be perfectly possible, however, to argue either (a) that very little changed when South Africa moved to majority rule, or (b) that the move to majority rule was itself the result of a prolonged and painful revolution. February 1990 will nonetheless remain a key symbolic date, marking as it does the release from jail of Nelson Mandela. For an example of the former argument, see Patrick Bond's *Elite Transition: From Apartheid to Neoliberalism in South Africa*; for an example of the latter reading, see Patti Waldmeir's *Anatomy of a Miracle: The End of Apartheid and the Birth of the New South Africa*.

24. The references are to Bhabha's essay, "The World and the Home." A modified version of that essay forms the introduction to Bhabha's book *The Location of Culture*. In addition to the house in *My Son's Story*, Bhabha refers to the house of Naipaul's Mr. Biswas and 124 Bluestone Road from Morrison's *Beloved*. As in much of Bhabha's work, such transcontinental comparison results in considerable abstraction, despite his ostensible interest in "location."

25. Mashinini's autobiographical account resonates with the difficulty Baby Suggs has in Morrison's *Beloved* in trying to remember her children, separated from her by slavery. See Hirsch, "Maternity and Rememory."

26. See also Dennis Brutus's poem "For My Sons and Daughters" in which he writes, "not to condemn me, you will need / forgetfulness of all my derelictions," derelictions that were driven by a "continental sense of sorrow" (Maja-Pearce 8).

27. In addition to Mandela's own account of Zindzi's unsatisfactory visit (*Long Walk to Freedom* 559–61), see Lynne Bryer's "Through a Glass Quietly" and de Kok's "Small Passing."

28. In the postapartheid era, the scourge of AIDS is producing more and more orphans and putting further strain on South Africa's social fabric. In one of her most recent poems, "The Child at the Lights," de Kok concludes, "For two hundred orphans / will soon be there, waiting for red. / In a long line their needs already sway. / Their satchels are packed with / two thousand brothers and sisters. / Two million more are in the wings" (*Terrestrial Things* 62).

29. The formulation of the proverb in the epigraph is from Plaatje's collection of Setswana proverbs. The formulation I have quoted here is a rather more familiar one, translated from the Sesotho version used, for example, by Jeremy Cronin in his fine poem in *Inside*, "Motho ke Motho ka Batho Babang."

Chapter 4. Stories of African Farms and the Politics of Landscape

1. Lise Kure-Jensen notes that there are intriguing differences between Blixen's original English texts and her translations into Danish, the latter frequently involving what Kure-Jensen calls verbal "amplification" (317). The effort of such translation appears to indicate an awareness on Blixen's part that she played different roles in Danish and British culture (literary and otherwise).

2. Much of my comment on mapping and naming anticipates the content of part 3, my discussion of the European historical/geographical invention of Africa. Helgerson's article "The Land Speaks: Cartography, Chorography, and Subversion in Renaissance England" points to a twin emergence—"of the author and the land, of the self and nation" (67)—which resonates with my discussion in chapter 8 of the invention of Africa and Africans as Other in European discourse.

3. See Bindman, *Thames and Hudson Dictionary of British Art* 140.

4. This chapter concentrates on Schreiner and the self-conscious originality of her descriptions of her African farm. Blixen's greater conventionality in landscape representation is perhaps illustrated by comments in her letters to the effect that there is "no better expression of the English spirit than a park" (*Letters* 235), in her using Turner's pictures as emblematic of what is distinctively English (*Letters* 162), and in her seeing the Kenyan landscape in terms of European paintings (e.g., "An absolutely enchanting 'romantic' landscape, like Claude Lorrain's," *Letters* 59). Thurman quotes an early unpublished work in which Blixen wrote: "I have always had difficulty seeing how a landscape looked if I had not first had the key to it from a great painter. . . . Constable, Gainsborough and Turner showed me England" (92).

5. This is the case not just in Williams's work on literary pastoral but also in Barrell's on eighteenth- and nineteenth-century poetry and painting, Bermingham's on painting from that period, and in Pratt's or JanMohamed's writing on colonialist travel writing and fiction.

Said's descriptions of the "relationship between knowledge and geography" in the specific context of Orientalism are also relevant here. Not only does Said insist on the "imaginative" nature of geographical knowledge (*Orientalism* 53–55), but he also shows how, in the nineteenth century, "scientific geography soon gave way to 'commercial geography'" (218). Thus Western geographical representations of all kinds, whether in fictional works, travel writing, or "pure" geographies are all to varying degrees involved in making foreign space knowable and hence usable by Western powers.

6. See also "The Mapping Impulse in Dutch Art," in which Alpers links the arts of painting, mapmaking, and surveying as forms of description that enable knowledge, possession, and control. Like Harley, Alpers insists on the political and economic value of maps (rather than seeing them as expressions of objective knowledge), pointing to the "jealous care with which the Dutch trading companies guarded their sea charts against competitors" (67). Alpers, however, distinguishes between the Dutch tradition and the English tradition, noting that whereas surveying "was greeted with suspicion by tenant farmers" in England, in the Netherlands, with its greater proportion of peasant-owned land, surveying appeared less threateningly proprietorial: "What [Dutch] maps present is not land possessed but land known in certain respects" (82).

7. It is also worth noting that Schreiner positively worshipped the former governor-general of the Cape, Sir George Grey, whose policies in the 1850s had laid the foundation for the 1894 Act. In his attempts to undermine and destroy the last remaining Xhosa institutions in Xhosaland, Grey had taken full advantage of the Cattle-Killing disaster (see chapter 8). In addition to confiscating land and goods, he also bought out chiefs—paying them as judges assisted by white magistrates—thereby subsuming them into white culture. (See also Peires, Switzer, Crais.) To be fair to Schreiner, it should be added that Grey's success depended on his own skillful misrepresentations of his own aims and achievements, so she might be forgiven for not knowing the truth about him. Switzer, who calls Grey "the final architect in the conquest of Xhosaland" (65), points to Grey's manipulation of the colonial authorities in London both before the Cattle-Killing, when he used a "bogus threat of a possible Mfengu-Xhosa alliance" (65) to get money for his policies, and after it, when he and his officials "*manufactured* a so-called chiefs' plot to destroy the power of the chiefs, force the Xhosa into migrant labor, and open up their territories to white settlement" (71). As Belich shows, Grey used similar tactics in his two governorships in New Zealand; in *The New Zealand Wars*, Belich calls Grey a "master of propaganda" (58), refers to the "conscious artifice" (68) of Grey's reports, and shows how Grey's concealment of facts led to a "paper victory" in the New Zealand Wars when in fact the British had suffered a military defeat (70). Elsewhere, Belich writes

that Grey "could certainly have taught Machiavelli a trick or two in methodology" (120); as in South Africa the "campaign of misinformation" involved "a near monopoly of the flow of information to the Colonial Office" (123). It is nonetheless extraordinarily ironic that Schreiner's highly politicized representation of British landgrabbing in Rhodesia in *Trooper Peter Halket of Mashonaland* (see chapter 7) should have been dedicated to Sir George Grey, a "great good man." Sally-Ann Murray draws attention to that irony in her article "Olive Schreiner: 'A Soul Struggling with Its Material Surroundings,'" where she points out that despite remarkable percipience, Schreiner's "comprehension had limitations pertaining to the entire presence of Britain in Africa, whether imperialistic or humanitarian" (31–32).

8. Bror Blixen was an active supporter of this scheme (*Letters* 71), and Karen Blixen even floated the idea that her ex-soldier brother Thomas might apply for land under it (*Letters* 96–97).

9. For details of land distribution in colonial Kenya and the creation of a Kenyan wage-labor force, see, e.g., Wolff, *The Economics of Colonialism* 47–131, and Kennedy, *Islands of White* 21–27, 42–47.

10. Writing about the hybridity of creole languages in *Colonial Desire*, Young links the ideas of Bakhtin with those of Homi Bhabha. Citing Bakhtin's claim for the cultural productivity of hybridized languages ("they are pregnant with potential for new world views, with new 'internal forms' for perceiving the world in words"), he goes on to show how for Bhabha the particular hybridity of colonial discourse "describes a process in which the single voice of colonial authority undermines the operation of colonial power by inscribing and disclosing the trace of the other so that it reveals itself as double-voiced" (Young 23).

11. In their anthology of Victorian writers, Bloom and Trilling write, for instance, that "by the pertinacity, passion, and brilliance of his teaching[,] . . . Ruskin had shaped the minds of three intellectual generations in their relation to art" (154).

12. In her essay on "The Boer," Schreiner describes Boer culture as a medieval hangover, resulting from the Boers' isolation geographically and linguistically from Europe and the European Enlightenment. Like Ruskin, she does not assume that this medievalness is grounds for mockery. Rather, a "discerning" person would approach Boer culture "not recklessly, but holding the attitude habitual to the wise man—that of the learner, not the scoffer" (*Thoughts* 93). "The Boer" is highly relevant to this chapter's discussion of landscape and nationalism in that Schreiner declares the landscape to be crucial in understanding Afrikaner nationalism: "The South African land became from the very moment he landed the object of a direct and absorbing religious veneration, excluding all other national feelings" (*Thoughts* 75).

13. In *The Tory View of Landscape*, Nigel Everett draws attention to the intellectual conflicts from the eighteenth century on within and between Tory notions of a "moral economy" and Liberal notions of a "free" market. Ruskin's position as a Tory who was "constantly seeking means of composing society, reluctant to relinquish it to individual greed and taste or to a natural tendency towards improvement" (Everett 7) is not only central to his argument but also evocative of Schreiner's

attack in *Trooper Peter Halket* and elsewhere on "King Gold," Cecil Rhodes, and capitalist expansion generally in southern Africa.

14. First person pronouns are frequently problematical with Schreiner; her "we" here seems more like an advertiser's interpellation of audience than a statement of identity; in other words, "we" really means "you" English readers who need to know the real truth about "us" in "Africa."

15. In a letter to Havelock Ellis in 1888 she writes, "I *hate* Zola and that school more and more" (*Letters* 129).

16. Blixen, who had had some formal art school training in Copenhagen, makes the same sort of slip very consciously in a letter to her Aunt Bess in 1928 when she comments on having learned "out here . . . the value of distance or perspective" something which initially "dawned on me when I attended the Academy and learned to draw perspective, which I count as one of the experiences of my life, but whose significance I have only recently understood how to apply to practical life" (*Letters* 356).

17. Coetzee points to specific features that preclude a picturesque representation: the absence of deep greens; the foliage's lack of luster; the dazzling brightness and evenness of the light which makes transitions from light to dark harshly abrupt; the absence of reflective surface water and of diffusive atmospheric moisture (42).

18. Again, see the *Thames and Hudson Dictionary of British Art*, which states that the earliest landscapes in British painting were "topographical views" such as Hollar's "carefully drawn and etched 'prospects.'" Such "prospects" depended on an "elevated viewpoint" from which to present their detailed pictures of country houses (Bindman 140).

19. The proprietorial sense is not quite so overt in *Out of Africa* as it is in Blixen's letters. In a relatively early letter to Thomas Dinesen (February 1918) she writes, "I have a feeling that this country belongs to us," and she goes on to describe the country in terms of its "dryness, colorlessness, monotony" (*Letters* 60), suggesting that she sees Kenya as a landscape, like a painting one might acquire.

20. Blixen, too, explicitly declares Africans to be a *part* of the landscape: "The Natives," she writes, "were Africa in flesh and blood" (*Out of Africa* 28).

21. See, e.g., Itala Vivan's essay "The Treatment of Blacks in *The Story of an African Farm*," where she observes that "the only instance where a black character actually articulates words and chooses a line of behaviour" only "confirms the character's fixed and dependent role, that of a servant and satellite" (100). In that scene, the saintly Otto, about to be turfed off the farm by Tant' Sannie as a result of Blenkins's calumnies, turns for support to the "Hottentot woman" whom he has always treated well. Instead of setting the record straight as Otto had expected, she responds with "a loud ringing laugh" and urges Tant' Sannie, "Give it him, old missis! Give it him!" (*African Farm* 90).

22. This was precisely the logic used by the British Foreign Office in overcoming opposition to the idea of selling land in Kenya that did not belong to them. The Foreign Office "pleaded for 'jurisdiction over waste and uncultivated land in places

where the native Ruler is incompetent, whether from ignorance or otherwise, to exercise that jurisdiction'" (Wolff 62). They duly won that jurisdiction in the guise of the Crown Lands Ordinance of 1902, after which the alienation of lands to Europeans gathered momentum: 4,991 acres were alienated to Europeans in 1903, 571,368 in 1907, and 639,640 in 1914 (Wolff 57). Jomo Kenyatta satirizes Foreign Office language in his pseudo-folktale "Gentlemen of the Jungle" when he has the invading elephant explain to his fellow animals: "I considered it necessary, in my friend's own interests, to turn the undeveloped space to a more economic use by sitting in it myself" (49-50).

23. The consequences of this "unnaturalness" for Schreiner's depiction of and reception by the Boers are no less complex. Catherine Barnes Stevenson points out that Schreiner's pro-Boer stance at the end of the century is prefigured by Tant' Sannie's dismissal of the British with "Dear Lord! . . . all Englishmen are ugly" (53); she cites Schreiner as the only woman writer of the time to be "aware of her own cultural biases or the valid reasons for the Boers' hostility to the British" (69). The Boers, however, were not flattered. Many felt patronized and insulted by their depiction in the novel and in Schreiner's later nonfictional descriptions of Boer life. An editorial in *Ons Land* "expressed indignation that Olive had chosen as a type of the Afrikaner the 'despised white frontiersman'—the dour, barely literate farmer—or (as in the case of *The Story of an African Farm*) the formidable Tant' Sannie" (Rive 274).

24. *African Farm* 262; *Undine* 278. The smooth white sand on the bottom of the kloof, the silver bell-like sound of the little stream, and the quivering of leaves in the peaceful evening air appear in both descriptions. Schoeman further suggests that the similar intensity of Waldo's and Undine's emotions links these fictional descriptions to Schreiner's almost mystical recollection of just such an experience in just such a kloof when Schreiner was a child and living at Healdtown in the Eastern Cape (Schoeman 104–8).

25. See the discussion of Stevenson and Mills in chapter 3.

26. Assessments of target audience for a previously unpublished author are perhaps harder to determine than I suggest here. In a letter to Karl Pearson, for instance, Schreiner describes *African Farm* as a novel "written altogether for myself, when there seemed no possible chance that I should ever come to England or publish it" (Rive 109). That collocation of coming to England and publishing does suggest, however, that the latter would have been impossible without the former. As I have delineated elsewhere, Schreiner was widely read once published; Krebs describes her as "perhaps the South African most well-known in Britain during the Boer War, apart from Boer president Paul Kruger" (109).

27. According to Jacobson's introduction to the Penguin edition of *The Story of an African Farm*, even "some sixty years after it was first published" the Karoo landscape was still so infrequently encountered in books that he [Jacobson] had to "struggle with [his] own incredulity that the kopjes, *kraals* and cactus plants she

mentions were of the same kind as those I was familiar with" (*African Farm* 18). Both Plaatje and Jacobson, like Schreiner, lived in Kimberley for extended periods.

28. Plaatje actually uses "hairbreadth escape" on page 36; the three encounters with lions occur on pages 34–36, 64, 77 (where the animal is called a "tiger"). Plaatje also has Mzilikazi relate a folktale concerning one Zungu's ill-fated attempt at taming a lion to provide an analogy for the Bechuana alliance with the Boers (*Mhudi* 175).

29. The significance of Bamford Smales's bakkie and gun in *July's People* is analogous to the wagon and rifle here: Using these icons of the technology of transport and weaponry (together with the technology of communication—the radio—in *July's People*) locates precisely the source of European power in Southern Africa.

30. See also Chrisman, *Rereading the Imperial Romance.* Chrisman's entire book is relevant to my arguments here; in particular, her reading of the narrative strategy of *Mhudi* echoes my account of the multiple possible readings of *Mhudi.*

31. See chapter 7 for a discussion of Schreiner's descriptions of British military activity in Rhodesia.

32. One might draw a parallel with Julius Nyerere's translation of Shakespeare into Kiswahili as a kind of nationalist statement, demonstrating the literary range and value of the Swahili language.

33. We might think of the unlikely alliance, in the period leading up to the 1994 elections, between Buthelezi's Inkatha Freedom Party and the Afrikaner Vryheidsfront. The situation with Afrikaans is all the more complicated owing to its status as a vehicle of anticolonialism, a status Nelson Mandela stressed in a speech on June 11, 1997, at the Rand Afrikaans University, reassuring Afrikaners that they still had invaluable contributions to make in building the new South Africa (http://www.anc.org.za:80/ancdocs/briefing/nw19970612/82.html).

34. See Ndebele's essay, "The English Language and Social Change in South Africa."

35. Or we might consider the case of Salman Rushdie and Indian literature. Rushdie argues, "To conquer English may be to complete the process of making ourselves free" (Thieme 899).

36. See Heywood, "*The Story of an African Farm:* Society, Positivism, and Myth" 31–32. Even if the specifically Comtean nature of Heywood's hierarchies may be dubious, the hierarchies themselves—and the tendency to impose hierarchies—seem accurate reflections of late Victorian (metropolitan and colonial) habits of thought.

37. Classifying Bonaparte Blenkins as "English" raises further questions regarding the racial, rather than national, marking of Irishness, particularly in the Victorian period. I read Schreiner as intending Blenkins's "difference" from Englishness as negligible. She has him disclaim Englishness in order to overcome Tant' Sannie's anglophobia, professing himself to be "Irish every inch of me" (53), yet he claims kin with Napoleon as well as the duke of Wellington (58–59). Irishness appears to be a kind of flag of convenience. Given his mendacity and opportunism, few of his claims

are to be trusted, and Heywood is probably justified in concurring with Tant' Sannie's identification of him as "You vaggabonds se Engelschman" (*African Farm* 52), despite the one narrative reference to the young Bonaparte's "playing in an Irish street gutter" (111). Schreiner appears to have been taken by surprise that her representation of Blenkins might have been racially motivated and thus undercut her support for Irish Home Rule (see her letter to her brother W. P. Schreiner in Rive 273).

38. We might also draw attention to Schreiner's bleak short story, "Dream Life and Real Life," in which Jannita, a "poor indentured child . . . living with Boers" (12) but apparently hailing from Denmark, falls victim to an unholy alliance of a Bushman, an English navvy, and her coworker, Dirk the Hottentot. Although the Boer family has treated her appallingly, Jannita risks, and loses, her life in warning them of the transracial trio's impending attack on the Boer homestead. Like *The Story of an African Farm*, "Dream Life and Real Life" thoroughly confounds conventional contemporary racial and ethnic hierarchies.

39. Krog has continued to raise the ire of right-wing Afrikaners by her rejection of nonracial models of nationalism. See *Country of My Skull*, her controversial autobiographical account of her work reporting on the Truth and Reconciliation Commission (TRC).

40. See the essay by Kelwyn Sole ("Oral Performance and Social Struggle in Contemporary Black South African Literature") and the section introduced by Ari Sitas ("From *Black Mamba Rising: South African Worker Poets in Struggle*") in *From South Africa: New Writing, Photographs and Art* 254–304.

41. In 1996, 65 percent of primetime viewing on the South African Broadcasting Corporation's three national television channels was in English. Multilingual viewing took up 14.5 percent, Zulu and Xhosa both took up 4.1 percent, and Afrikaans took up 3.86 percent of programming. The rights of South Africa's eleven official languages are protected by the country's new constitution. The significance of English as a lingua franca, however, more acceptable to more people for whom it is not the first language, is widely apparent, not least in the recent decision to make English the sole language of command and instruction in the armed forces (Beresford). A similar attitude toward English led to the establishment of English as the sole official language in Namibia, despite the slightly greater use of Afrikaans in that country before independence.

42. Fransen is presumably referring to the Cape Peninsular area rather than Schreiner's Karoo.

Chapter 5. Culture, Cultivation, and Colonialism in *Out of Africa* and Beyond

1. One obvious example might be the publication and filming of Kuki Gallmann's memoir, *I Dreamed of Africa*, a work which bears striking similarities with Blixen's.

2. For a discussion of the two authors' versions of Kenya, see Annie Gagiano's article "Blixen, Ngugi: Recounting Kenya."

3. In addition, in approaching Blixen's work in terms of its ideology I am fully aware that I am undervaluing the sheer gorgeousness of much of Blixen's word painting.

4. I have noted elsewhere that one of the unexpected consequences of the end of apartheid has been the unabashed recycling of colonialist language and iconography in the advertising of safaris to South Africa. One company, INTRAV, even offers the ultimate imperialist fantasy holiday of a three-week "Cape to Cairo" trip by private jet and the "legendary" Blue Train. See my "Sanitising South Africa."

5. In *Chronicles of Darkness,* David Ward gives a potted history of the murder and extortion (49–51) in the twenty or so years of British colonization of Kenya prior to the Blixens' arrival that made possession of their farm possible. See also Kennedy, *Islands of White,* Wolff, *The Economics of Colonialism,* and Ambler, *Kenyan Communities in the Age of Imperialism.* Kenyatta writes, "The Gikuyu lost most of their lands through magnanimity, for the Gikuyu country was never wholly conquered by force of arms, but the people were put under the ruthless domination of European imperialism through the insidious trickery of hypocritical treaties" (47).

6. The nostalgia of *Shadows on the Grass,* written well after the defeat of Nazism and published in 1960, is even more pronounced than that of *Out of Africa.*

7. For further discussion of this point, see chapter 8 for an analysis of Patrick Brantlinger's term *imperial Gothic.* Cain and Hopkins's theory that "gentlemanly capitalism" provided the basis for imperialism is also relevant here.

8. We might contrast, for instance, the way that Blixen responds to her farm manager Dickens (Nichols in *Out of Africa*) over the killing of lions. In *Out of Africa* Nichols's pragmatic request to poison the lions is dismissed pretty much out of hand, and serves as the catalyst for one of Blixen's grandest gestures, going out and shooting the lions in the dark with Finch Hatton, marked by her most flamboyantly romantic statements, "Let us go and risk our lives unnecessarily. For if they have got any value at all it is this that they have got none. *Frei lebt wer sterben kann"* (*Out of Africa* 200). In her letters, Blixen treats Dickens's approach much more carefully, using his attitude as a starting point for a much more balanced discussion on married responsibility and her rejection of it (*Letters* 364–68, 369–74).

9. For Ngugi's justifiably outraged comments on this comparison, see the essay "Her Cook, Her Dog: Karen Blixen's Africa" (*Moving the Centre* 132–35).

10. See also the opening to the previous chapter in which Williams traces the etymology of the word *farm* back to leasing arrangements.

11. Much the same can be said with regard to white settlement in Southern Rhodesia at the same time. Wolff cites an official 1903 British handbook on the colony that explicitly "discouraged prospective immigrants from contemplating farming, suggesting that Africans were more efficient producers" (29).

12. While increasing population pressure in the reserves drew the Kikuyu into the available grazing land of the "White Highlands" as squatters, their exploitation once there, fully sanctioned by colonial law, made their situation intolerable. Wolff

records a proposed 1924 ordinance, for instance, that would have allowed plantation owners not to pay their squatters "in a state of emergency" for their mandatory 180 days of work (Wolff 127). Tabitha Kanogo's *Squatters and the Roots of Mau Mau, 1905–1963* examines precisely the way in which the Kikuyu people were transformed from a nation of farmers first into "squatters" and thence into rebels by colonial law. More recently, Wunyabari Maloba in *Mau Mau and Kenya* has attempted to place Mau Mau in a wider context of peasant revolts. Maloba stresses that the goals of Mau Mau, though far from even, were unlike previous European peasant movements in their mix of looking backward to an ideal society when land had been available and in looking forward to a period free from colonial and racist control. Both the nationalism of Mau Mau and its apparent class-specific nature are less to do with a specifically political consciousness than with the materiality of land availability. The resultant lack of "a common concrete idea as to the shape of [the] future" was, Maloba argues, "one of Mau Mau's major weaknesses" (4).

The underdevelopment of rural Africa generally has been described by numerous historians (e.g., Walter Rodney's classic *How Europe Underdeveloped Africa;* but see also Palmer and Parsons, *The Roots of Rural Poverty in Central and Southern Africa,* or Colin Bundy, *Rise and Fall of the South African Peasantry*); the pervasiveness of the evolutionary model in European thinking about all aspects of African "development" is evident not just in agricultural matters but also, as we have seen in Young's analysis, in regard to "culture" and "civilization" generally and, specifically, in attitudes toward religion (see Valentin Mudimbe's analysis of the aims and roles of Christian missionaries in Africa in *The Invention of Africa* 44–64).

13. See Keegan, *Rural Transformation in Industrializing South Africa,* esp. chapter 4, "Interventions of the Capitalist State and the Development of the Arable Highveld."

14. Blixen records the actual events in a letter to her mother on January 3, 1928, quite coolly (by contrast with the purple prose of the published versions) reporting that having debated whether or not to shoot the second lion "we came to the conclusion that we had to have it, so just as it was about to take itself off Denys shot it" (*Letters* 332–33); in an aside in a letter home two years later (18 May 1930) she insists that her having not shot the lion "must for ever be the most strictly kept secret" (*Letters* 407).

15. There is an unusual degree of indignation in her memoirs at the charge that she and Finch Hatton killed the giraffe on which they shot the lion whose skin was presented to King Christian; balanced against the apparent arbitrariness of bureaucracy, represented by the regulations of the impersonal "Game Department," and its need of "proof" is Blixen's notion that "hunting is ever a love-affair" (*Shadows* 53) and that her shooting the lion was "a declaration of love" (*Out of Africa* 198). That any bureaucratic organization should claim authority over her or, worse, accuse her of impropriety is presented as absurd, as the principles by which the two operate are incommensurable.

16. Blixen's attitude toward riding and hunting exemplifies the typically upper-

class attitudes that Bourdieu identifies in outdoor sports as combining the "purely health-oriented function of maintaining the body . . . with all the symbolic gratifications associated with practising a highly distinctive activity. This gives to the highest degree the sense of mastery of one's own body as well as the free and exclusive appropriation of scenery inaccessible to the vulgar" ("How Can One Be a Sports Fan?" 355).

17. In fact, Jardine's phrasing may be a diplomat's avoidance of pointing the finger at the citizens of another country. Upper-class British snobbery against tourists in general, and American tourists in particular, must have been rife. In 1914, Blixen wrote to her brother about "a ghastly American woman . . . whose safari had been financed by a magazine and given immense publicity, and who travels with seven white men and 200 bearers" who pitched camp at the Blixen camp, "shot all around us against all the rules, put a kill out herself and built a boma and chased all the lions away so that we were obliged to clear out and go eastward" (*Letters* 20). Even in Hemingway's "The Short, Happy Life of Francis Macomber," the professional hunter Wilson (presented as English but reputedly based on Bror Blixen) is outraged by the ignorant behavior of the wealthy Macomber and his society wife. After Macomber's display of cowardice, Wilson imagines himself "seeing them through the safari on a very formal basis" (*Short Stories of Ernest Hemingway* 7), a coded phrase indicating distance and disapproval.

18. Race also plays a significant role. Jane Carruthers argues that in South Africa "upper- and middle-class European values about sport-hunting and the cruelty of snares and trapping were imposed on Africans whose values were the opposite. . . . The issue of cruelty was frequently raised in order to stop Africans from hunting" (5).

19. See Ranger's essay "The Invention of Tradition in Colonial Africa" in which he writes, for example: "With the coming of formal colonial rule it was urgently necessary to turn the whites into a convincing ruling class, entitled to hold sway over their subjects not only through force of arms, but also through the prescriptive status bestowed by neo-tradition" (215). See also the discussion of Gregory Rose in chapter 3 and of Tony Marston in chapter 6.

20. In 1890 Schreiner complained in a letter to Havelock Ellis: "Harry, you don't know what Philistines the people in Africa are. . . . Fancy a whole nation of *lower* middle-class Philistines, without an aristocracy of blood or intellect or of muscular labourers to save them!" (*Letters* 168). Similarly, in a letter to J. X. Merriman in 1896, Schreiner writes of the Boers that "they have had no Job; but they have had no language in which a Job could express his thoughts!" (*Letters* 278). The specific absence of a *literary* culture also gets in the way of Schreiner's seeing Africans as "cultured."

21. Gordimer reproduces a similar farm in *None to Accompany Me* where one of Vera Stark's husband's businessman friends owns a farm which is really a "weekend fishing retreat" (163), one of the perks of white privilege that may be lost in the transition from apartheid. On the other hand, the farmer Odendaal—a thoroughly

boorish Boer—whose own farming brings in scarcely enough revenue to sustain his white advantage, plans to cash in on the transition of power by "convert[ing] the farm into cash as a landlord; he would divide it into plots for rent to blacks. He was going to turn their invasion to profit" (21–22). Gordimer's recent work, in particular, shows a very astute awareness of the politics and ideology of landownership. See also chapter 8 for further discussion of *The Conservationist*.

22. Post-apartheid South Africa has had to come to terms with the legacy of the apartheid era's environmental policies, and despite some greater sensitivity to the needs of local people, it has not performed uniformly well. In the late 1990s, a number of scandalous deals made local headlines. In 1997 the South African Mpumalanga Parks Board struck a secret deal, giving the Dubai-based Dolphin Group exclusive rights to develop six game reserves in return for guaranteeing any shortfall in the Parks Board's budget as state funding decreases over the next ten years. Public outcry at the secrecy of this deal led to a renegotiation cutting the lease to twenty-five years and reducing Dolphin's rights to just three reserves. Just across the border in Mozambique, a Louisiana-based businessman, James Blanchard, signed a fifty-year lease with the government to develop the coastline south of Maputo by constructing "four 'Club-Med-style' holiday resorts, nine 'beach resorts,' two holiday villages, 350 private holiday homes, a railway line, two casinos and a yacht marina" (*Economist*, May 3, 1997, 37). The secrecy and haste with which the deal was struck left ecologists and locals very anxious. Blanchard claimed he would let the locals stay, having ringed their villages with protective fences. The rights of locals appeared to be a low priority, however. In attempting to make local people part of the draw to his development, Blanchard conceived of a number of "cultural villages" where tourists would visit the "natives." Blanchard's disregard for the locals was exemplified by the fact that these plans initially included the building of a "Bushman village" despite the geographical incongruity. Not all theme-park tourism is necessarily exploitative, though. In a separate initiative in Mpumalanga, the South African Press Association on July 1, 1997, reported that eleven game farmers were working together with several families of the Matsamo people in the Onderberg region to set up a 15,000-hectare game reserve. The project, described as a "first" by Parks Board chairman Alan Gray, would include the establishment of a nursery for medicinal plants used by traditional healers as well as tourist facilities. Ketan Somaia, Dolphin's boss, and James Blanchard may be more overtly driven by a profit motive than Karen Blixen ever was, either as a farmer or as a writer, but it is difficult to conceive of an adequate criterion that would distinguish their land deals from those of the Blixens and Westenholtzes from 1913 on.

23. One thinks of such places as Florida's Busch Gardens, stocked to high density with African big game, or of Britain's first safari park, Longleat, which combined the nostalgic tourist attraction of the country house with the thrill of imported lions. More insidiously, we might think of the American Museum of Natural History in New York (among other such museums), whose dioramas designed by the husband-

and-wife team of Martin and Osa Johnson include Africans as part of the natural history.

24. Among the many ironies of the representations of wild Africa in these films I might just mention that the "jungle" sequences in *Congo* were shot in Costa Rica, while the lions in *Out of Africa* were imported from California. At least there were no horses painted with black and white stripes as in the 1984 *Sheena, Queen of the Jungle!*

25. See the 1995 television and print ads for Nissan Pathfinder and the 1995 television ads for American Express featuring Kent of the classiest of Kenya's safari companies, Abercrombie and Kent. A 2002 Land Rover ad repeats the trope, with a bored turnpike toll collector fantasizing about the Serengeti as soon as a Land Rover pulls up alongside the tollbooth.

26. In the age of ecotourism, this situation is not confined to Africa. The Burmese government has apparently been involved in "razing entire Karen villages, killing, raping, enslaving, to make way for the biggest nature reserve in the world." (See the article "Save the Rhino, but Kill the People" by Adrian Levy, Cathy Scott-Clark, and David Harrison in *Manchester Guardian Weekly*, March 30, 1997, 5).

27. In *Africa on Film*, Kenneth Cameron takes the moviemakers to task for presenting Blixen's "sweet behavior toward 'her' Kikuyu" as showing us "her goodness and modernity" (173). Cameron criticizes the film for presenting Blixen's poetic creations as historical realities, thereby "smudg[ing] . . . the real reason why there was money to be made in 'British East': land and labor were deliberately undervalued." See also Gurnah's "Settler Writing in Kenya," where he critiques the film for taking "Blixen's text out of its time" and adding "what a contemporary reader would have been unlikely to know" (289).

28. Indeed, Blixen's and Schreiner's deep attachment to their pet dogs puts one in mind of Mphahlele's definitive debunking of the white liberal woman in his story "Mrs. Plum," which opens: "My madam's name was Mrs. Plum. She loved dogs and Africans and said that everyone must follow the law even if it hurt" (*In Corner B* 164). When I have taught this story in England and the United States, an alarming number of my (mainly white) students have failed to see the sarcasm.

29. In defense of Blixen's use of animal similes, it might be noted that (a) she tends to use similar comparisons for white folks, too, and (b) she could claim to be using a technique common in African story-telling. See also my references to Blixen's use of animal imagery in chapters 3 (with regard to the Somali matriarch) and 7 (with regard to Kinanjui).

Chapter 6. Violence and Voluntarism: The Will to Power and the Will to Die

1. See, e.g., Doris Lessing's essay "In Defence of the Underground," in which she revels in London's "variety, its populations from everywhere in the world, its transitoriness" (119).

2. The only person in the novel whose speech is represented as radically divergent from standard English is Wendlandt, the Nazi Bund member. His speech is marked by heavy-handed reversals of standard word order. The speech of the Africans in the novel, by contrast, has no such indication of "abnormality," even though their articulacy is severely restricted.

Casual British racism is represented by the anti-Irish sentiment of sarcastic comments such as "Irish logic" regarding the part-Irish Edward Corcoran. Likewise, "Irish charm" characterizes the hotheaded settler Donovan Popple in *Murder at Government House*.

3. See Young's *Colonial Desire*, esp. chapter 3, "The Complicity of Culture: Arnold's Ethnographic Politics." Young reproduces illustrations of "A Celtic Group" from Knox's *Races of Men* and of "English types" from Beddoes's *Races of Britain*, and shows that one of Arnold's chief sources for his beliefs was W. F. Edwards, whose *Des caractères physiologiques des races humaines* (1829) "assimilat[ed] history to physiology and natural history" (Young 76). Young's explanation of how Matthew Arnold's sense of Englishness comes rather paradoxically to be a forerunner of multiculturalism, "proposing a fusion [of the Celtic and Saxon] at the same time as he makes a claim for the permanence of the two racial types" (71), also has relevance to my argument here of differences within sameness.

4. Even here, though, we might note some transatlantic hybridity in Huxley's use of the detective genre, with Vachell seeming to owe as much to Philip Marlowe as to the more ascetic Lord Peter Wimsey or Hercule Poirot.

5. See, e.g., Conrad, *Heart of Darkness*, where the vegetation stands "higher than the wall of a temple," making Marlow ask himself: "What were we who had strayed in here? Could we handle that dumb thing, or would it handle us? I felt how big, how confoundedly big, was that thing that couldn't talk, and perhaps was deaf as well. What was in there?" (56).

Along the same lines, attention might also be drawn to one of Mary Turner's fantasies at the end of *The Grass Is Singing*, where she imagines her house being destroyed in a few years "by the bush, which had always hated it, had always stood around it silently, waiting for the moment when it could advance and cover it, for ever, so that nothing remained" (Lessing 231). This passage, like the one quoted from Conrad, mixes fantasies of the defeat of cultivation/culture by nature with disintegration of the self. The suggestion that "Africa" is antithetical to civilization and the human further prompts the suggestion that "Africans" cannot themselves be civilized or human. Achebe's critique in "An Image of Africa: Racism in Conrad's *Heart of Darkness*" (*Hopes and Impediments* 1-20) of the attribution of inscrutability, incomprehensibility, muteness, and malevolence to Africans and African landscape remains the locus classicus of criticism that shows the canonical status of racism in English literature. See also chapter 7 of this study.

6. Young's notion of the constitution of "colonial desire," with its mix of simultaneous attraction to and repulsion from the object of desire, draws explicitly on

Bhabha's notion of ambivalence. Young agrees with Bhabha that "colonial discourse of whatever kind operated not only as an instrumental construction of knowledge [Said's insight as defined in *Orientalism*] but also according to the ambivalent protocols of fantasy and desire" (*Colonial Desire* 161).

7. Abiola Irele calls *Things Fall Apart* the "master text in the case of Africa" of "literary expression dedicated to the promotion of nationalist consciousness" (22), and one in which the "claim to self-determination thus becomes grounded in a cult of difference all the more plausible in that it seems ratified by the visible imprint of racial and ethnic characteristics" (23). I cite this because of the peculiar similarity between pan-African nationalism and Arnold's "theory of English culture as multicultural" (Young 17).

8. Perhaps typical of such settler reactionariness would be Lord Delamere's role in the Vigilance Committee, a group which was formed to counter moves in the British Parliament from 1923 on to define the interests of Africans in Kenya as paramount. Judith Thurman records that the Vigilance Committee "met in secret and made plans for an Ulster-like resistance" (205).

9. The District Officer's attitude toward anthropologists and settlers clearly does not prevent him from belittling traditional African ways of life. While the secret society is dismissed as "schoolboy"-ish, the D.O. seems intent on imposing his own schoolboy values on his district, introducing British sports "to replace the old thrills of tribal war, you know, and to give the young men some incentive to keep fit" (147). His naïveté toward secret societies is all the more obvious in the light of the Mau Mau movement of the 1950s (see previous chapter), while the British advancement of the boxing champion Idi Amin highlights a rather differently nuanced relationship between organized sport and war (see Ranger, "Invention" 217–26).

10. And this whole study is concerned in one way or another with the double meaning of the phrase "the occupation of the land." Like "colonization," it implies both inhabitation of a foreign space and the *job* of tilling soil. See introduction.

11. Gordimer's Toby Hood plays a similar role in her 1958 novel, *A World of Strangers*.

12. Wendy Webster argues that Huxley's memoirs reproduce this sort of gendering of settlers as male, with metropolitan English as female: "white (home) men are less adventurous than white (colonial) women" (535).

13. The trial is, of course, a mere formality and scarcely represented in the novel. The radicalism of Lessing's work is again perhaps revealed by the way she resists another literary convention—the trial scene. Compare with Alan Paton's *Cry, the Beloved Country* (1948) and Harper Lee's *To Kill a Mockingbird* (1960), where good, honest, white liberal lawyers defend black clients in racist situations.

14. The suggestion that Moses might be seen as Mary's victim is troubling in its apparent blaming of the actual murder victim. What Lessing has very acutely caught is the way in which racist patriarchy tends to exonerate itself through self-fulfilling prophecies regarding racial and gender others. Her accuracy in representing the

nexus of racism, sexism, and colonialism does indeed make *The Grass Is Singing* a troubling book to write about. Almost as much as Schreiner's impolite *Trooper Peter Halket of Mashonaland*, it presents a model of political incorrectness (see chapter 7).

15. Although Belsey does not make the point, it is probably worth remembering that Conan Doyle was a staunch proponent of British imperialism who actively supported the British war effort in the Anglo-Boer War by offering his services as a physician. See Krebs, *Gender, Race, and the Writing of Empire* 80–108.

16. I have found relatively little comment on Blixen's account of Kitosch's death, an omission which in itself is telling. Ngugi, however, in *Detained: A Writer's Prison Diary* takes the account as typifying a "hideous colonial aesthetic" (35), a phrase that resonates with Achebe's condemnation of *Heart of Darkness* and my discussion of the separation of aesthetic and political considerations in western canon formation (see chapter 7). Ward briefly elaborates on Ngugi's comments in *Chronicles of Darkness* 48–49.

Kennedy reads Blixen's attitude as illustrating the extraordinary extent of the racial boundaries that white settlers erected in order to protect their prestige. In a situation which frequently demanded dependence as well as almost constant physical proximity, Kennedy argues that the settlers relied on these racial boundaries for "emotional assuagement" as much as economic advantage (149); "even so universal a matter as death, then, set sharp and steadfast boundaries between the two races" (166).

17. The locus classicus of such medical fudging would probably be the case of Steve Biko in South Africa in 1977. Beaten semiconscious by police in Port Elizabeth, Biko was examined by two district surgeons, Benjamin Tucker and Ivor Lang. They disregarded the obvious symptoms of brain damage that Biko manifested and eventually allowed the security police to transport Biko, naked on the floor of a Land Rover, 750 miles to Pretoria, where he died. Biko's postmortem examination "showed brain damage and necrosis, extensive head trauma, disseminated intravascular coagulation, renal failure, and various external injuries" (*Truth and Reconciliation Commission Report* 4:112). The magistrate in the case referred the findings to the South African Medical and Dental Council, who determined after two and a half years that the doctors had not been guilty of any professional misconduct and/or negligence. For further details, see the conclusions concerning the South African institutional health sector in *Truth and Reconciliation Commission Report* 4:109–64.

18. Elsewhere in *Out of Africa* Blixen twice acknowledges that the phrase translated as "I want to die" (*nataka kufa* in Kiswahili) can be synonymous with a simple future tense, not necessarily implying volition. Both occasions involve imminent death, and Blixen gives a literal translation merely as a gloss to her own English versions "was about to die" (108) and "was dying" (286). The literal translations, modified by almost identical phrasing—"wished to die, they have it in Swaheli" (108), and "he wants to die—the Natives have it" (286)—appear to point to a quirk of expression in Kiswahili rather than to fundamentally different European and

African attitudes to death. Ward in *Chronicles of Darkness* concludes from this that Blixen "elects to *pretend* to believe the false interpretation" (49).

Chapter 7. X-ing Out Africa to Produce Something New

1. For fuller accounts of the history of this discourse, see Brantlinger, *Rule of Darkness* (esp. chapter 6, "The Genealogy of the Myth of the 'Dark Continent'"); Curtin, *The Image of Africa: British Ideas and Action, 1780–1850;* Hammond and Jablow, *The Africa That Never Was;* Hansberry, *Africa and Africans as Seen by Classical Writers;* Jones, *Othello's Countrymen;* Miller, *Blank Darkness;* and Mphahlele, *The African Image.* The debate over Bernal's *Black Athena* is also relevant.

2. *Heart of Darkness* makes this point explicit. Marlow tells his audience, "Going up that river was like traveling back to the earliest beginnings of the world" (35) and "We were wanderers on a prehistoric earth" (37). The trope reappears widely in the novella.

3. Johannes Fabian coined the term *allochronic discourse* in his *Time and the Other: How Anthropology Makes Its Object.* As a Belgian anthropologist with considerable experience in the Congo, Fabian's work is of particular relevance to this chapter. See also his *Remembering the Present: Painting and Popular History in Zaire,* in which Fabian discusses the sequence of paintings by local artist Tshibumba Kanda Matulu, illustrating the history of the Congo from the sixteenth century to the present.

4. I feel confident it would be possible to establish the veracity of this claim in a duly scientific way by reference to works of popular culture dealing with Africa. Such a study would be way beyond the scope of this chapter and this work; however, I think it is valid to mention that whenever I have taught *Heart of Darkness,* before introducing the text I have run a word-association "test" on my (mainly white) students, asking them to respond to the words *Europe, Africa, America, science,* and *progress.* In broad outline, the results have confirmed that my students tend to assume that "Europe" is the site of "culture" and "history," now in decline, that "Africa" is characterized by "jungle," "disease," "starvation," and "poverty," while America is still the land of the free and the home of the brave. "Progress" and "science" are, of course, just as Sellars and Yeatman have it, "a good thing." The number of titles that play on Conrad's phrase—e.g., *Blank Darkness, Chronicles of Darkness, Rule of Darkness*—gives further evidence of the catchiness of the phrase. A websearch for the phrase yields numerous hits covering topics from photography techniques, to Boris Yeltsin's health, to the genocide in Rwanda.

5. See, e.g., Ngugi's *Decolonising the Mind*—"It seems it is the fate of Africa to have her destiny always decided around conference tables in the metropolises of the western world: her submergence from self-governing communities into colonies was decided in Berlin; her more recent transition into neo-colonies along the same boundaries was negotiated around the same tables in London, Paris, Brussels and Lisbon" (4); or Rodney's *How Europe Underdeveloped Africa*—"The development

of political unity in the form of large states was proceeding steadily in Africa. But even so, at the time of the Berlin Conference, Africa was still a continent of a large number of socio-political groupings who had not arrived at a common purpose. Therefore, it was easy for the European intruder to play the classic game of divide and conquer" (144).

6. Basil Davidson, commenting in *The Black Man's Burden* on the simultaneous rise of nationalism in Europe in the second half of the nineteenth century and European imperialism in Africa, describes the resultant African nation-formation as "the curse of the nation-state." The crisis of decolonized Africa he sees primarily as a "crisis of institutions," specifically "the nationalism that became nation-statism. This nation-statism looked like a liberation, and really began as one. But it did not continue as a liberation. In practice, it was not a restoration of Africa to Africa's own history, but the onset of a new period of indirect subjection to the history of Europe. The fifty or so states of the colonial partition, each formed and governed as though their peoples possessed no history of their own, became fifty or so nation-states formed and governed on European models, chiefly the models of Britain and France. Liberation thus produced its own denial. Liberation led to alienation" (10). Davidson's statement may represent a nostalgic yearning for an impossibly authentic "Africa," but his point is clear.

7. South Africa's Truth and Reconciliation Commission might be seen as representing a formalized version of just such a "forgetting." Those who confessed any pre-1994 crimes were to be granted amnesty; those who did not were liable to be investigated by an unforgetting, unforgiving state. If you call the memory up, we will forget it; if we call it up, you won't forget it. This odd mix of purging and repression surely captures the essence of South Africa's national neurosis, especially when combined with the emotions of those who can neither forget nor forgive. In addition to its own archive and five-volume report, recording and synthesizing the thousands of testimonies it heard, the Truth and Reconciliation Commission has spawned a huge quantity of secondary material—autobiographical, critical, and imaginative—including Desmond Tutu's *No Future without Forgiveness,* Antjie Krog's *Country of My Skull,* and Jane Taylor's *Ubu and the Truth Commission.* Extrapolating from the South African situation to the worldwide situation of black Africans, Wole Soyinka has pondered the implications of extending the principle of forgiving and forgetting to the longer history of Euro-American involvement with Africa and the possibility of Euro-American reparations for the horrors of the transatlantic slave trade.

8. For further discussion of this claim, see Chinua Achebe's essay "An Image of Africa" in *Hopes and Impediments* and Brantlinger's discussion of it in *Rule of Darkness.* In his analysis of Conrad in *Maps of Englishness,* Simon Gikandi argues that Conrad's departure from realism produces a "state of temporal limbo, in which neither Africa nor Europe can provide the European subject, be it Marlow or Kurtz, with secure places of emplacement or a set of redemptive values" (178).

9. See chapter 5, note 7.

10. "Stone age," of course, is a racist smear that underestimates African technological know-how and equates contemporary Africans with those genuinely stone age remains found in East Africa.

11. The idea of a new dark age, reminiscent of Churchill's wartime rhetoric, suggests that, other cyclical notions of history notwithstanding, such an idea may have its own very specific history at the end of the 1930s when Blixen was writing *Out of Africa*.

12. Judith Thurman traces one of Blixen's earliest references to "destiny" to about 1904 (i.e., before she was twenty), linking her attitudes toward the "unshakeable justice and regularity in the laws of perspective" in drawing to the equally exacting workings of destiny (*Isak Dinesen* 67). In her more than stoical response to her syphilis, Thurman ascribes to Blixen a Nietzschean *amor fati* which allowed her to see the sickness as both necessary and useful (258).

In the section titled "Of Pride," Blixen herself writes that a proud man's "success is the idea of God, successfully carried through, and he is in love with his destiny. As the good citizen finds his happiness in the fulfilment of his duty to the community, so does the proud man find his happiness in the fulfilment of his fate" (*Out of Africa* 224). Here, as clearly as anywhere, we can see how Blixen valorizes the proud, fatalistic individual—in direct relation with God—over the dutiful citizen.

13. See also Ward, *Chronicles of Darkness* 50.

14. Charles H. Ambler points out that European assumptions about the discrete and monolithic nature of various "tribes," and the presumed animosity between them, actually produced that "inter-tribal" animosity. By using Masai warriors as mercenaries on raids into Kikuyuland, the British "generated precisely the kind of generalized ethnic antipathy that [they] assumed was the product of ancient tribal antagonism" (Ambler 112).

15. Blixen resists the drive of her own writing and the conclusions of her own experience by insisting that "Kabero must have had Masai blood in him, the habits and discipline of Masai life could not in themselves have worked the metamorphosis" (121).

16. Equally typically, Blixen attempts to reverse the slave/slave owner binarism: "Upon the long track of blood and tears, the sheep, deep in their dark dumb hearts, had made for themselves a bobtailed philosophy, and thought not highly of the shepherds or the dogs. 'You have no rest either day or night,' they said, 'you run with your hot tongues out, panting, you are kept awake at night so that your dry eyes smart in the daytime, all on our account. You exist for our sake, not we for your sake.' The Kikuyu of the farm at times had a flippant manner towards Farah, as a lamb may skip in the face of the sheepdog just to make him get up and run" (134).

17. At least Blixen does have some idea of the grandeur that was Africa, the glory that was Arabia. Although in an admittedly highly "Orientalist" manner, she does recognize the length of European-free Arab-African history: "Farah's attitude to the Natives of the country was a picturesque thing. No more than the attire and countenance of the Masai warriors, had it been made yesterday, or the day before; it was

the product of many centuries. The forces which had built it up had constructed great buildings in stone as well, but they had crumbled into dust a long time ago" (*Out of Africa* 131)

18. See also chapter 3.

19. The cultural associations of "refined" link culture and nature in a way not uncommon in Blixen. See especially chapter 5.

20. In the sense that she had never proselytized; as a "friend of the Native" she had, rather, attempted to uphold "authentic" African customs and beliefs.

21. See also chapter 5.

22. I use "politer" as an allusion to the etymological connection between *politeness, politics,* and *police,* a familiar poststructuralist connection drawn attention to, for example, by Jacques Derrida (*Limited, Inc.* 112–13). Derrida's general insistence on the violence of discourse, not least academic and intellectual discourse, with its policing conventions of politeness, suggests that the epigraph taken from Bond's preface to *Lear* plays on a false distinction between manners and violence.

23. Cf. Thomas Knipp's article, "Kenya's Literary Ladies," in which he talks about the "triple nostalgia" involved in the reception of the film of *Out of Africa,* nostalgically recalling Karen Blixen nostalgically recalling a lifestyle in Kenya that was already anachronistic in her native Denmark. Abdulrazak Gurnah's article "Settler Writing in Kenya" is also apropos here; Gurnah suggests that both Blixen and Huxley propose Africa as "a site of authenticity outside the fragmented self. It suggests a lost self or essence of self, and a wholeness that cannot be retrieved with Western discourses of modernity. Gurnah's fictional work, notably his 1994 novel *Paradise,* writes Africa in very different ways than those used by Blixen or Conrad.

24. Blixen understood "Isak" as meaning "one who laughs."

25. Conrad's famous opening with the Thames at London being declared "one of the dark places of the earth" is an obvious case in point. It is notable that even Ngugi—generally less of a liberal humanist than Achebe—displays more caution in dealing with Conrad, finding his *"ambivalence* towards imperialism" the limiting factor that "could never let him go beyond the balancing acts of liberal humanism" (Ngugi, *Decolonising the Mind* 76).

26. The epigraph for section 3 of *Out of Africa,* "Visitors to the Farm," is "post res perditas."

27. See, e.g., Ross C. Murfin's 1989 edition of *Heart of Darkness* for the Case Studies in Contemporary Criticism series (Boston: Bedford, 1989). The edition comes closest to a postcolonial critique in the essay by Brook Thomas ("Preserving and Keeping Order by Killing Time in *Heart of Darkness*") used as an example of New Historicist criticism.

28. South African activist-poet Jeremy Cronin uses this pun in his poem "Even the Dead" critiquing the complacent amnesia that has allowed the continuation of ruling-class attitudes in postapartheid South Africa—"Perhaps the aesthetic should be defined in opposition to anaesthetic. // Art is the struggle to stay awake."

29. Patrick Brantlinger in *Rule of Darkness* estimates the number of people "up-

rooted, tortured, and murdered through the forced labor system" as 6 million (257). More recently, Adam Hochschild in *King Leopold's Ghost* puts the figure at 10 million.

30. The publishing history of *Trooper Peter Halket of Mashonaland* is markedly different from *Heart of Darkness*. After wide circulation when the book was first published in 1897 (by Unwin in London, Tauchnitz in Leipzig, and Roberts Brothers in Boston), it reappeared twice from Unwin in 1899 and 1905, twice more in 1926 (in Adelphi Library and Cabinet Library editions), before vanishing for thirty years. In 1959, shortly after the centenary of Schreiner's birth, Benn (London) put out an edition with a foreword from the prominent anti-apartheid priest Bishop Trevor Huddleston. The book has since reappeared twice from South African publisher Ad. Donker, once with an introduction by Marion Friedmann (1974), and most recently with an introduction by Sally-Ann Murray (1992). After 1897, the photograph used as frontispiece appeared only in the two Ad. Donker editions. Very few scholars have devoted full-length articles to the book. In prioritizing *Trooper Peter Halket* over *The Story of an African Farm* by giving the former two chapters and the latter none in *Rereading the Imperial Romance,* Laura Chrisman specifically aimed to counter the tendency in the Euro-American academy to privilege books which can be understood at a level of "colonial generality" at the expense of regionally and historically specific texts which insist on the "stubbornly local" (2).

31. Most obviously because of Conrad's marginal status as a Polish-born émigré for whom English—which he spoke with a marked "foreign" accent—was a third language.

32. This feature which I describe as creating a "comfort zone" for Conrad's readership, Achebe describes as a "*cordon sanitaire* between himself [Conrad] and the moral and psychological *malaise* of his narrator" (*Hopes and Impediments* 10).

33. In fact, if this statement is true for first-time readers, it must also be true for all readers. In stressing first-time readers I am trying to establish the point that Conrad has established a kind of "comfort zone" which allows readers to feel a considerable distance between themselves and the experience described (or suggested!) by the text.

34. The question of the "puerility of evil" (Brantlinger) in British imperialism is one I return to in chapter 8. Martin Green's work on the status of boys' adventure stories in late Victorian England as "primers of Empire" is relevant here (see, e.g., "Adventurers Stake Their Claim: The Adventure Tale's Bid for Status, 1876–1914"). Green's argument that the overt imperialism of boys' adventure stories pushes them out of the canon represents the obverse of my own argument that *Trooper Peter* is disqualified on account of the overtness of its anti-imperialism.

35. At its most explicit, this exoneration of the contemporary British reader occurs when Conrad has Marlow contrast the specifically British imperialism with other European varieties. The "vast amount of red" on the map of Africa is "good to see at any time, because one knows that some real work is done in there" (36).

36. Cf. Chrisman, *Rereading the Imperial Romance:* "No reader can take refuge

in the notion that there is a legitimate narrative of settler colonialism and liberal free trade capitalism against which Rhodes's company and murderous expansionism can be judged as mere parasitic aberrations. . . . The spectacular pathology of a Kurtz . . . allows readers a more comfortable self-location" (141).

37. Houghton, in his compendious book *The Victorian Frame of Mind*, opens his section on "Work" thus: "Except for 'God,' the most popular word in the Victorian vocabulary must have been 'work'" and "it . . . became an end in itself, a virtue in its own right" (242–43). The attitude reveals itself in all sorts of ways. The proverb "The devil finds work for idle hands" more explicitly than anything else suggests that those who are already working are on the side of the angels. Furthermore, those who *put* others to work, especially those previously idle, must likewise be on the side of the angels. The implications of this attitude for the practice of imperialism are enormous. J. M. Coetzee devotes a chapter to the issue in *White Writing*. For an example from the texts immediately under discussion, we might turn to the brief anecdote "Fellow-Travellers" told by Karen Blixen in *Out of Africa*. Unwittingly having asked a Belgian fellow passenger whether he has worked much in his life (she used the French *travailler* for English *travel*), Blixen has to listen not only to the Belgian's tales of his own labor but also of the grand purpose of it all: "Notre mission. Notre grand mission dans le Congo" (262). In discussion of education for Africans, the man is convinced that there is only one thing that Europeans need to teach Africans: "Il faut enseigner aux nègres à être honnêtes à travailler. Rien de plus" (262). The man's combination of attitudes toward "work," "mission," and "education" reveals as tellingly as Louis Althusser could have dreamed of the operation of church and school as ideological state apparatuses.

38. Cf. Houghton: "A religion of work, with or without a supernatural context, came to be, in fact, the actual faith of many Victorians: it could resolve both intellectual perplexity and psychological depression" (251). Or cf. Brook Thomas: "It is work, then, that constructs the lie of civilization that hides humanity, necessarily, from the prehistoric truth about itself" (253).

39. Writing this, I'm reminded of all the racist language about work that I grew up with. In Afrikaans, a physical task such as cleaning or digging might be considered demeaning and hence termed "kaffirwerk," in a perfect colloquial discursive analogue to the legal discourse of actual job reservation. Similarly, to "work like a black" meant to work incredibly hard physically, but, weirdly, such work was completely undervalued because it didn't require *mental* activity. I say "weirdly" because the whole anti-intellectual, rugger-bugger, macho construction of white South African masculinity appeared to endorse Victorian attitudes toward physical work as an inherently good thing. This irrational, self-contradicting set of attitudes toward work and race has an interesting bearing on this chapter's subsequent discussion of the irrationality of the application of terror in the imposition of an economic order. Even in the new South Africa, the officialese of immigration forms draws a distinction between "work" and "business."

40. Schreiner's comment puts one in mind of Sartre's doubts as to whether Picasso's *Guernica* had won any support for the Spanish cause (cited in Adorno 93).

41. Taussig takes the phrasing from Frederick Karl's biography *Joseph Conrad: The Three Lives.*

42. And, one might add, following Jameson, popular, too.

43. Consider, for example, the attack on the steamer shortly before it reaches Kurtz's Inner Station. Conrad brilliantly catches Marlow's and the "pilgrims'" bewilderment at the attack by describing the arrows as "sticks, little sticks . . . flying about," and concentrating on Marlow's need to steer the boat. The smoke from the pilgrims' Winchesters therefore causes Marlow a practical problem—how to see to steer—and ignores the materiality of African casualties.

44. See, e.g., First and Scott, who quote a good six pages' worth from the original (*Trooper Peter* 33–39; First and Scott 226–28) with a lengthy footnote devoted to the frontispiece (229); or Brantlinger, who, referring to "Schreiner's fictional diatribe against Cecil Rhodes" ("Victorians and Africans" 189), includes the photograph and comments on it as "unfortunately a summary of much of the history of Southern Africa" (189). Neither text offers much else on *Trooper Peter Halket,* as if indeed the initial text and photograph did say all that needed saying. Laura Chrisman discusses Schreiner's bolstering of fictional with documentary truth-claims in *Rereading the Imperial Romance* (155–57).

45. In fact, Keppel-Jones's claim that spies (however that term might be defined) "were not executed out of hand" is belied by his own admission, within a paragraph, that "justice may often have miscarried," by his recognition that law is not the same as justice, and by his own accounts of the frequent absence of official control on "unofficial" executions and atrocities in the field. Eyewitness accounts, although full of the horror of African attacks on whites, also tell of the ferocity and cruelty of the white fighters. Selous, in true *Heart of Darkness* fashion, urged his readers to look sympathetically on his tales of battles in which "no quarter was either given or asked for," commenting that "it is possible for a man to live a long life without ever becoming aware that below the surface conventionality there exists in him an ineradicable leaven of innate ferocity" (cited in Taylor 240).

46. On the question of Rhodesian belief/admission, Schreiner wrote to Betty Molteno in 1897 that her husband had received a letter from "a leading man at Bulawayo in the employ of the Chartered Company on some business. At the end of his letter he sent his kind regards to me and said, 'Tell Mrs Schreiner *Peter Halket is quite true,* but she would find it very hard to get anyone here to stand to it.' He is a hard man of the world and not at all a friend of the native" (Rive 322; original emphasis).

47. Personal anecdotes may not count for much, but I cannot imagine that Monsman's experience has been that much more sheltered than mine from the casual brutishness and brutality of sexist and racist talk and behavior. And even from my very bourgeois experience I can recall a British squaddie telling me with great

glee of the delights of a posting to Mombasa, where you could get a "whore" to be your "wife" for the duration of your posting. For a few shillings a week, he claimed, squaddies bought women who gratefully provided them with sex and housework. In Tanzania I came across a number of cases where white male ex-pats were actually married (in at least one case bigamously) to Tanzanian women without ever having any intention of taking their wives "home" with them to Europe. Muriel Spark uses such a situation as chief plot-device in her short story "Portobello Road." During my schoolboy years in South Africa (and remember Peter Halket is only nineteen), macho conversations about the relative merits and "efficiency" of the South African and Rhodesian armies were commonplace among my peers for whom conscription loomed but for whom the idea of conscientious objection was scarcely thinkable. As far as language use is concerned, the phrase "to swear like a trooper" would suggest that Schreiner has considerably euphemized Peter's language.

48. For a graphic account of the economic imbalance between European and American universities on the one hand and African universities, see Moore, "Where Are All the African and Caribbean *Critics?* The MLA, Honorary Members, and Honorary Fellows," in which Moore notes that even the wealthiest African university he is aware of (the University of Cape Town) had an annual budget in 1998 of "under 200 million dollars—that is, around that of a typical middle-ranking U.S. university, of which several hundred exist" (120). As Moore demonstrates by analyzing the MLA's list of honorary members and honorary fellows, the effect of that imbalance on the production, circulation, evaluation, and valorization of knowledge is profound.

49. The body of literature on this topic is large and growing larger. For a contextualized discussion and bibliography, see the introduction to Chrisman's *Rereading the Imperial Romance*, esp. 21–22.

Chapter 8. Graves with a View: Atavism and the European History of Africa

1. This comment is perhaps interesting in light of my focus on women writers, as feminists have been suspicious of the theoretical notion of the death of the subject at the very moment when a feminist subject appeared to be claiming her rights of speech and agency. While Fukuyama's politics may not coincide with Foucault's in many other respects, they do both seem to limit the theoretical impact available to previously marginalized Others. Both Hegel's and Fukuyama's positions strike me as examples of the "solipsistic absurdity" of mainstream Western academic historiography as critiqued by Hammond and Jablow in *The Africa That Never Was*.

2. See Crais, "The Vacant Land: The Mythology of British Expansion in the Eastern Cape, South Africa"; Pratt, *Imperial Eyes* 43–67.

3. First and Scott point to the fact that while Cronwright-Schreiner may have ignored or been high-handed with regard to some of the directives of Olive's will, he was assiduous in carrying out her wishes regarding the burial (330–32). The sugges-

tion that he wrote himself into history with her also arises in the phrase used by some of Olive's close women friends regarding his "autobiography of his wife" (20).

4. The process of establishing a vantage point and then claiming the land below it by writing is compressed in the work of the Victorian traveler-writers working in the "monarch-of-all-I-survey" mode identified by Mary Louise Pratt. She has pointed out how the Victorians opted for "a brand of verbal painting whose highest calling was to produce for the home audience the peak moments at which geographical 'discoveries' were 'won' for England" (201). Pratt also plays on the multiple associations of the "prospect" through that word's cognate in the verb "to prospect" (61). She shows how John Barrow's description of the Cape presents landscape from an aesthetic prospect in such a way as to stress its mineral prospects and its future prospects as colonizable. See also chapter 4.

5. See, e.g., Terence Ranger's article "'Great Spaces Washed with Sun': The Matopos and Uluru Compared" in which he argues that the sacred places of the Matopos not only control the environment but "propagate a linear version of a long historical past. This narrates a sequence of the rise and fall of successive regimes in southwestern Zimbabwe, reaching back to the seventeenth century. It constitutes an elaborate statement of how rulers legitimate themselves by 'making peace' with the land—and how they lose legitimation through arrogance and greed" (160). See also chapter 4 for comments on Plaatje's use of Mzilikazi both as invader of African space and victim of European invasion.

6. W. T. Stead is an interesting intermediary here, as he was both a close ally of Schreiner on such issues as prostitution and the Anglo-Boer War and yet such a close friend and admirer of Rhodes that he was at one point chosen by Rhodes as an executor of his will. Stead's fame as pioneering editor (of the *Pall Mall Gazette* and the *Review of Reviews*) and social campaigner is matched by the notoriety of his belief in the spirit world. Closely associated with various occultist movements around the turn of the century, Stead anticipated the tabloid journalism of our own day by publishing interviews with the dead (see Brantlinger 247–49). For Stead's opposition to the Anglo-Boer War, see Krebs 80–108.

7. See also Chrisman's careful rereading of the imperial romance in Rider Haggard's works, in which she argues that Haggard uses fantasies of Britishness and Africanness, particularly Zulus, and "British *as* Zulus" (119), in order to avoid the instrumentality of British economic nostrums. Particularly relevant to this section, and my claims in chapters 5 and 6 that European inventions of Africa come at the expense of Africans, is Chrisman's comment that in *King Solomon's Mines* "the pursuit of material acquisition by British imperialists does . . . lead to the death of black Africans. . . . white gain is equated with black death" (54).

8. See esp. the section entitled "Hard Times" (275–86).

9. See the last two chapters of Williams, *The Country and the City* 278–306.

10. See Thurman, *Isak Dinesen* 233–34, 246; Pelensky, *Isak Dinesen* 117–18, 127; Trzebinski, *Silence Will Speak* 434–35.

11. For the cause of the crash, see Trzebinski 446. For the idea of its being fated, see also Trzebinski 440–41, where she quotes Beryl Markham's claim that "both Arap Ruta, her personal servant, and Tom Campbell Black, her flying instructor, had strange premonitions" (440), and 443. Blixen records, "This was the only time that I asked Denys to take me with him on his aeroplane that he would not do it" (297). If Finch Hatton really did know, as Yeats imagines Major Robert Gregory knowing, that he would "Meet [his] fate / Somewhere among the clouds above" (Yeats 152), then one has to ask about the "fate" of Kamau, "his own boy," who also died in the crash. According to Blixen, he "was terrified of flying" (298), anyway; his silence is perhaps the most eloquent example of the violence of the European versions of Africa mentioned in this chapter.

12. In light of my subsequent discussion of specifically war-related elegies, it is also interesting to speculate whether or not Blixen had Horace and/or Wilfred Owen in mind when she wrote, "It was fit and decorous."

13. Cf. Gurnah, "Settler Writing in Kenya": "The ambivalence in settler writing derives from . . . two sources, the tribal imperatives of the imperialist narrative and the yearning for a wholesome self—which, paradoxically, depends on turning the European into the native" (277).

14. Cf. Chrisman on the "gentlemen" heroes of Haggard's fiction who seem to be throwbacks to preindustrial English (or Zulu) models of warrior heroism in which gentlemen are ultimately defined as "those who fight bravely and kill heroically for a just cause" (52).

15. In fact, Blixen's comment about the "Natives'" affection for Finch Hatton should be modified by the fact that their nickname for him meant "To tread upon" (see Pelensky, *Isak Dinesen* 102, Thurman, *Isak Dinesen* 127, Trzebinski, *Silence Will Speak* 210).

16. See Mangan, *The Cultural Bond,* esp. the essay by Anthony Kirk-Greene (179–201).

17. See E. M. Forster's "Notes on the English Character" in *Abinger Harvest:* "It is not that the Englishman can't feel—it is that he is afraid to feel. He has been taught at his public school that feeling is bad form" (5). Judith Thurman describes Finch Hatton as having "an almost morbid aversion to emotional demands" (*Isak Dinesen* 246).

18. Schreiner's representation of Trooper Peter Halket may be a case in point. Further devious links between Finch Hatton, Peter Halket, and Tom Brown might be made via the hunter Frederick Selous (see also chapter 5). Selous was educated at Rugby in the 1860s and 1870s, but was notorious, like Tom Brown, for his bird-nesting activities, a penchant for which he shared with Schreiner's fictional Peter. Selous considered writing an updated version of Thomas Hughes's novel, and drafted part of a manuscript whose provisional title, *Fred LeRoux's Schooldays,* suggests that the novel would have been highly autobiographical.

19. In *The Darkened Room: Women, Power, and Spiritualism in Late Victorian England,* Alex Owen points out the various connections between spiritualism and

dissenting religion, socialism, and abolitionism; he contends that "women's rights formed an integral, although not dominant part of the progressive spiritualist programme" (27), and that "Victorian mediumship was a form of protest and dissent which predated 'political' awareness" (240). Similarly, Ann Braude in *Radical Spirits: Spiritualism and Women's Rights in Nineteenth-Century America* draws attention to "spiritualism's association with abolition" (29) and contends that "Spiritualism held two attractions that proved irresistible to thousands of Americans: rebellion against death and rebellion against authority" (30). (I am grateful to Professor Dan Cottom for this insight.) By contrast, Paul Carter has a rather different take on the connection between occultism and colonialism, seeing in the various messages from "beyond" a "shadow narrative of domestic spaces where the colonized world was being dreamed, theorized, modelled and re-enacted" ("Turning the Tables" 32).

20. See also Crais, *White Supremacy and Black Resistance,* esp. chapter 10, "Empire and the Ancestors." Crais points out that the symbolism of the prophetesses' dreams "stressed, if only implicitly, the pre-colonial order and the return to the beginning of time," but goes on to say that "the prophecies seamlessly incorporated symbols of Christian eschatology" and that incorporation makes the movement "a case in which the essentially conservative teachings of evangelical mission Christianity were subverted into an ideology of resistance" (207). Peires stresses that it is a misconception to see the Cattle Killing as a "pagan reaction" (as colonialist historians had tended to do); instead, the movement was, according to Peires, "one which combined Christian and pre-Christian elements fused under the heroic leadership of the expected redeemer, the son of Sifubasibanzi, the Broad-Chested One" (*The Dead Will Arise* 123). Zakes Mda's Commonwealth Writers Prize–winning novel, *Heart of Redness,* highlights these complications not just by splitting the Xhosa into Red and School camps (Believers and Unbelievers) but also by including in the nineteenth-century Believers' camp the significant presence of Khoikhoi belief and in the contemporary Believers' camp the white man John Dalton. With its concern with theme park–style conservation, *Heart of Redness* is also relevant to my discussion in chapter 5.

21. Ironically, the epigraphs that Gordimer reuses describing the Zulu beliefs are from the nineteenth-century missionary Henry Callaway's 1868 book *The Religious System of the Amazulu.*

22. "Memory is a weapon" comes from Don Mattera's autobiographical account of Sophiatown in the 1950s in which he recalls a period of heterogeneity and uninhibited cultural expression (151). While this book has concentrated on rural rather than urban landscape, it seems pertinent to point out that Mattera's romanticization of Sophiatown and of his own gangsterism evinces another kind of nostalgia, another memorial reconstruction of relative innocence in a less viciously complicated but no less masculinist age.

23. Etienne van Heerden's story is itself resurrected in slightly different form in his novel *Kikuyu.*

24. I mention Sachs in part because of his violent disarming and his disarming of violence, and in part because in *The Soft Vengeance of a Freedom Fighter* one of the key ancestral ghosts he brings back is Ruth First: she who most impressively resurrected the rebel Olive Schreiner, but who paid for her own rebellion against apartheid with her own life, assassinated in a letter-bomb attack.

25. See, e.g., Sachs's caution in *Soft Vengeance* that a Bill of Rights might "simply be a means of entrenching white privilege" (165). Critics of South Africa's neoliberal economics such as Patrick Bond have repeatedly made similar points; I address these contemporary issues more fully in "'This Land South Africa': Rewriting Time and Space in Postapartheid Poetry and Property."

Works Cited

Achebe, Chinua. *Anthills of the Savannah.* New York: Doubleday, 1988.

———. *Hopes and Impediments.* New York: Doubleday, 1989.

———. *Things Fall Apart.* New York: Doubleday, 1994.

Adler, Michelle. "'Skirting the Edges of Civilization': Two Victorian Women Travellers and 'Colonial Spaces' in South Africa." *Text, Theory, Space: Land, Literature, and History in South Africa and Australia.* Ed. Kate Darian-Smith, Liz Gunner, and Sarah Nuttall. London: Routledge, 1996. 83–98.

Adorno, Theodor. *Aesthetics and Politics.* London: New Left Books, 1977.

Ahmad, Aijaz. *In Theory: Classes, Nations, Literatures.* London: Verso, 1992.

———. "Jameson's Rhetoric of Otherness and the 'National Allegory.'" *Social Text* 17 (Fall 1987): 3–25.

Aiken, Susan Hardy. "Consuming Isak Dinesen." *Isak Dinesen and Narrativity: Reassessments for the 1990s.* Ed. Gurli Woods. Ottawa: Carleton University Press, 1994. 3–24.

Alpers, Svetlana. "The Mapping Impulse in Dutch Art." *The Art of Describing: Dutch Art in the Seventeenth Century.* Chicago: University of Chicago Press, 1983.

Ambler, Charles H. *Kenyan Communities in the Age of Imperialism: The Central Region in the Late Nineteenth Century.* New Haven: Yale University Press, 1988.

Arkins, Brian. "The Role of Greek and Latin in Friel's Translations." *Colby Quarterly* 27 (1991): 202–9.

Barrell, John. *The Dark Side of the Landscape: The Rural Poor in English Painting, 1730–1840.* Cambridge: Cambridge University Press, 1980.

———. *The Idea of Landscape and the Sense of Place, 1730–1840: An Approach to the Poetry of John Clare.* Cambridge: Cambridge University Press, 1972.

Barthes, Roland. *Mythologies.* New York: Hill and Wang, 1994.

Baucom, Ian. *Out of Place: Englishness, Empire, and the Locations of Identity.* Princeton: Princeton University Press, 1999.

Beer, Gillian. "The Death of the Sun: Victorian Solar Physics and Solar Myth." *The Sun is God: Painting, Literature, and Mythology in the Nineteenth Century.* Ed. B. Bullen. Oxford: Clarendon, 1989.

Belich, James. *The New Zealand Wars and the Victorian Interpretation of Racial Conflict.* Auckland: Penguin, 1988.

Belsey, Catherine. *Critical Practice.* London: Routledge, 1992.

Benjamin, Walter. *Illuminations.* New York: Schocken, 1969.

Beresford, David. "Afrikaans Loses Battle for Airtime on South African TV." *Guardian Weekly,* December 10, 1995, 7.

Berkman, Joyce Avrech. *The Healing Imagination of Olive Schreiner: Beyond South African Colonialism.* Amherst: University of Massachusetts Press, 1989.

Berlinerblau, Jacques. *Heresy in the University: The Black Athena Controversy and the Responsibilities of American Intellectuals.* New Brunswick, NJ: Rutgers University Press, 1999.

Berman, Esme. *Art and Artists of South Africa: An Illustrated Biographical Dictionary and Historical Survey of Painters and Graphic Artists since 1875.* Cape Town and Rotterdam: A. A. Balkema, 1974.

Bermingham, Ann. *Landscape and Ideology.* Berkeley: University of California Press, 1986.

Bernal, Martin. *Black Athena: The Afroasiatic Roots of Classical Civilization.* Vol. 1, *The Fabrication of Ancient Greece, 1785–1985.* New Brunswick: Rutgers University Press, 1987.

Bertelsen, Eve. "Ads and Amnesia: Black Advertising in the New South Africa." *Negotiating the Past: The Making of Memory in South Africa.* Ed. Sarah Nuttall and Carli Coetzee. Cape Town: Oxford University Press, 1998. 221–41.

Bhabha, Homi. Conference Presentation. *Critical Fictions: The Politics of Imaginative Writing.* Ed. Philomena Mariani. Seattle: Bay Press, 1991. 62–65.

———. *The Location of Culture.* London: Routledge, 1994.

———. "The World and the Home." *Social Text* 31/32 (1992): 141–53.

———, ed. *Nation and Narration.* London: Routledge, 1990.

Bindman, David, ed. *The Thames and Hudson Encyclopaedia of British Art.* London: Thames and Hudson, 1985.

Bjorhovde, Gerd. *Rebellious Structures.* Oslo: Norwegian University Press, 1987.

Blake, Susan L. "A Woman's Trek: What Difference Does Gender Make?" *Western Women and Imperialism: Complicity and Resistance.* Ed. Nupur Chaudhuri and Margaret Strobel. Bloomington: Indiana University Press, 1992. 21–33.

Blixen, Karen. *Letters from Africa, 1914–1931.* London: Picador, 1983.

———. *On Modern Marriage.* 1977. New York: St. Martin's, 1986.

———. *Out of Africa.* 1937. Harmondsworth: Penguin, 1984.

———. *Seven Gothic Tales.* London: Putnam, 1934.

———. *Shadows on the Grass.* New York: Random House, 1961.

———. *Winter's Tales.* 1942. New York: Vintage, 1993.

Bloom, Harold, and Lionel Trilling, eds. *Victorian Prose and Poetry.* New York: Oxford University Press, 1973.

Bond, Edward. *Plays: Two.* London: Methuen, 1978.

Bond, Patrick. *Elite Transition: From Apartheid to Neoliberalism in South Africa.* London: Pluto, 2000.

Bourdieu, Pierre. "How Can One Be a Sports Fan?" *The Cultural Studies Reader.* Ed. Simon During. London: Routledge, 1993. 339–56.

———. *Language and Symbolic Power.* Cambridge: Harvard University Press, 1991.

Brantlinger, Patrick. *Rule of Darkness.* Ithaca, N.Y.: Cornell University Press, 1988.

———. "Victorians and Africans: A Genealogy of the Myth of the Dark Continent." *"Race," Writing, and Difference.* Ed. Henry Louis Gates Jr. Chicago: University of Chicago Press, 1986. 185–222.

Braude, Ann. *Radical Spirits: Spiritualism and Women's Rights in Nineteenth-Century America.* Boston: Beacon, 1989.

Brittain, Vera. *Testament of Youth: An Autobiographical Study of the Years 1910–1925.* Harmondsworth: Penguin, 1989.

Brontë, Emily. *Wuthering Heights.* Harmondsworth: Penguin, 1978.

Bryer, Lynne. "Through a Glass Quietly." *Illuminations* 9 (1990): 1.

Bundy, Colin. *The Rise and Fall of the South African Peasantry.* Berkeley: University of California Press, 1979.

Bunn, David, and Jane Taylor, eds. *From South Africa: New Writing, Photographs, and Art.* Evanston, Ill.: Northwestern University Press, 1987.

Burdett, Carolyn. *Olive Schreiner and the Progress of Feminism: Evolution, Gender, Empire.* Basingstoke: Palgrave, 2001.

Cain, P. J., and A. G. Hopkins. *British Imperialism: Crisis and Deconstruction, 1914–1990.* London: Longman, 1993.

Callaway, Henry. *The Religious System of the Amazulu.* Cape Town: Struick, 1970.

Cameron, Kenneth. *Africa on Film: Beyond Black and White.* New York: Continuum, 1994.

Cantalupo, Charles, ed. *Ngugi wa Thiong'o: Texts and Contexts.* Trenton, N.J.: Africa World Press, 1995.

Carby, Hazel. "'On the Threshold of Woman's Era': Lynching, Empire, and Sexuality in Black Feminist Theory." *"Race," Writing, and Difference.* Ed. Henry Louis Gates Jr. Chicago: University of Chicago Press, 1986. 301–16.

Carruthers, Jane. "National Parks and Game Reserves, the Transvaal and Natal: Protected for the People or against the People?" South African Historical Society 16th Biennial Conference: "Land, Violence, and Social Problems in the History of Southern Africa." University of Pretoria, July 6–9, 1997.

Carter, Paul. "Turning the Tables, or Grounding Post-Colonialism." *Text, Theory, Space: Land, Literature, and History in South Africa and Australia.* Ed. Kate Darian-Smith, Liz Gunner, and Sarah Nuttall. London: Routledge, 1996. 23–36.

Cederborg, Else. Introduction. *On Modern Marriage.* By Karen Blixen. 1977. New York: St. Martin's, 1986. 1–31.

Célestin, Roger. *From Cannibals to Radicals: Figures and Limits of Exoticism.* Minneapolis: University of Minnesota Press, 1996.

Chapman, Michael, Colin Gardner, and Es'kia Mphahlele, eds. *Perspectives on South African English Literature*. Parklands: Donker, 1992.

Chaudhuri, Nupur, and Margaret Strobel, eds. *Western Women and Imperialism: Complicity and Resistance*. Bloomington: Indiana University Press, 1992.

Chodorow, Nancy. *The Reproduction of Mothering: Psychoanalysis and the Sociology of Gender*. Los Angeles: University of California Press, 1978.

Chrisman, Laura. *Rereading the Imperial Romance: British Imperialism and South African Resistance in Haggard, Schreiner, and Plaatje*. Oxford: Oxford University Press, 2000.

Clayton, Cherry, ed. *Olive Schreiner*. Johannesburg: McGraw-Hill, 1983.

Clifford, James. *The Predicament of Culture*. Cambridge: Harvard University Press, 1988.

Coetzee, J. M. *White Writing: On the Culture of Letters in South Africa*. New Haven: Yale University Press, 1988.

Comaroff, Jean, and John Comaroff. *Of Revelation and Revolution: Christianity, Colonialism, and Consciousness in South Africa*. Vol. 1. Chicago: University of Chicago Press, 1991.

Conrad, Joseph. *Heart of Darkness*. Ed. Robert Kimbrough. 3rd ed. New York: Norton, 1988.

Cooper, Ann Laura, and Frederick Stoler, eds. *Tensions of Empire: Colonial Cultures in a Bourgeois World*. Berkeley: University of California Press, 1997.

Cosslett, Tess. *Woman to Woman: Female Friendship in Victorian Fiction*. Atlantic Highlands, N.J.: Humanities Press International, 1988.

Coundouriotis, Eleni. *Claiming History: Colonialism, Ethnography, and the Novel*. New York: Columbia, 1999.

Crais, Clifton. "The Vacant Land: The Mythology of British Expansion in the Eastern Cape, South Africa." *Journal of Social History* 25.2 (1991): 255–75.

———. *White Supremacy and Black Resistance in Pre-industrial South Africa: The Making of the Colonial Order in the Eastern Cape, 1770–1865*. Cambridge: Cambridge University Press, 1992.

Cronin, Jeremy. "Even the Dead." *New Coin* 32.2 (December 1996): 5–11.

———. *Inside*. Johannesburg: Ravan Press, 1983.

Cronwright-Schreiner, S.C. *The Life of Olive Schreiner*. Boston: Little, Brown, 1924.

———. *The Re-interment on Buffelskop*. Ed. Guy Butler with N.W. Visser. Grahamstown, South Africa: Institute for the Study of English in Africa, Rhodes University, 1983.

Cunningham, Gail. *The New Woman and the Victorian Novel*. New York: Barnes and Noble, 1978.

Curtin, Philip. *The Image of Africa: British Ideas and Action, 1780–1850*. Madison: University of Wisconsin Press, 1964.

Dangarembga, Tsitsi. *Nervous Conditions*. Seattle: Seal Press, 1988.

Darian-Smith, Kate, Liz Gunner, and Sarah Nuttall, eds. *Text, Theory, Space: Land, Literature, and History in South Africa and Australia*. London: Routledge, 1996.

Davidson, Basil. *The Black Man's Burden: Africa and the Curse of the Nation-State.* New York: Random House, 1992.

Davin, Anna. "Imperialism and Motherhood." *Tensions of Empire: Colonial Cultures in a Bourgeois World.* Ed. Ann Laura Cooper and Frederick Stoler. Berkeley: University of California Press, 1997. 87–151.

de Kock, Leon. "South Africa in the Global Imaginary: An Introduction." *Poetics Today* 22.2 (Summer 2001): 263–98.

de Kok, Ingrid. *Familiar Ground.* Johannesburg: Ravan Press, 1988.

———. *Terrestrial Things.* Roggebaai and Plumstead [Cape Town]: Kwela/Snailpress, 2002.

de Kok, Ingrid, and Karen Press, eds. *Spring Is Rebellious: Arguments about Cultural Freedom by Albie Sachs and Respondents.* Cape Town: Buchu Books, 1990.

Derrida, Jacques. *Limited, Inc.* Evanston: Northwestern University Press, 1988.

———. *Of Grammatology.* Baltimore: Johns Hopkins University Press, 1976.

———. "Racism's Last Word." *"Race," Writing, and Difference.* Ed. Henry Louis Gates Jr. Chicago: University of Chicago Press, 1986. 329–38.

Donelson, Linda. "Karen Blixen." http://www.karenblixen.com.

Dumett, Raymond E., ed. *Gentlemanly Capitalism and British Imperialism: The New Debate on Empire.* Afterword by P. J. Cain and A. G. Hopkins. London: Longman, 1999.

Du Plessis, Rachel Blau. *Writing beyond the Ending: Narrative Strategies of Twentieth-Century Women Writers.* Bloomington: Indiana University Press, 1985.

During, Simon, ed. *The Cultural Studies Reader.* London and New York: Routledge, 1993.

Engle, Lars. "The Political Uncanny: The Novels of Nadine Gordimer." *Yale Journal of Criticism* 2.2 (1989): 101-27.

Everett, Nigel. *The Tory View of Landscape.* New Haven: Yale University Press, 1994.

Fabian, Johannes. *Remembering the Present: Painting and Popular History in Zaire.* Berkeley: University of California Press, 1996.

———. *Time and the Other: How Anthropology Makes Its Object.* New York: Columbia University Press, 1983.

Fanon, Frantz. *Black Skin, White Masks.* New York: Grove Press, 1967.

Felski, Rita. *The Gender of Modernity.* Cambridge: Harvard University Press, 1995.

Fernando, Lloyd. *"New Women" in the Late Victorian Novel.* University Park: Pennsylvania State University Press, 1977.

First, Ruth, and Ann Scott. *Olive Schreiner.* New Brunswick: Rutgers University Press, 1990.

Fishburn, Katherine. "The Manichean Allegories of Doris Lessing's *The Grass Is Singing.*" *Research in African Literatures* 25.4 (Winter 1994): 1–15.

Forster, E. M. *A Passage to India.* Harmondsworth: Penguin, 1980.

———. *Abinger Harvest.* New York: Harcourt, 1964.

Fransen, Hans. *Three Centuries of South African Art: Fine Art, Architecture, Applied Arts.* Johannesburg: Donker, 1982.

Fukuyama, Francis. *The End of History and the Last Man.* New York: Free Press, 1992.

Fuss, Diana. *Essentially Speaking: Feminism, Nature, and Difference.* New York: Routledge, 1989.

Gagiano, Annie. "Blixen, Ngugi: Recounting Kenya." *Ngugi wa Thiong'o: Texts and Contexts.* Ed. Charles Cantalupo. Trenton, N.J.: Africa World Press, 1995. 95–110.

Gagnier, Regenia. *Subjectivities: A History of Self-Representation in Britain, 1832–1920.* New York: Oxford University Press, 1991.

Gallmann, Kuki. *I Dreamed of Africa.* London: Penguin, 1991.

Gates, Henry Louis, Jr. ed. *"Race," Writing, and Difference.* Chicago: University of Chicago Press, 1986.

Gikandi, Simon. *Maps of Englishness: Writing Identity in the Culture of Colonialism.* New York: Columbia University Press, 1996.

Gilbert, Sandra M., and Susan Gubar. *The Madwoman in the Attic: The Woman Writer and the Nineteenth-Century Literary Imagination.* New Haven: Yale University Press, 1979.

Gilman, Sander L. "Black Bodies, White Bodies: Toward an Iconography of Female Sexuality in Late Nineteenth-Century Art, Medicine, and Literature." *"Race," Writing, and Difference.* Ed. Henry Louis Gates Jr. Chicago: University of Chicago Press, 1986. 223–61.

Gorak, Irene. "Olive Schreiner's Colonial Allegory: *The Story of an African Farm.*" *ARIEL* 23.4 (October 1992): 53–74.

Gordimer, Nadine. *Burger's Daughter.* New York: Viking, 1979.

———. *The Conservationist.* London: Cape, 1974.

———. *Crimes of Conscience.* London: Heinemann, 1991.

———. *The Essential Gesture: Writing, Politics, and Places.* New York: Farrar, Straus and Giroux, 1990.

———. *July's People.* Harmondsworth: Penguin, 1982.

———. *My Son's Story.* New York: Farrar, Straus and Giroux, 1990.

———. *None to Accompany Me.* New York: Farrar, Straus and Giroux, 1994.

———. "The Prison-House of Colonialism." *Olive Schreiner.* Ed. Cherry Clayton. Johannesburg: McGraw-Hill, 1983. 95–98.

———. *A Sport of Nature.* New York: Knopf, 1987.

———. *Writing and Being.* Cambridge: Harvard University Press, 1995.

Gray, Stephen. "The Trooper at the Hanging Tree." *Olive Schreiner.* Ed. Cherry Clayton. Johannesburg: McGraw-Hill, 1983. 198–207.

Green, Martin. "Adventurers Stake Their Claim: The Adventure Tale's Bid for Status, 1876–1914." *Decolonizing Tradition: New Views of Twentieth-Century "British" Literary Canons.* Ed. Karen Lawrence. Urbana: University of Illinois Press, 1992. 70–87.

Gurnah, Abdulrazak. *Paradise.* New York: New Press, 1994.

———. "Settler Writing in Kenya: 'Nomenclature Is an Uncertain Science in These Parts.'" *Modernism and Empire*. Ed. Howard J. Booth and Nigel Rigby. Manchester: Manchester University Press, 2000. 275–91.

Hall, Edith. "When Is a Myth not a Myth?: Bernal's 'Ancient Model.'" *Black Athena Revisited*. Ed. Mary Lefkowitz and Guy MacLean Rogers. Chapel Hill: University of North Carolina Press, 1996. 333–48.

Hammond, Dorothy, and Alta Jablow. *The Africa That Never Was: Four Centuries of British Writing about Africa*. Prospect Heights, Ill.: Waveland. 1992. (1970)

Hannah, Donald. "Art and Dream in 'The Dreaming Child' and 'The Dreamers.'" *Isak Dinesen: Critical Views*. Ed. Olga A. Pelensky. Athens: Ohio University Press, 1993. 54–63.

———. *"Isak Dinesen" and Karen Blixen: The Mask and the Reality*. New York: Random House, 1971.

Hansberry, William Leo. *Africa and Africans as Seen by Classical Writers*. Washington, D.C.: Howard University Press, 1981.

Harley, J. B. "Silences and Secrecy: The Hidden Agenda of Cartography in Early Modern Europe." *Imago Mundi* 40 (1988): 57–75.

Hay, Jean. "Historical Context." *Coming to Birth*. Ed. Marjorie Oludhe Macgoye. New York: Feminist Press, 2000.

Hegel, G. F. *Lectures on the Philosophy of History*. Atlantic Highlands, N.J.: Humanities Press, 1983.

Helgerson, Richard. "The Land Speaks: Cartography, Chorography, and Subversion in Renaissance England." *Representations* 16 (1986): 50–85.

Hemingway, Ernest. *The Short Stories of Ernest Hemingway*. New York: Scribner's, 1955.

Heywood, Christopher. "*The Story of an African Farm*: Society, Positivism, and Myth." *The Flawed Diamond: Essays on Olive Schreiner*. Ed. Itala Vivan. Sydney: Dangaroo Press, 1992. 26–39.

Hirsch, Marianne. "Maternity and Rememory: Toni Morrison's *Beloved*." *Representations of Motherhood*. Ed. Donna Bassin, Margaret Honey, and Meryle Mahrer Kaplan. New Haven: Yale University Press, 1994.

Hobman, Daisy Lucie. *Olive Schreiner: Her Friends and Times*. London: Watts, 1955.

Hobsbawm, Eric, ed. *The Invention of Tradition*. Cambridge: Cambridge University Press, 1986.

Hochschild, Adam. *King Leopold's Ghost: A Story of Greed, Terror, and Heroism in Colonial Africa*. Boston: Houghton Mifflin, 1998.

Horton, Susan. *Difficult Women, Artful Lives: Olive Schreiner and Isak Dinesen, in and out of Africa*. Baltimore: Johns Hopkins University Press, 1995.

Houghton, Walter E. *The Victorian Frame of Mind, 1830–1870*. New Haven: Yale University Press, 1978.

Huston, Nancy. "Novels and Navels." *Critical Inquiry* 21.4 (Summer 1995): 708–21.

Huxley, Elspeth. *The African Poison Murders*. New York: Penguin, 1989.

————. *Back Street New Worlds: A Look at Immigrants in Britain*. London: Chatto and Windus, 1964.

————. *Murder at Government House*. New York: Penguin, 1989.

Imbo, Samuel Oluoch. *An Introduction to African Philosophy*. Lanham, Md.: Rowman and Littlefield, 1998.

Irele, Abiola. "Dimensions of African Discourse." *Order and Partialities: Theory, Pedagogy, and the "Postcolonial."* Ed. Kostas Myrsiades and Jerry McGuire. Albany: State University of New York Press, 1995. 15–34.

Jacobson, Dan. Introduction. *The Story of an African Farm*. By Olive Schreiner. Harmondsworth: Penguin, 1982. 7–23.

Jameson, Fredric. *The Political Unconscious: Narrative as a Socially Symbolic Act*. Ithaca, N.Y.: Cornell University Press, 1981.

————. "Third-World Literature in the Era of Multinational Capitalism." *Social Text* 15 (Fall 1986): 65–88.

JanMohamed, Abdul A. "The Economy of Manichean Allegory: The Function of Racial Difference in Colonialist Literature." *"Race," Writing, and Difference*. Ed. Henry Louis Gates Jr. Chicago: University of Chicago Press, 1986. 78–106.

————. *Manichaean Aesthetics*. Amherst: University of Massachusetts Press, 1983.

Jones, Eldred. *Othello's Countrymen: The African in English Renaissance Drama*. Oxford: Oxford University Press, 1965.

Juhl, Marianne, and Bo Hakon Jorgensen. "Why Gothic Tales?" *Isak Dinesen: Critical Views*. Ed. Olga A. Pelensky. Athens: Ohio University Press, 1993. 88–99.

Kahane, Claire. *Passions of the Voice: Hysteria, Narrative, and the Figure of the Speaking Woman, 1850–1915*. Baltimore: Johns Hopkins University Press, 1995.

Kanogo, Tabitha. *Squatters and the Roots of Mau Mau, 1905–1963*. Nairobi: Heinemann, 1987.

Karl, Frederick. *Joseph Conrad: The Three Lives*. New York: Farrar, Straus and Giroux, 1979.

Keegan, Tim. *Facing the Storm: Portraits of Black Lives in Rural South Africa*. London: Zed Books, 1988.

————. *Rural Transformation in Industrializing South Africa*. Braamfontein: Ravan, 1986.

Kennedy, Dane. *Islands of White: Settler Society and Culture in Kenya and Southern Rhodesia, 1890–1939*. Durham: Duke University Press, 1987.

Kenyatta, Jomo. "Gentlemen of the Jungle." *Facing Mount Kenya*. New York: Random House, 1937. 47–51.

Keppel-Jones, Arthur. *Rhodes and Rhodesia: The White Conquest of Zimbabwe, 1884–1902*. Montreal: McGill-Queen's University Press, 1983.

Kimbrough, Robert, ed. *Heart of Darkness*, by Joseph Conrad. 3rd ed. New York: Norton, 1988.

Kirk-Greene, Anthony. "Badge of Office: Sport and His Excellency in the British Empire." *The Cultural Bond: Sport, Empire, Society*. Ed. J. A. Mangan. London: Frank Cass, 1992. 179–201.

Klausen, Susanne. Review of *Long Night's Journey into Day: South Africa's Search for Truth and Reconciliation*. <H-SAfrica@h-net.msu.edu> (January 2002).

Knipp, Thomas R. "Kenya's Literary Ladies and the Mythologizing of the White Highlands." *South Atlantic Review* 55.1 (January 1990): 1–16.

Knox, Alice. "No Place like Utopia: Cross-Racial Couples in Nadine Gordimer's Later Novels." *ARIEL* 27.1 (January 1996): 63–80.

Krebs, Paula. *Gender, Race, and the Writing of Empire: Public Discourse and the Boer War*. Cambridge: Cambridge University Press, 1999.

Krog, Antjie. *Country of My Skull: Guilt, Sorrow, and the Limits of Forgiveness in the New South Africa*. New York: Random House, 1998.

Kure-Jensen, Lise. "Isak Dinesen in English, Danish, and Translation: Are We Reading the Same Text?" *Isak Dinesen: Critical Views*. Ed. Olga A. Pelensky. Athens: Ohio University Press, 1993. 314–21.

Langbaum, Robert. "Autobiography and Myth in the African Memoirs." *Isak Dinesen: Critical Views*. Ed. Olga A. Pelensky. Athens: Ohio University Press, 1993. 38–50.

Lasson, Frans. "The Rain at Ngong: An Introduction to the Letters of Isak Dinesen (Karen Blixen)." *Letters from Africa, 1914–1931*. Ed. Karen Blixen. London: Picador, 1983. ix–xxvii.

Lawrence, Karen, ed. *Decolonizing Tradition: New Views of Twentieth-Century "British" Literary Canons*. Urbana: University of Illinois Press, 1992.

Lee, Judith. "The Mask of Form in *Out of Africa*." *Isak Dinesen: Critical Views*. Ed. Olga A. Pelensky. Athens: Ohio University Press, 1993. 266–82.

Lefkowitz, Mary. *Not Out of Africa: How Afrocentrism Became an Excuse to Teach Myth as History*. New York: Basic Books, 1996.

Lefkowitz, Mary, and Guy MacLean Rogers, eds. *Black Athena Revisited*. Chapel Hill: University of North Carolina Press, 1996.

Lessing, Doris. *The Grass Is Singing*. New York: Plume, 1978.

———. "In Defense of the Underground." *Extravagant Strangers: A Literature of Belonging*. Ed. Caryl Phillips. Vintage: New York, 1997.

Lewis, Simon. "Sanitising South Africa." *Soundings* 16 (Autumn 2000): 45–55.

———. "This Land South Africa: Rewriting Time and Space in Postapartheid Poetry and Property." *Environment and Planning A* 33.12 (December 2001): 2095–108.

Magona, Sindiwe. *Mother to Mother*. Boston: Beacon, 1998.

Maja-Pearce, Adewale, ed. *The Heinemann Book of African Poetry in English*. Oxford: Heinemann, 1990.

Maloba, Wunyabari O. *Mau Mau and Kenya: An Analysis of a Peasant Revolt*. Bloomington: Indiana University Press, 1993.

Mandela, Nelson. *Long Walk to Freedom*. Boston: Little, Brown, 1994.

Mangan, J. A., ed. *The Cultural Bond: Sport, Empire, Society*. London: Frank Cass, 1992.

Mariani, Philomena, ed. *Critical Fictions: The Politics of Imaginative Writing*. Seattle: Bay Press, 1991.

Mashinini, Emma. *Strikes Have Followed Me All My Life.* New York: Routledge, 1991.

Mattera, Don. *Sophiatown.* Braamfontein: Ravan, 1988.

McClintock, Anne. *Imperial Leather: Race, Gender, and Sexuality in the Colonial Contest.* New York: Routledge, 1995.

Mda, Zakes. *The Heart of Redness.* Cape Town: Oxford University Press, 2000.

Merrington, Peter. "A Staggered Orientalism: The Cape-to-Cairo Imaginary." *Poetics Today* 22.2 (Summer 2001): 323–64.

Miller, Christopher L. *Blank Darkness: Africanist Discourse in French.* Chicago: University of Chicago Press, 1985.

Mills, Sara. *Discourses of Difference: An Analysis of Women's Travel Writing and Colonialism.* New York: Routledge, 1991.

Mitchell, Sally. *The New Girl: Girls' Culture in England, 1880–1915.* New York: Columbia University Press, 1996.

Monsman, Gerald. *Olive Schreiner's Fiction: Landscape and Power.* New Brunswick: Rutgers University Press, 1992.

Moore, David Chioni. "Where Are All the African and Caribbean Critics? The MLA, Honorary Members, and Honorary Fellows." *Research in African Literatures* 32.1 (Spring 2001): 110–21.

Morrison, Toni. *Playing in the Dark: Whiteness and the Literary Imagination.* Cambridge: Harvard University Press, 1992.

———. *Beloved.* New York: Knopf, 1987.

Mphahlele, Ezekiel. *The African Image.* New York: Frederick A. Praeger, 1962.

———. *In Corner B.* Nairobi: East African, 1967.

Mtwa, Percy, and Mbongeni Ngema. *Woza, Albert!* London: Methuen, 1983.

Mudimbe, V. Y. *The Idea of Africa.* Bloomington: Indiana University Press, 1994.

———. *The Invention of Africa: Gnosis, Philosophy, and the Order of Knowledge.* Bloomington: Indiana University Press, 1988.

———. "Letters of Reference." *Transition* 53 (1991): 62–78.

Murray, Sally-Ann. "Olive Schreiner: 'A Soul Struggling with Its Material Surroundings.'" *Perspectives on South African English Literature.* Ed. Michael Chapman, Colin Gardner, and Es'kia Mphahlele. Parklands: Donker, 1992. 19–36.

Myrsiades, Kostas, and Jerry McGuire, eds. *Order and Partialities: Theory, Pedagogy, and the "Postcolonial."* Albany: State University of New York Press, 1995.

Ndebele, Njabulo S. "The English Language and Social Change in South Africa." *From South Africa: New Writing, Photographs, and Art.* Ed. David Bunn and Jane Taylor. Evanston: Northwestern University Press, 1987. 217–35.

———. *Essays on South African Literature and Culture: Rediscovery of the Ordinary.* Manchester: Manchester University Press, 1994.

Ngcobo, Lauretta. "A Black South African Woman Writing Long after Schreiner." *The Flawed Diamond: Essays on Olive Schreiner.* Ed. Itala Vivan. Sydney: Dangaroo Press, 1992. 189–99.

Ngugi wa Thiong'o. *Decolonising the Mind.* London: James Currey, 1986.

————. *Detained: A Writer's Prison Diary.* London: Heinemann, 1981.

————. *Moving the Centre: The Struggle for Cultural Freedoms.* London: James Currey, 1993.

Nixon, Rob. *Homelands, Harlem, and Hollywood: South African Culture and the World Beyond.* New York: Routledge, 1994.

Nuttall, Sarah, and Carli Coetzee, eds. *Negotiating the Past: The Making of Memory in South Africa.* Cape Town: Oxford University Press, 1998.

Nuttall, Sarah, and Cheryl-Ann Michael, eds. *Senses of Culture: South African Culture Studies.* Cape Town: Oxford University Press, 2000.

O'Brien, Anthony. *Against Normalization: Writing Radical Democracy in South Africa.* Durham: Duke University Press, 2001.

Owen, Alex. *The Darkened Room: Women, Power, and Spiritualism in Late Victorian England.* Philadelphia: University of Pennsylvania Press, 1990.

Palmer, Robin, and Neil Parsons, eds. *The Roots of Rural Poverty in Central and Southern Africa.* London: Heinemann, 1977.

Peires, Jeff. *The Dead Will Arise: Nongqawuse and the Great Xhosa Cattle-Killing Movement of 1856–57.* Johannesburg: Ravan, 1989.

Pelensky, Olga A. *Isak Dinesen.* Athens: Ohio University Press, 1991.

————. *Isak Dinesen: Critical Views.* Athens: Ohio University Press, 1993.

Phillips, Caryl, ed. *Extravagant Strangers: A Literature of Belonging.* New York: Vintage, 1997.

Plaatje, Solomon T. *Mhudi.* London: Heinemann, 1978.

————. *Native Life in South Africa.* Harlow: Longman, 1987.

Pratt, Mary Louise. *Imperial Eyes: Travel Writing and Transculturation.* London: Routledge, 1992.

Probyn, Elspeth. *Sexing the Self: Gendered Positions in Cultural Studies.* London: Routledge, 1993.

Raiskin, Judith L. *Snow on the Cane Fields: Women's Writing and Creole Subjectivity.* Minneapolis: University of Minnesota Press, 1996.

Ranger, Terence. "'Great Spaces Washed with Sun': The Matopos and Uluru Compared." *Text, Theory, Space: Land, Literature, and History in South Africa and Australia.* Ed. Kate Darian-Smith, Liz Gunner, and Sarah Nuttall. London: Routledge, 1996. 157–72.

————. "The Invention of Tradition in Colonial Africa." *The Invention of Tradition.* Ed. Eric Hobsbawm. Cambridge: Cambridge University Press, 1986. 211–62.

Read, Alan, ed. *The Fact of Blackness: Frantz Fanon and Visual Representation.* London: ICA Press, 1996.

Renan, Ernest. "What Is a Nation?" *Nation and Narration.* Ed. Homi Bhabha. London: Routledge, 1990. 8–22.

Rive, Richard, ed. *Olive Schreiner Letters.* Vol. 1, *1871–1899.* Oxford: Oxford University Press, 1988.

Robins, Steven. "Silence in My Father's House: Memory, Nationalism, and Narratives of the Body." *Negotiating the Past: The Making of Memory in South Africa.*

Ed. Sarah Nuttall and Carli Coetzee. Cape Town: Oxford University Press, 1998. 120–40.

Rodney, Walter. *How Europe Underdeveloped Africa.* Washington, D.C.: Howard University Press, 1982.

Ross, Robert. *A Concise History of South Africa.* Cambridge: Cambridge University Press, 1999.

Ruskin, John. *Praeterita: Outlines of Scenes and Thoughts Perhaps Worthy of Memory in My Past Life.* London: Rupert Hart-Davis, 1949.

———. "Pre-Raphaelitism." *The Works of John Ruskin.* Ed. E. T. Cook and Alexander Wedderburn. London: George Allen, 1904. 12:134–64.

———. *The Stones of Venice.* London: George Allen, 1904.

———. *Unto This Last.* Harmondsworth: Penguin, 1985.

Sachs, Albie. "Preparing Ourselves for Freedom." *Spring Is Rebellious: Arguments about Cultural Freedom by Albie Sachs and Respondents.* Ed. Ingrid de Kok and Karen Press. Cape Town: Buchu Books, 1990. 19–29.

———. *The Soft Vengeance of a Freedom Fighter.* London: Grafton, 1990.

Said, Edward. *Joseph Conrad and the Fiction of Autobiography.* Cambridge: Harvard University Press, 1965.

———. *Orientalism.* New York: Random House, 1979.

Schipper, Mineke. *Source of All Evil: African Proverbs and Sayings.* Chicago: Ivan R. Dee, 1991.

Schoeman, Karel. *Olive Schreiner: A Woman in South Africa, 1855–1881.* Johannesburg: Jonathan Ball, 1991.

Schreiner, Olive. *Dream Life and Real Life.* 1891. Chicago: Academy, 1981.

———. *Dreams.* New York: Mershon, 1891.

———. *From Man to Man.* 1926. Chicago: Academy, 1977.

———. *The Letters of Olive Schreiner, 1876–1920.* Ed. S. C. Cronwright-Schreiner. London: Unwin, 1924; Westport, Conn.: Hyperion Press, 1976.

———. *Olive Schreiner Letters.* Vol. 1, *1871–1899.* Ed. Richard Rive. Oxford: Oxford University Press, 1988.

———. *The South African Question.* Chicago: Charles H. Sergel, 1899. Also published as *An English South African's View of the Situation: Words in Season.* London: Hodder and Stoughton, 1899.

———. *The Story of an African Farm.* 1883. Harmondsworth: Penguin, 1982.

———. *Thoughts on South Africa.* 1923. Parklands: Donker, 1992.

———. *Trooper Peter Halket of Mashonaland.* Boston: Roberts Brothers, 1897.

———. *Undine.* New York: Harper and Brothers, 1928.

———. *Woman and Labour.* London: T. Fisher Unwin, 1911.

Senghor, Léopold Sédar. *On African Socialism.* Translated and with an introduction by Mercer Cook. New York: Praeger, 1964.

Serequeberhan, Tsenay. *The Hermeneutics of African Philosophy: Horizon and Discourse.* London: Routledge, 1994.

Showalter, Elaine. *Sexual Anarchy: Gender and Culture at the Fin de Siècle.* New York: Viking, 1990.

Silkin, Jon, ed. *The Penguin Book of First World War Poetry.* Harmondsworth: Penguin, 1979.

Sitas, Ari. "From *Black Mamba Rising: South African Worker Poets in Struggle.*" *From South Africa: New Writing, Photographs, and Art.* Ed. David Bunn and Jane Taylor. Evanston: Northwestern University Press, 1987. 273–306.

Sole, Kelwyn. "Oral Performance and Social Struggle in Contemporary Black South African Literature." *From South Africa: New Writing, Photographs, and Art.* Ed. David Bunn and Jane Taylor. Evanston: Northwestern University Press, 1987. 254–72.

Soyinka, Wole. "Neo-Tarzanism: The Poetics of Pseudo-Tradition." *Transition* 45 (1974): 9–11.

Spark, Muriel. *The Stories of Muriel Spark.* London: Dutton, 1985.

Spillers, Hortense. "Mama's Baby, Papa's Maybe: An American Grammar Book." *Diacritics* 17.2 (1987): 62–85.

Spivak, Gayatri Chakravorty. "Can the Subaltern Speak?" *Marxism and the Interpretation of Culture.* Ed. Lawrence Grossberg and Cary Nelson. Urbana: University of Illinois Press, 1988.

———. *The Postcolonial Critic: Interviews, Strategies, and Dialogues.* New York: Routledge, 1990.

Stambaugh, Sara. *The Witch and the Goddess in the Stories of Isak Dinesen: A Feminist Reading.* Ann Arbor: UMI Research Press, 1988.

Stape, J. H., ed. *The Cambridge Companion to Joseph Conrad.* Cambridge: Cambridge University Press, 1996.

Stead, W. T., ed. *The Last Will and Testament of Cecil J. Rhodes.* London: Review of Reviews, 1902.

Stevenson, Catherine Barnes. *Victorian Women Travel Writers in Africa.* Boston: Twayne, 1982.

Switzer, Les. *Power and Resistance in an African Society: The Ciskei Xhosa and the Making of South Africa.* Madison: University of Wisconsin Press, 1993.

Taussig, Michael. *Mimesis and Alterity: A Particular History of the Senses.* New York: Routledge, 1993.

———. *Shamanism, Colonialism, and the Wild Man.* Chicago: University of Chicago Press, 1987.

Taylor, Jane. *Ubu and the Truth Commission.* Cape Town: University of Cape Town Press, 1998.

Taylor, Stephen. *The Mighty Nimrod: A Life of Frederick Courteney Selous, African Hunter and Adventurer, 1851–1917.* London: Collins, 1989.

Thieme, John. *The Arnold Anthology of Post-Colonial Literatures.* London: Edward Arnold, 1996.

Thomas, Brook. "Preserving and Keeping Order by Killing Time in *Heart of Darkness.*" *Heart of Darkness.* Ed. Ross C. Murfin. Boston: Bedford, 1989.

Thompson, John B. Editor's Introduction. *Language and Symbolic Power.* By Pierre Bourdieu. Cambridge: Harvard University Press, 1991. 1–31.

Thurman, Judith. *Isak Dinesen: The Life of a Storyteller.* New York: St. Martin's Press, 1982.

Truth and Reconciliation Commission of South Africa Report. 5 vols. London: Macmillan, 1999 (International edition).

Trzebinski, Errol. *Silence Will Speak.* London: Grafton, 1985.

Tutu, Desmond. *No Future without Forgiveness.* New York: Doubleday, 1999.

van Heerden, Etienne. *Kikuyu.* Cape Town: Kwela, 1998.

———. *Mad Dog and Other Stories.* Cape Town: David Philip, 1992.

van Onselen, Charles. *Studies in the Social and Economic History of the Witwatersrand, 1886–1914* (2 vols.). Harlow: Longman, 1982.

Vivan, Itala. "The Treatment of Blacks in *The Story of an African Farm.*" *The Flawed Diamond: Essays on Olive Schreiner.* Ed. Itala Vivan. Sydney: Dangaroo Press, 1992. 95–106.

Waldmeir, Patti. *Anatomy of a Miracle: The End of Apartheid and the Birth of the New South Africa.* New York: Norton, 1997.

Walton, Jean. "Re-Placing Race in (White) Psychoanalytic Discourse: Founding Narratives of Feminism." *Critical Inquiry* 21.4 (Summer 1995): 775–804.

Ward, David. *Chronicles of Darkness.* London: Routledge, 1989.

Ware, Vron. *Beyond the Pale.* London: Verso, 1992.

Webster, Wendy. "Elspeth Huxley: Gender, Empire, and Narratives of Nation, 1935–1964." *Women's History Review* 8.3 (1999): 527–45.

Wheatcroft, Geoffrey. *The Randlords: South Africa's Robber Barons and the Mines That Forged a Nation.* New York: Simon and Schuster, 1987.

Whissen, Thomas R. "The Bow of the Lord: Isak Dinesen's 'Portrait of the Artist.'" *Isak Dinesen: Critical Views.* Ed. Olga A. Pelensky. Athens: Ohio University Press, 1993. 64–74.

White, Andrea. "Conrad and Imperialism." *The Cambridge Companion to Joseph Conrad.* Ed. J. H. Stape. Cambridge: Cambridge University Press, 1996. 179–202.

Wicomb, Zoë. *You Can't Get Lost in Cape Town.* New York: Feminist, 2000.

Wilentz, Gay. *Binding Cultures: Black Women Writers in Africa and the Diaspora.* Bloomington: Indiana University Press, 1992.

Willan, Brian. *Sol Plaatje: South African Nationalist, 1876–1932.* Berkeley: University of California Press, 1984.

Williams, Raymond. *The Country and the City.* Oxford: Oxford University Press, 1979.

Wolff, Richard D. *The Economics of Colonialism: Britain and Kenya, 1870–1930.* New Haven: Yale University Press, 1988.

Woods, Gurli, ed. *Isak Dinesen and Narrativity: Reassessments for the 1990s.* Ottawa: Carleton University Press, 1994.

Woolf, Virginia. "Olive Schreiner: Review of *The Letters of Olive Schreiner.*" *Olive Schreiner.* Ed. Cherry Clayton. Johannesburg: McGraw-Hill, 1983. 93–94.

Yeats, W. B. *Collected Poems of W. B. Yeats.* London: Macmillan, 1979.

Young, Robert J. C. *Colonial Desire: Hybridity in Theory, Culture, and Race.* London: Routledge, 1995.

Yurco, Frank. "*Black Athena:* An Egyptological Review." *Black Athena Revisited.* Ed. Mary Lefkowitz and Guy MacLean Rogers. Chapel Hill: University of North Carolina Press, 1996. 62–100.

Index

academic funding, 180, 232n. 48
Achebe, Chinua, 102, 106, 135, 168–69, 180–81, 183, 222n. 5, 223n. 7, 224n. 16, 226n. 8
Ackroyd, Annette, 48
Aden, Farah. *See* Farah Aden
Adorno, Theodor, 165, 192
adventure novels, 170, 185, 229n. 34
Africa: African reclamation of, 192–97; as Eden or inferno, 166, 167–69; erasure of African experience in, 2, 154; European invention of, 2, 3, 6, 9, 34–35, 77, 166; as female, 71; as home for whites, 1, 59–60, 72–77; as lacking history, 183–84; opacity of, 134; representation of, in films, 112, 125, 221n. 24; as safari park, 112, 125; as shaped by European control, 18, 153–54; as site of difference, 153–54, 165; as site of European adventure, 71; use in advertising, 125, 221n. 25; Western stereotype of, 112, 125, 153, 180. *See also* European discourses, power of
African family structure, disruption of, 59–60, 77–80, 206n. 1
African literature, 5, 8
African Literature Association (ALA), 8
African National Congress (ANC), 29, 100, 180
African nationalism, 5, 226n. 6
African philosophy, 9
African studies, 8
Afrikaans, 108, 215n. 33, 216n. 41
Afrikaners. *See* Boers
Afrocentrism, 8, 200n. 12

agriculture, 113, 121, 139. *See also* farming in Africa; farms
Aidoo, Ama Ata, 8
AIDS, 207n. 5, 210n. 28
Aiken, Susan Hardy, 36, 64, 111
allegory, 30–31, 91, 98, 169, 194, 195
allochronic discourse, 153, 154, 165, 180, 225n. 3. *See also* Fabian, Johannes
Alpers, Svetlana, 85, 211n. 6
Ambler, Charles H., 158, 227n. 14
anarchy, 113, 205n. 9
Anglo-Boer War, 1, 2, 26–27, 100, 176, 191, 201n. 7, 203nn. 11, 13, 205n. 13, 224n. 15, 233n. 6
anthropology, 113–14, 134–37. *See also* ethnography; European discourses, power of
anti-lynching movement. *See* lynching
apartheid, 6, 135, 196. *See also* colonial laws
Arnold, Matthew, 12, 113, 115, 205n. 9, 222n. 3, 223n. 7
Arnold, Thomas, 50
atavism, 114, 115, 184, 185, 190, 195
atheism, 23
autobiography, 10, 13, 19, 59, 68, 78, 203n. 14

Baartman, Sara, 206n. 18
Barolong, 102–3
Barrell, John, 85, 94, 211n. 5
Barrow, John, 86, 101, 233n. 4
Barthes, Roland, 39, 203n. 15
Bechuana (Batswana), 104–5
Beddoes, John, 133, 222n. 3

Simon Lewis is associate professor of English at the College of Charleston, where he teaches African and post-colonial literature. He edits the little literary magazine *Illuminations* and has published articles on a number of South African writers.